Parliaments in the Czech and Slovak Republics

Party competition and parliamentary institutionalization

PETR KOPECKÝ
University of Sheffield

Ashgate
Aldershot • Burlington USA • Singapore • Sydney

Published by
Ashgate Publishing Limited
Gower House
Croft Road
Aldershot
Hampshire GU11 3HR
England

Ashgate Publishing Company
131 Main Street
Burlington, VT 05401-5600 USA

Ashgate website: http://www.ashgate.com

British Library Cataloguing in Publication Data
Kopecký, Petr
Parliaments in the Czech and Slovak republics : party competition and parliamentary institutionalization
1. Czech Republic. Parliament. Poslanecka snemovna
2. Slovakia. Narodna rada 3. Political parties - Czech Republic 4. Political parties - Slovakia 5. Democratization - Czech Republic 6. Democratization - Slovakia 7. Czech Republic - Politics and government - 1993- 8. Slovakia - Politics and government - 1993 -
I. Title
328.4'371

Library of Congress Control Number: 2001086239

ISBN 0 7546 1644 4

Printed and bound in Great Britain by
Antony Rowe Ltd., Chippenham, Wiltshire

90 0469183 7

PARLIAMENTS IN THE CZECH AND SLOVAK REPUBLICS

To Tineke

Contents

List of Figures — *vi*
List of Tables — *vii*
Preface — *x*
Acknowledgments — *xii*
List of Acronyms — *xiii*

1 Introduction: Transition, Consolidation and Parliamentary Institutionalization — 1

2 The Institutional Origins of the Modern Czech and Slovak Parliaments — 22

3 Parliaments, Parties and Electorate: Organizing Representation — 53

4 Executive-Legislative Relations: Parliaments and Governments — 96

5 Executive-Legislative Relations: Presidents — 145

6 Inside the Parliaments: Parliamentary Parties — 171

7 Conclusion: Growing Apart? — 206

Appendix: Survey Information — *244*
Bibliography — *246*
Index — *261*

List of Figures

Figure 1:	Institutionalization of parliaments: key topics	15
Figure 2.	Voting Distances between Individual Parties I	100
Figure 3:	Voting Distances between Individual Parties II	100

List of Tables

Table 2.1:	Key constitutional and institutional proposals between June 1990 and June1992	32
Table 2.2:	Structure of institutions as embodied in the 1992 Czech and Slovak constitutions: Compared with the First Republic	44
Table 3.1:	Features of Czechoslovak, Czech and Slovak electoral systems	56
Table 3.2:	Satisfaction with the electoral system	64
Table 3.3:	Most negative aspects of the electoral system	65
Table 3.4:	Most positive aspects of the electoral system	66
Table 3.5:	The most important task of an MP	68
Table 3.6:	Focus of Representation	69
Table 3.7:	Main Czech parties between 1990 and 1996	76
Table 3.8:	Main Slovak parties between 1990 and 1994	77
Table 3.9:	State premiums for Czech and Slovak political parties according to electoral results and number of seats	79
Table 3.10:	Party membership in the Czech and Slovak Republics	82

Table 3.11:	Party membership	83
Table 4.1:	Perceptions of relations between ministers and MPs	99
Table 4.2:	Frequency of meetings between ministers and parliamentary parties: Czech coalition parties	111
Table 4.3:	Actual and desired influence of parliamentary party over 'own' ministers: Czech coalition parties	112
Table 4.4:	Frequency of meetings between ministers and parliamentary parties: Czech opposition parties	113
Table 4.5:	Permanent Committees in Czech and Slovak parliaments, 1994	119
Table 4.6:	Committee Structures, Powers and Procedures	120
Table 5.1:	Views of Czech MPs on presidential powers	161
Table 5.2:	Views of Slovak MPs on presidential powers	162
Table 6.1:	Czech and Slovak parliamentary parties and number of seats	173
Table 6.2:	Main advantages of membership of parliamentary party	176
Table 6.3:	Main disadvantages of membership of parliamentary party	177
Table 6.4:	Voting Cohesion of the Czech parliamentary parties	179
Table 6.5:	How should an MP vote in case of a difference of opinion with his parliamentary party? (Czech Republic)	185
Table 6.6:	How should an MP vote in case of a difference of opinion with his parliamentary party? (Slovak Republic)	186

Table 6.7:	Who should have the final say in case of conflicts between parliamentary party and party executive?	191
Table 6.8:	Frequency of party national executive instructions to parliamentary parties	192
Table 7.1:	Parliamentary Institutionalization and Democratic Consolidation in the Czech and Slovak Republics	241

Preface

The establishment and consolidation of democracy in contemporary Eastern Europe is proving both problematic and arduous. The postcommunist totalitarian legacy appears much less favourable for successful democratization than the legacy left by non-democratic regimes in Southern Europe and Latin America. In addition to combatting severe social and economic problems caused by the hitherto unprecedented transformation from a centrally planned economy to a market one, political leaders in Eastern Europe have been simultaneously engaged in the process of establishing the rules, procedures and norms which should sustain the institutional structures within which democracy is to function. This book is primarily concerned with examining these political-institutional problems in two East-Central European countries: the Czech and Slovak Republics. In particular, the book explores and evaluates the process of *parliamentary institutionalization* and, by doing so, also explores and evaluates a broader process of *democratic consolidation* in both countries. It intends not only to fill a void in the research on parliaments in the Czech and Slovak Republics, but also to contribute to studies of democratization in general, and to cross-national legislative studies in particular.

The book provides a comparative analysis of the Czech and Slovak parliaments - *Parlament* (*Poslanecká Sněmovna a Senát*) in the Czech Republic and *Národná Rada* in Slovakia - with the main empirical focus on their first and partly on their second legislative terms (1992-1998). It shows the development of these two parliaments in their full political contexts. It views parliaments not so much as institutions on their own, as rather as arenas within which other major political actors, such as political parties or interest groups, interact. Parliaments are seen as an important partial regime of a new political system, which encompasses a wide range of institutions, rules, procedures, and political organizations, and around which crucial questions of political style, legitimacy and democratic accountability revolve. The book is organized so as to analyze parliaments both in their relations with polity (both the electorate and other state institutions, such as governments and presidents), and in their internal functioning (role of individual MPs, parliamentary parties and parliamentary committees). In addition, it also offers an interesting perspective on two relatively understudied countries which appear to differ substantially in the way in which parliamentary institutionalization and democratic consolidation have developed, yet which both started with a more or less identical institutional design and a similar social, economic and political environment.

The book originates from a comparative project - The Institutionalization of Parliamentary Democracy in Poland, Hungary, the Czech Republic and Slovakia - carried out in the Department of Political Science of Leiden University. The project was set up as a comparative study. However, it was not set up as a single study, executed by a single person, or tied to a single analytical framework. Rather, the project was an umbrella under which three distinct (case) studies were undertaken, each carried out by a single person completing a PhD. thesis, but connected by a set of common themes and broadly defined questions. A common questionnaire was developed within the project, with the aim of conducting interviews with parliamentarians in all countries researched, gathering cross-nationally comparable data. The core data for this book is thus derived from a unique set of structured interviews with large samples of parliamentarians in the Czech and Slovak Republics, which were conducted in 1993 and 1994 (see Appendix 1about the survey). These interviews are complemented by data derived from the study of both primary and secondary sources, involving material on constitutions, formal parliamentary and party rules and procedures and so forth, as well as additional interviews with MPs, party leaders and activists which I conducted in both countries.

The book's contribution to both comparative legislative studies, and to the studies of democratization in Central and Eastern Europe, centers around three key issues. First, it shows that parliamentary institutionalization is not so much determined by different configurations of formal institutional procedures but rather by their comformity with the values and expectations of political actors who act within them. Second, it substantiates the importance of democratization theories working with assumptions of elite and political autonomy. Third, it refutes the three oft-cited broad explanations - economic, cultural, and institutional - for the differences in parliamentary institutionalization and democratic consolidation between the Czech and Slovak Republics, instead offering a more complex explanation based on the understanding of the (different) nature of party competition in these two countries.

Acknowledgments

A number of institutions and people helped me to bring the study to this point. To start with my research would have been impossible on such a scale without generous financial support from the Dutch Organization for Scientific Research (NWO), which I gratefully acknowledge. Within the project and the Department of Political Science of Leiden University, I greatly benefited from the guidance and insightful comments of Rudy Andeweg and Peter Mair, as well as from my collaboration with Heleen den Haan, Ania van der Meer, Marc van den Muyzenberg and Ingrid van Biezen. In the Czech Republic, my thanks go to Jan Herzmann and his team, as well as to Pavel Hubáček and Petr Plecitý. In Slovakia, I am indebted to Darina Malová and her students of politics from the Comenius University, as well as to Danica Siváková and Peter Učeň. At Sheffield University, I would particularly like to thank Jean Grugel, Martin Smith and all the office staff at the Department of Politics, as well as to Neil Bermel, from the Department of Russian and Slavonic Studies.

My friend and academic colleague Cas Mudde deserves a special mention, for his help, entertainment and company ever since we met in Leiden. Throughout all these years, he uncomplainingly read many drafts of my work and discussed any problems. He also provided me with a lot of encouragement. Finally, I wish to express my many thanks to Tineke Griffioen. She suffered through an endless series of deadlines and worries about the book. But perhaps most importantly, her presence and understanding helped me to put my academic career in a healthy perspective. I would like to dedicate this work to her.

List of Acronyms

Acronym	Original Name	English Name
Czech Parties		
ČMSS	Česko-Moravská strana středu	Czech-Moravian Party of the Center
ČMSS	Česko-Moravská strana středu	Czech-Moravian Party of the Center
ČMUS	Česká-Moravská unie středu	Czech-Moravian Union of the Center
ČSS	Českosovenská strana socialistická	Czechoslovak Socialist Party
ČSSD	Československá sociální demokracie / Česká strana sociálně demokratická	Czechoslovak/Czech Social Democratic Party
HSD-(S)MS	Hnutí za samosprávnou demokracii	Movement for Self-Governing
(HSDMS/HSD-SMS)	Společnost pro Moravu a Slezsko	Democracy- Association for Moravia and Silesia
KDS	Křest'ansko-demokratická strana	Christian Democratic Party
KDU	Křest'ansko-demokratická unie	Christian Democratic Union
KDU-ČSL	Křest'ansko-demokratická unie - Československá strana lidová	Christian Democratic Union - Czechoslovak People's Party
KSČ	Komunistická strana Československá	Communist Party of Czechoslovakia
KSČM	Komunistická strana Čech a Moravy	Communist Party of Bohemia and Moravia

LB	Levý blok	Left Bloc
LSNS	Liberálně sociální národní strana	Liberal Social National Party
LSU	Liberálně sociální unie	Liberal Social Union
ODA	Občanská demokratická aliance	Civic Democratic Alliance
ODS	Občanská demokratická strana	Civic Democratic Party
OF	Občanské forum	Civic Forum
SD-LSNS	Svobodní demokraté-Liberálně sociální národní strana	Free Democrats-Liberal Social National Party
SLB	Strana levý blok	Party Left Block
SPR-RSČ	Sdružení pro republiku-Republikánská strana Československa	Association for the Republic - the Republican Party of Czechoslovakia

Slovak Parties

DU	Demokratická Únia	Democratic Union
ESWMK	Egyuttélés a Mad'arské křest'ansko democratické hnutie	Egyutteles and Hungarian Christian Democratic Movement
HZDS	Hnutie za demokratické Slovensko	Movement for a Democratic Slovakia
KDH	Křest'ansko-demokratické hnutie	Christian Democratic Movement
KNP	Klub nezávislých poslancov	Group of Independent Representatives
KSČ	Komunistická strana Československa	Communist Party of Czechoslovakia
KSS	Komunistická strana Slovenska	Communist Party of Slovakia

MK	Magyar koalicio	Hungarian Coalition
MKDH	Mad'arské křest'ansko-demokratické hnutie	Hungarian Christian Democratic Movement
MOS	Mad'arská občianská strana	Hungarian Civic Party
NDS-NA	Národno-demokratická strana-Nová alternativa	National Democratic Party-New Alternative
SDL	Strana demokratickej lavice	Party of the Democratic Left
SNS	Slovenská národná strana	Slovak National Party
SV	Spoločná volba	Common Choice
VPN	Verejnost' proti násiliu	Public Against Violence
ZRS	Združenie robotníkov Slovenska	Association of Workers of Slovakia

1 Introduction: Transition, Consolidation and Parliamentary Institutionalization

The attempts to establish democracy and market economy in the Czech and Slovak Republics and in the countries of the former Eastern block have now lasted well over ten years. In the light of the complicated post-communist legacy, this may not have been enough time for democracy and markets to take firm root. But it has been sufficient time to observe general patterns of change and to detect an increasing variety among the ex-communist countries, whether in the development of political institutions, such as parliaments, or in the forms of governance and economic management or, indeed, in their levels of democratic consolidation. Why, then, do some countries succeed in consolidating their democracy and others fail? What accounts for their different forms and levels of institutionalization? Do similiar institutional characteristics lead to the same form of institutionalization? Or does that form of institutionalization depend on economic performance, elite behavior, political culture or any other contextual factor? These are the broader questions this book intends to address, drawing on empirical explorations of the origins and functioning of the Czech and Slovak parliaments in their crucial formative years following the breakdown of the communist regime in 1989.

Why Parliaments?

The focus on parliaments in this book is important in both practical and theoretical sense. It is important in practical sense because one of the key characteristics of parliaments - or legislatures - is the pivotal position they occupy among other democratic institutions. Parliaments are not so much institutions on their own as they are arenas which other actors, such as political parties or interests groups, interact in and cut across (Di Palma, 1990b). This view has two consequences. On the one hand, it emphasizes the interaction of parliaments with intermediary agencies: the parties, interest groups, or other elements that link them to society. On the other hand, it also highlights the importance of parliaments in linking society with other democratic institutions, the executive, judiciary or state bureaucracy. The parliaments are, to use Phillipe Schmitter's term, an important and large "partial regime" of a new political system, which encompasses a wide range of institutions, rules and procedures, as well as political organizations. They can thus be viewed as a focal point around which all crucial questions of political style, legitimacy and democratic accountability revolve, and it is precisely this understanding which drives the interest in parliament in this book.

This view has been adopted in earlier legislative studies situated in the context of democratization. For example, Close (1995:9), in his study on Latin American legislatures, notes that parliament is a subject of inquiry in terms of its own structure and operations, and that it is also an input to inquiry in terms of its role in the broader political system and its impact on democratic construction. However, even in much of the literature on established democracies, parliaments are thought to occupy a central position among democratic institutions of governance, because "of all political institutions, none is more vital to the process of linking governors and governed in relationships of authority, responsibility, and legitimacy, than the modern legislature" (Wahlke and Eulau, cited in Kornberg and Musolf, 1970:7).

Certainly it is questionable whether the centrality of parliaments is a valid empirical premise beyond the context of US democracy (and functionalist orthodoxy) in which it was originally formulated. Political parties and other intermediary agencies can be viewed as providing basically the same function. Moreover, many studies of European politics and government have for a long time advocated a thesis of the parliaments in decline. Parliaments came to be seen no longer as supreme legislative and representational institutions - a view heavily biased toward 19th-century democratic theory - but instead became stigmatized as rubber-stamping bodies, dominated by executives, bureaucracies and strong political parties.[1]

This notwithstanding, it is striking to see the universality of parliaments across the globe. They are to be found in almost all countries, whether democratic or non-democratic, which testifies to the extent to which parliaments still dominate thinking and conceptions about representative government, and to how important they are for the legitimacy of political systems.[2] Moreover, parliaments are also multifunctional. As Polsby notes, "what in the end seems most intriguing about legislatures is their all-purpose flexibility... they do the job of gaining legitimacy for government tolerably well and in addition serve as training grounds for future elites" (Polsby, 1975:302). And, as Packenham pointed out, parliaments may also perform other functions: they legislate (hence the oft-used term *legislatures*); that is, they make laws, release tensions stemming from the political process, socialize and train elites, oversee administration, and help to articulate interests (see Packenham, 1970). They are thus important in a modern democracy, as well as in the context of non-democratic regimes, in which they seemingly perform a minimum of functions.[3] As some authors argue, parliaments may also perform specific and important functions in countries undergoing a process of democratic transition and consolidation.[4]

On a more theoretical level, parliaments deserve close attention because they are institutions or, as we argued, cross-sections of various institutions. The study of institutions, of course, has been an enduring concern in political science, and even more so in recent years, with the emergence of 'new institutionalism'. The literature trying to explain both the occurrence of transition from a non-democratic regime to democracy, as well as its subsequent stability (or lack of it), has not been spared that theoretical influence either. Indeed, at certain point, democratization studies witnessed an almost paradigmatic shift from the preoccupation with social preconditions of democracy, associated with modernization theory of the 1950s and 1960s,[5] to the emphasis on elite behavior and institutional choices, associated with the so-called transition or "process-oriented" (Kitschelt, 1992) school of the 1970s and 1980s.[6]

Although scholars still argue about the relative explanatory weight of various variables - and we shall return to this in the concluding chapter - much contemporary writing on democratization does not see modernization or transition perspectives anymore in a strictly dichotomous fashion.[7] Perhaps most importantly, it is widely recognized that institutions matter, and that the study of how they develop and what effects they have is a very important, if not pivotal, aspect of the study of democratization. Institutions, both in the sense of rules of a political game and as political organizations acting within such a framework contribute to crafting the new regime. On a more fundamental level, they shape actors' powers and identities, they privilege certain policy alternatives over others and give rise to particular behaviors. In other words, institutions act as independent variables. Among the set of questions addressed in this book will thus be: to what extent did institutions such as relations between the parliaments and presidents contribute to political stability; how do electoral systems affect the representative roles performed by the MPs; did a change in the rules governing state support for parties affect the internal balance of power within them?

However, not enough attention is paid to the fact that institutions are designed and implemented in specific historical, cultural and socioeconomic contexts. Various informal rules, conventions and traditions either exist or develop as extensions of formal rules, and these may produce different institutional outcomes, or might profoundly affect the functioning of political organizations. This is a second set of questions running through this study. Institutions can be taken as dependent variables. It is then perfectly legitimate and theoretically important to explore the extent to which institutions are affected by their immediate social context, be that purposeful behavior of political elites, the nature of political competition, the strength of traditions or even the forces of the international environment. These are all questions fundamental to our understanding of the processes of democratic consolidation and parliamentary institutionalization - concepts we shall now try to clarify.

Transition and Consolidation

The literature on democratization frequently refers to three key concepts: transition, consolidation and institutionalization. The first step will be to distinguish between these concepts. For although these concepts are closely connected, their original meaning and assumptions are often either ignored, stretched, or used interchangeably, rendering many studies fuzzy. Too often we read about 'non-consolidated party systems', 'less institutionalized democracies', without much specification of what the labels really mean. As with many frequently used terms, these too became part of political science's common vocabulary, and are used in an uncritical way as if their meaning was self-evident. In part, this is not surprising, given the confusion and the disagreements within the academic community on what exactly democratic transition and consolidation mean and the wide variety of different definitions currently in use (see Munck 1994; Plasser, Ulram and Waldrauch 1998: 44-45; Schedler 1998). Even the very notion of democratization - technically referring to the entire, complex process of political change from an authoritarian regime toward democracy - is problematic, carrying its own assumptions and bias (see Mainwaring, 1992).

Transition

The concept of transition should pose the least trouble, both theoretically and in the empirical context of this book. Originally, transitions were defined as the interval between the dissolution of the old regime and the installation of a new regime (O'Donnell & Schmitter 1986). Transitions were thought to be highly uncertain processes, dependent on individuals and various political groups, as well as on strategic choices made by these actors as they struggle over the rules of the game constituent of a new regime. It was defined as a process delimited on both ends by different (types of) regimes: if *successful*, this came to mean an authoritarian regime on the one end, and a democratic regime on the other (e.g. O'Donnell 1992; Plasser, Ulram & Waldrauch 1998). More specifically, the transition to democracy is over when an agreement on democratic rules is reached successfully (Di Palma 1990a). The study of transition was not suppose to indicate exactly what kind of democracy is to emerge, or how deep-rooted or stable it will be. It was supposed to provide insights into the dynamics of change in the initial stages of political change and to define the outcomes of this process in broad generic terms, such as democracy, *democradura*, *dictablanca* etc. (see Munck, 1994; Schmitter, 1994).

Transition are thus processes in which the rules likely to govern a new democratic political order are crafted.[8] The emphasis placed on *an agreement* is crucial here. It indicates both that some democratic rules have been established to guide political conflicts and that these rules are not necessarily the same as those under which democracy will function in the future. They can be adjusted or changed as the situation develops, for instance, in the process of consolidation. Empirically, the end of *successful* transition often coincides with the conduct of the first free elections and, as we shall see in the second chapter, Czechoslovakia is arguably a good example of this.[9] In other words, our concern with transition to democracy in Czechoslovakia (and the Czech and Slovak Republics) in this book will be brief, as it was completed in a relatively short period of time after the breakdown of the communist regime in 1989.

Consolidation

Consolidation will be a more substantial concern in this book. Unlike transition, consolidation is also a more difficult concept to define, although, in an attempt to free its meaning of excessive conceptual overload, many authors cautiously tried to construct what are referred to as minimal definitions. The first minimal definition is that of democracy itself. The comparative democratization literature seems to share a consensus that both transition to and consolidation of democracy refer to the procedural minimum of democracy, rather than to the substantive, complex, and normatively strong underpinnings often to be found in democratic theory (see Weiner, 1987; O'Donnell and Schmitter, 1986; Valenzuela, 1992). How minimal even minimal definitions must be is, however, open to debates, and conceptualizations of democracy represent a constant challenge to students of democratization and their research strategies (see Collier and Levitsky, 1997). In order to establish the smallest possible number of characteristics producing a 'democracy', minimalists focused on procedures and, consequently, they see democracy as a system of procedural rules for governance and as an institutional framework.[10]

In contrast to transition, the essence of consolidation was originally thought to be the defining and fixing of the core rules of democratic competition (Di Palma 1990a); i.e. transforming the set of democratic rules and institutions agreed upon in the transition phase into regular, acceptable and predictable patterns (Schmitter 1994). Therefore, the phase of consolidation is primarily characterised by the increased importance of routinised (institutional) structures that start to influence the behavior of political actors, rather than, as in the more volatile process of transition, by voluntaristically behaving actors defining and struggling over the rules in a series of events seemingly unbound by structures (Munck 1994). Consolidation is based on partial redefining of agreements, arrangements and institutions which emerged from the process of transition, or on the affirmation, strengthening and routinization of these provisions. The process of consolidation can also involve both partial altering and partial affirmation of the existing agreements in some proportion. It also involves the removal of all provisions which are inimical to democracy but were necessary to make transition possible; for example, reserving a certain number of parliamentary seats for members of the previous ruling Communist Party, as happened in the first post-1989 parliaments in Czechoslovakia.

The question crucial for our empirical exploration is, however: when can we say that democracy is consolidated? How do we recognize this point? What are the measures; what are the criteria? Drawing on the minimal conception of democracy, i.e. that democracy is equal to a procedural minimum, Valenzuela (1992:69) suggests the following definition:

> "(...) a democracy is consolidated when elections following procedures devoid of egregious and deliberate distortions designed to underrepresent systematically a certain segment of opinion are perceived by all significant political forces to be unambiguously the only means to create governments well into the foreseeable future, and when the latter are not subjected to tutelary oversight or constrained by the presence of reserved domains of state policy formulation."

Conversely, a non-consolidated democracy is, for example, a system which satisfies formal procedural criteria of democracy while at the same time the major political actors consider alternatives to elections as viable or possible, or where the army or some other agency has an effective veto over state policy and the electoral process. In this respect, Valenzuela's notion of consolidated democracy shares a common ground with many other definitions, namely that to speak of consolidated democracy, in an ideal-typical and minimal sense, is to recognize that all politically significant groups adhere to democratic rules of the game (see Linz, 1990; Burton, Gunther and Higley, 1992; Diamondouros, Puhle and Gunther, 1995). Consolidated democracy, in minimal terms, is thus understood in terms of the behavioral compliance of political actors with the established rules, i.e. compliance is a sufficient indicator of consolidation, and non-compliance is a sufficient indicator of non-consolidation.[11]

It is a relatively simple definition, providing a clear cutoff point between consolidated and non-consolidated democracies. It is also a definition which implicitly underscores the fact that consolidated democracies are not necessarily immune to complete breakdowns, political crises, ethnic tensions and other sorts of potentially destabilizing events. Indeed, as Valenzuela himself argues, the definition of consolidation should not be grounded in the presence or absence of these destabilizing elements. Crises of the state, for example, should be distinguished from crises of democracy. It is important to remember this point when studying postcommunist Europe, because many such problems have already been labelled as problems of democratic consolidation or interpreted as the signs of non-consolidation.

Linz and Stepan (1996:6) adopt a similar view to Valenzuela's and argue that any eventual breakdown of democracy or re-emergence of non-democratic alternatives must be related to new and different political dynamics from those specific to the historical process of democratic consolidation. Furthermore, they also introduce a 'more than minimal' definition of democratic consolidation and democracy. Accordingly, democracy is consolidated when, first, "no significant national, social, economic, political, or institutional actors spend significant resources attempting to achieve their objectives by creating a nondemocratic regime or turning to violence or foreign intervention to secede from the state"; when, second, "a strong majority of public opinion holds the belief that democratic procedures and institutions are the most appropriate way to govern collective life in a society..."; and, third, "when governmental and non-governmental forces alike, throughout the territory of the state, become subjected to, and habituated to, the resolution of conflict within the specific laws, procedures, and institutions sanctioned by the new democratic process" (Linz and Stepan, 1996:6).

The feature that distinguishes this definition of consolidation from the one(s) mentioned above is as follows: not only must the main political actors *comply* with democratic rules of the game, but these rules must also be seen as *legitimate* (as opposed to, say, *tolerated without conviction*), by the actors themselves and by a large section of the public. To the previous elite's behavioral element, Linz and Stepan thus add an element of attitudinal compliance, and also step down from the elite to the mass level. Moreover, as the authors argue, in a consolidated democracy there must exist a free and lively civil society and a relatively autonomous political society; political actors must be subjected to the rule of law; and a functioning bureaucracy and an institutionalized economic society must be in operation. Linz and Stepan define these as supporting conditions, or arenas of consolidated democracy. However, later on they also refer to the first three of these supporting conditions as definitional pre-requisites for consolidation (p.10). Some of these arenas thus actually become part of the definition itself and, consequently, both authors depart significantly from their original aim to construct a narrow definition, arriving instead at a relatively broad definition of consolidation and democracy.

This extended definition of democratic consolidation is likely to be difficult for both practical empirical research, and its eventual theoretical interpretations. However, it clearly reflects recent concerns about relying solely on minimal electoralist and institutionalist definitions in assessing the consolidation of democracy. Standards used to evaluate any given democracy were defined in excess, so that almost no existing democracy could fully qualify. Scholars therefore opted for minimal definitions, in order to construct less problematic cutoff points. As it turns out now, with democratic regimes becoming more widespread and enduring in our times, at least in minimal procedural terms, scholarly attention has now turned again to investigate more closely the fit between their formal rules and actual political practice. As O'Donnell (1996:42) argues, scholars overlooking a discrepancy between the two "attach the label 'consolidated' to cases that clearly do not fit its arguments but that have endured for a significantly longer period than the new polyarchies have so far....It deals with these cases by relegating them to a theoretical limbo, as if, because they are somehow considered 'consolidated', the big gap between their formal rules and behavior were irrelevant"[12] (for similar views see Schmitter, 1994).

The recent writings of O'Donnell, and Linz and Stepan, therefore represent attempts to construct analytical tools and categories to differentiate between cases of regimes which fall within the bounds of a minimal definition of democracy. They have launched what Linz and Stepan (1996:6) argue is "an exciting new area of research ..... on the variety of consolidated democracies". Indeed, O'Donnell (1996) goes so far as to reject the term 'consolidation' altogether and, in a similar vein as Linz and Stepan, makes a plea for the study of variations among polyarchies - that is, between regimes which fit minimal definitions but which differ in other important aspects of their functioning.

Taking both a minimalist procedural definition of democracy, as well as minimalist (behavioral) definition of consolidation as the useful starting point, this study will show - in the final chapter - that concerns of these scholars are indeed warranted. While both the Czech and Slovak Republics might appear to be minimally consolidated democracies, a close exploration of political practices, elite behavior and institutions centered around the parliament will reveal substantial differences in the way these new political systems function - differences which would be foolish to ignore. Employing Linz and Stepan's definition, even in a cursory fashion, will then help us to summarize these differences effectively. However, it will also reopen the question as to whether these differences are then to be subsumed under problems of democratic consolidation, or rather under problems of an already consolidated democracy. We shall offer a view on this in the final chapter.

Parliamentary Institutionalization

As the title of the book suggests, the institutionalization (of parliaments) will be our most important concern. We will evaluate and explain the differences in democratic consolidation between the Czech and Slovak Republics; however, it is only through the study of parliamentary institutionalization that we will assemble enough material to evaluate the process of consolidation as it applies to these two countries. Having said that, the first inevitable question when one is concerned with the institutionalization in the context of democratization is the relationship between institutionalization and the concepts of transition and consolidation. The first distinction is that whenever we analyze concrete institutions - and parliaments are the focus of this work - we will talk about their institutionalization, rather than about their transition or consolidation. The terms "transition" and "consolidation" are linked to the concept of democracy or to particular regimes, and thus will be reserved in this study for a system-wide level of analysis. In contrast, the term "institutionalization" will refer to a particular institution, such as parliament, or a partial institutional system, such as a party system. This is to say that, unlike transition and consolidation, institutionalization will be applied to the sub-systemic level of analysis. It will be a concept related here to the study of a concrete institution or a set of linked institutions.

Huntington's seminal work on political stability, which defines institutionalization as the process which gives institutions (organizations and procedures) value and stability, does not seem to support our distinction between different levels of analysis (see Huntington, 1968). Huntington's treatment of institutionalization seems to suggest that it is possible to speak about the institutionalization of a whole democracy or political system and not only of particular institutions, just as we speak about the transition or consolidation of a whole democracy or political system. Nevertheless, the author does not give any clear example of how political systems as a whole differ in their level of institutionalization. Instead, the criteria of adaptability, complexity, autonomy, and coherence, which Huntigton identifies as defining characteristics of institutionalization, are specified only with examples of particular organizations. This gives the impression that the level of institutionalization of a political system somehow consists of a cumulative effect of levels of institutionalization of its constituent institutions and procedures - a concern which is clearly reflected in distinction between different levels of analysis made above.[13]

This all said, there is an important theoretical relationship between consolidation and institutionalization. If consolidation of democracy as a process is all about routinizing formal rules into actual patterns of behavior, then institutionalization is, as we shall clearly see below, a concept almost synonymous to it. Di Palma realizes this problematic relationship and notes that it would not make much sense to focus on institutionalization should the process of consolidation (or transition) be at its very beginning, or worse, failing. In his perspective, "consolidation logically precedes institutionalization. If successful, we may well claim consolidation well before institutionalization is advanced. If unsuccessful, then the longer process of institutionalization is itself stalemated" (Di Palma, 1990b:38). If the main political actors show no consensus and no behavioral compliance with established rules of the game, then there will be no move towards longer process of institutionalization; that is, toward turning the formal nominal rules into valued and routine behavioral patterns.

However, another important fact which follows from this is that a consensus on the rules of the game (e.g. consolidation) is generated by the process of institutionalization itself, because if rules become habitual and internalized, this would imply the existence of a widespread consensus on them. And this is exactly why a clear conceptual and theoretical distinction between consolidation and institutionalization is difficult to sustain. Furthermore, Di Palma also implicitly sets a specific desired standard for institutionalization, binding it to democracy, and ignoring a possibility that, as in many new democratic regimes, institutionalization might actually proceed according to informal rules, non-universalistic relationships and patronage exchanges, which are perhaps not explicitly sanctioned by the formal standards of polyarchy, but equally are not in sharp contradiction with them (see O'Donnell, 1996). In other words, there can be different types of institutionalization, not necessarily at odds with minimal behavioral definition of consolidation of democracy. We shall see in this book that such a situation may well be already in place in Slovakia.

How, then, can we understand the concept of institutionalization, and in particular that of parliamentary institutionalization? In the first major study on this topic, Polsby develops a series of measures to analyze the institutionalization of the US House of Representatives: one, institutional autonomy defined in terms of ease of identification of members, difficulty of entry, and internal recruitment of leadership; two, complex internal organization defined in terms of role specificity and widely shared performance expectations; three, regularized recruitment roles, and regularized patterns of movement from role to role; and four, universal criteria applied in the conduct of internal business and impersonal codes that supplant personal preferences as prescriptions for behavior (Polsby, 1968). Similarly, Loewenberg and Patterson use the term "institutionalization" to refer to "the process by which legislatures acquire a definite way of performing their functions that sets them apart" (Loewenberg and Patterson, 1979:21). The authors suggest two factors as the main contributors to the institutionalization of legislature over time: human habit as the tendency to perform identical tasks in the same way; and organizational complexity as embodied in a number of structural features of a given legislature.

These understandings of parliamentary institutionalization developed by Polsby and by Lowenberg and Patterson represent a very useful starting point for our analysis, and have also proved so in other attempts to analyze parliaments. However, we shall attempt to move a step beyond them. The main reason is that both of these notions of parliamentary institutionalization tend to neglect links between changes within parliaments and the external environment. In particular, Polsby's concept was criticized for being only descriptive, and not attempting to answer questions regarding the nature of the relationships between legislative change and the environment in which the legislature is evolving (see Hibbing, 1988). Both concepts are primarily, though not exclusively, concerned with describing developmental trends within the parliaments, illustrating general tendencies by selecting measures centered mainly around structural (formal and legal) characteristics of parliaments.

Sisson provides a more developed conceptualization of institutionalization. His understanding of the essence of institutionalization is similar to the previously mentioned work:

> "political institutionalization refers to the creation and persistence of valued rules, procedures, and patterns of behaviour that enable the successful accommodation of new configurations of political claimants and/or demands within a given organization whether it be a party, a legislature, or a state" (Sisson, 1973:19).

However, Sisson argues that any analysis of institutionalization must address the relationship and the character of interaction between the relevant institution and its environment, as well as the relevance and implications of this interaction for the internal structure of the institution. By "environment" he means a bureaucratic system that includes those institutions of public authority subordinate and responsible to the authoritative head of state; a constitutive system that includes the party political format and an electoral system; and the system of social stratification, including both class and status group (Sisson, 1973:24). The author then goes on to analyze both the external and internal structure of legislative institutions in terms of three criteria, which are nevertheless partly derived from, and similar to, the abovementioned features. These are: 1) structural: the autonomy of an institution and its complexity; 2) cultural: value systems that connect the institution and its environment and that govern behavior within the institution; 3) the character of elite and public obligation and compliance, i.e. the structure of compliance and support for public institutions.

Sisson's attempt is thus a more elaborate concept of institutionalization of parliaments. As a theory it has merits in synthesizing previous efforts into a more complex picture, with the specification of links between different aspects of institutionalization. Despite the large number of variables, which will inevitably complicate any empirical study employing this concept of institutionalization, it directs attention to the relationship between the internal structure of parliament and the external environment. Perhaps most importantly, it also directs attention to the relationship between structural characteristics (i.e. formal and legal features) of parliaments and the value systems, norms and expectations that underpin them. For these reasons, Sisson's conceptualization will form the basis for understanding and evaluating institutionalization of Czech and Slovak parliaments. Two central points should be emphasized.

Firstly, there are two broad analytical issues related to the institutionalization of parliament. One is parliament's internal workings and the other is parliament's external environment. Focusing exclusively on one of the two issues, as Polsby does with his concentration on the internal life of the US House of Representatives, seems justifiable only when each can be considered to be neutral with respect to the other - which is perhaps the case in an 'established democracy' or an 'institutionalized parliament'. However, in a situation typical of the early phase of democratization - when constitutional rules affecting the status of parliament can still be modified, and where political parties and interest groups rapidly change - focusing only on internal processes, for instance, would miss the point completely. This study will therefore take into account both issues. For example, we will be interested in the extent to which institutionalization of Czech and Slovak parliaments is affected by relationships between elites, or by the nature of emerging party systems. By the same token, however, we will also explore the extent to which the pressures and political processes internal to parliaments affect their wider constitutional and political position.

Secondly, the term 'institutionalization' refers to the process of establishing an institution; that is, to the process of creating social orders and patterns capable of reproducing themselves (see Jepperson, 1991). Parliamentary institutionalization is thus a process in which parliament acquires certain structural, behavioral and attitudinal characteristics which enhance its capacity to reproduce itself and to resist social intervention. In analytical terms, this means that we should ask about the direction of parliamentary institutionalization, as well as about the degree of parliamentary institutionalization. Each of these analytical dimensions point to slightly different sets of questions and slightly different sets of empirical measures or indicators.

The direction of parliamentary institutionalization follows the classical descriptive tradition in the study of institutions. When asking about direction of institutionalization, we tend to seek an answer to the questions: what sort of parliament, or a parliamentary institutional complex, is developing? What is the power and role of parliamentary committees? What are the rules guiding the activities of parliamentarians in their constituency work? To use Sisson's terminology, such assessment of parliamentary institutionalization centers primarily around the development of parliament's formal structural attributes, such as parliamentary committees, parliamentary parties, parliamentary rules of procedure, and relations to the executive branch. Without a doubt, these are standard variables addressed in any large scale legislative study and this one will not be an exception.

The degree of parliamentary institutionalization follows the more modern tradition of neo-institutional analysis. Parliamentary institutionalization, in this sense, directs attention to the capacity of parliament to reproduce itself and to resist social intervention. To use Sisson's terminology, such assessment of parliamentary institutionalization does focus on cultural criteria in addition to structural institutional configurations; that is, it focuses on political elites' consensus on institutional rules, roles and procedural regulations and the elite's conceptions and perceptions of them. These are perhaps less standard variables, if not only because their empirical measurement is complicated and often based on qualitative rather than quantitative techniques of assessment. But without an attempt to delve into these, the evaluation of institutionalization would be reduced to the study of various procedural components only. And, as was outlined above, the core of institutionalization is less a different configuration of procedures or powers of institutions than it is their degree of rootedness and conformity with values and expectations of actors who act within them. Therefore, in addition to structural attributes and formal rules, we will be interested in the development of informal authority structures which guide parliamentary processes and the evolution of norms and institutional identities which constitute parliamentary culture.

One final caveat. Can we ascertain the moment when the parliament is institutionalized? Our answer is affirmative, even though the interpretation of any particular case of parliament will always be controversial. However, it is important to note that while institutionalization can be said to be completed at some point, this does not mean an end to the institutional change or adaptation. Institutionalization is a long-term process. [14] It is also not quite the same as the acquisition of institutional stability. As Longley (1996:24) points out, "there are important change processes which occur, sometimes dramatically so, even in mature, 'institutionalized' parliaments. History does not end with institutionalization." Institutions based on solid structural foundations, and with stable and routine patterns of behavior and the capacity to reproduce themselves, can still change. But what distinguishes them from a non-institutionalized organization is the more predictable manner in which they cope with pressures for change, making them less expendable and vulnerable to social intervention (see Jepperson, 1991).

Figure 1: Institutionalization of parliaments: key topics

	EXTERNAL ENVIRONMENT constitutional structures electoral systems executive structures parties outside parliament
Characteristics of:	
	INTERNAL ENVIRONMENT individual members parliamentary parties parliamentary committees rules of procedure
Valued by:	members of parliament party political elites

The key relationships which will be analyzed in this study are listed in Figure 1. It should be stressed that these yield no simple formula for measuring overall parliamentary institutionalization. Just as institutionalization of democracy means institutionalization of its constituent organizations or 'partial institutional regimes', so here the study of parliamentary institutionalization will be evaluated through the study of several aspects (internal and external) of parliamentary life. Within any single study, there is obviously a degree of arbitrariness in choosing among the critical topics for evaluation. Several aspects of the parliaments' external environments often included in the studies of parliamentary institutionalization, such as administrative structures and the judiciary, or the internal environments, such as the parliaments' bureaucracies, are for the most part left out of our analysis.

All of these dimensions are, of course, very important. The relationships between parliaments and the judiciary system, for example, mirrors the degree of horizontal accountability between state institutions and, hence, the nature of democracy in a given polity. Similarly, parliament's capacity for autonomous action, especially in policy-making, depends to a large extent on its ability to employ the resources of the state administrative structures, as well as on the level of development of its own professional bureaucracy. Although we do not specifically focus on any of these dimensions, they will be referred to occasionally in all empirical chapters, and especially in the chapter devoted to the relationship between parliaments and governments (Chapter 4).

Citizens' perceptions of parliaments and their activities - another dimension through which parliamentary institutionalization might be analyzed are not included in this study either. As is apparent from Figure 1, the focus throughout this study is restricted to elite perceptions. In this respect, the study conforms to the now well- established theoretical tradition in democratization literature, which emphasizes the role of political elites in the processes of political change (e.g. Burton, Gunther and Higley, 1992). Certainly, parliaments are the highest and most visible representative bodies. They do reflect citizens' preferences more than any other state institutions. It is arguable that, especially in new democracies, parliaments ought to promote public confidence that they are capable of expressing and resolving political conflicts. They should be grounded in their constituency (an aspect which we shall analyze in great detail in Chapter 3), and they should be accorded widespread public support and confidence. In this sense, public evaluation of parliaments is critical for their level of institutionalization and it explains why Sisson included it in his concept.

However, if it is to be of a great theoretical significance, such support and trust should be diffused; that is, reflecting long-term influences based on citizens' cumulative experiences with the institution, rather than merely reflecting short-term (dis)satisfaction with their performance (see Loewenberg and Patterson, 1979). This distinction underscores the complexity of public support for representative institutions and its often ambiguous character. Indeed, the few studies conducted so far show that the generally low public confidence in the Central European parliaments is substantially influenced by citizens' current experiences, in particular by their feelings about the economic situation (see Hibbing and Patterson, 1994; Plasser, Ulram and Waldrauch, 1998; Miller, White and Heywood, 1998). At the same time, only a few Eastern Europeans would prefer their political system to be without a viable parliament (see Mishler and Rose, 1994). Thus, while it is reasonable to expect the public's confidence in the Czech and Slovak parliaments to fluctuate sharply during the period we studied (in itself not an insignificant phenomenon), we shall treat both institutions as essentially desired and grounded in the citizens' democratic conceptions, and will focus on elite conceptions only.

Plan of the Book

The set of topics outlined in Figure 1 forms the basic structure of this study. Each of the items listed represents a more or less separate research topic addressed in the study. The analysis of, and the sum of evidence brought to, these separate topics should then help us to paint a broad picture of both the direction and degree of parliamentary institutionalization, as well as the level of democratic consolidation in the Czech and Slovak Republics.

To lay the basis for that inquiry, we start with background material in Chapter 2. In this chapter we will concentrate on the origins of the modern Czech and Slovak parliaments and democracy, and investigate the basis for the institutional designs within which the Czech and Slovak parliaments began to function at the end of 1992. In particular, we will analyze the process of constitution-making in both countries, looking at the role played by parliament, institutions and political elites, and assessing the extent to which various competing models of democracy provided relevant starting points. We will also analyze both the pre-communist and the communist institutional traditions and the relevance of these for the new institutional structures, and assess the willingness of political elites to draw lessons from institutional, and particularly parliamentary, experiences within the established Western democracies. By the very nature of its focus, the chapter provides an overview of the institutional and democratic development between 1989 and 1992.

Chapter 3 is directly concerned with the institutionalization of parliaments. It is focused on the relationships between the Czech and Slovak parliaments and the electorate. It addresses the complexity of these relationships - often called 'representation' - from several different perspectives. The electoral system - the crucial channel by which popular preferences become translated into parliamentary and executive influence - is analyzed first, with particular attention to the type of electoral formula adopted and the reasons for the choice of systems and modifications thereof. The second section concentrates on representational links between individual parliamentarians and the electorate. It explores parliamentarians' own perceptions of their role in parliament and of their priorities as representatives. The chapter concludes with an analysis of the development of political parties - the collective agencies that link citizens with parliaments. It focuses on the organizational development of parties at the grass-roots level, thus exploring their ability to represent their constituencies.

The fourth and fifth chapters focus on the relationships between the parliaments and their respective executives in both countries. Chapter 4 analyzes the relationships between parliaments and governments, using an exploratory framework based on models initially developed by Anthony King. It looks at the appointment of cabinet ministers and the process of government formation and investigates the role of parliamentary parties, the various institutional links that exist between government and parliament, the role of parliamentary committees, and the powers of the House, tracing the overall effect of all of these factors on parliamentary institutionalization. Chapter 5 analyzes the position of the state presidents in executive-legislative relations, and their role in the political process more generally. It too traces the overall effect of presidential activities on parliamentary institutionalization

The final empirical chapter, Chapter 6, explores the developments inside the new parliaments. It is thus the chapter which is most directly concerned with the institutionalization of the internal functioning of parliaments. It complements Chapter 4, with its focus on government formation and parliamentary committees, and discusses the organization and behavior of parliamentary parties and their relationship both with individual parliamentarians and with extra-parliamentary party organizations. It examines the degree of party cohesion in parliament and the procedures which have been adopted to enhance internal discipline. It also assesses the extent to which parliamentary parties enjoy policy-making autonomy; the rules and regulations regarding state subventions for political parties; and the extent to which these factors are geared toward the parliamentary party in particular.

Chapter 7 summarizes the empirical material presented in the preceding chapters and, building on all these findings, provides a comparative analysis of the processes of parliamentary institutionalization and democratic consolidation in both countries. It emphasizes elements of our empirical inquiry that are generalizable and of a broader theoretical significance. The first section provides a summary of main findings on the process of parliamentary institutionalization, evaluating both its overall direction as well as its degree. The next section provides a closer look at the system level of emerging Czech and Slovak democracies and, using the definitions outlined in the first chapter, assesses the process of democratic consolidation. Finally, using theoretical insights from the democratization literature, the third and final section then focuses on possible explanations for the different trajectories of parliamentary institutionalization and democratic consolidation these two countries experienced.

Notes

1. On the decline of parliaments thesis see Norton (1990) and also a study by Damgaard (1994), which explicitly disputes the thesis with empirical material from Scandinavian countries.

2. Note that none of the Eastern European countries under communism abandoned parliaments, even though parliaments were subordinated to the party apparatus to the point of functional irrelevance and, most importantly, the prevailing ideology could easily have justified their replacement by another institution. The facade of democracy, linked to a parliament and the related concept of representation, was deemed necessary even for the communist leadership.

3. Specifically for communist legislatures, Nelson (1982:11) summarized these functions as follows: symbolic linkage function; educational and socialization activities designed to promote public support for the regime; the integration of diverse nationalities and social strata in one state; elite recruitment and training; and (a minimum of) law-affecting activities.

4. See studies by Liebert (1990), Close (1995), Ágh (1993), Norton and Olson (1996), Olson (1997). According to Liebert, for example, parliaments are the 'central' site in democratic consolidation due to three key functions they perform: first, the integration of political and social forces in the country; second, peaceful conflict regulation among the main political actors, providing the basis for effective decision-making capacity and governability of the new regime; and finally, building support among public at large. Close argued that (some) Latin American legislatures in the 1980s helped to reverse the region's long history of

centralized authority and executive dominance, because ambitious politicians turned parliament into an institution capable of challenging the agenda of the hitherto invincible executive.

5. The modernization paradigm focused on structural preconditions of democracy. It connected the emergence and sustainability of democracy to a certain level of economic development, of high level of literacy, education and urbanization, the existence of middle classes and the presence of civic culture. Influential studies by Lipset (1960) on the relations between levels of wealth and levels of democracy, Moore (1965) on the relations between the social structure and democracy, and Almond and Verba (1963) on the relations between political culture and the functioning of democratic institutions are classic examples of such approaches. For a more modern version see Rueschemeyer, Stephens and Stephens (1992).

6. The first theoretical position of the transition school was formulated by Rustow (1970) in his critique of the modernization school. He suggested that a) elite commitment to a democratic transition was (the only) necessary requirement for democracy, and b) that such a commitment was often a result of a stalemated conflict (rather than an intrinsic attachment to democracy) for which a democratic system was the only solution. See also O'Donnell and Schmitter (1986); Schmitter and Karl (1992). Studies by Lijphart (1990), Linz (1994) and Sartori (1994) are good examples of debates focusing on the link between political stability and the choice of institutional regimes.

7. For example, Lijphart and Waisman (1996:243) conclude a comparative exploration of institution-building in Latin America and Eastern Europe with a note that "it makes sense to think of structural and actional approaches as complementary rather than mutually exclusive" (see also Lipset et al., 1993; Pridham and Lewis, 1996).

8. It should be noted, however, that the agreement may only prove temporary. Transitions are dominated by actors making contingent and often highly unconstrained choices; their result is, therefore, uncertain (see Przeworski, 1991).

9. For a fuller discussion, applying the concept of transition to Czechoslovakia see Dvořáková and Kunc (1992).

10. These minimal procedural requirements usually refer to some form of Robert Dahl's list of eight institutional requirements for the existence of polyarchy (see Dahl, 1971). The definition of democracy often used in comparative democratization literature is also one offered by Schumpeter, who saw democracy purely in terms of elite competition for people's votes, and thus delimited democracy in terms of the existence of free elections (Schumpeter, 1976).

11. Who exactly are the most significant or relevant groups and political actors is nevertheless a moot point. Democratization literature often considers political parties and large interest groups as the main players, with the subsequent complaints that various civil society movements and associations are ignored even if their relative importance in a new democracy is significant.

12. Note that the author specifically refers in this quote to Italy, Japan and India.

13. Indeed, it is striking to see that many scholars tend to apply Huntington's concept mainly to particular institutions, for example competitive elections (see Özbudun, 1987), and not to political systems as a whole. Even where scholars depart from Huntington's original concept and measures, institutionalization clearly refers to organizational phenomena. Hopkin (1996), for example, attempts to define the institutionalization of (new) political parties and the conditions which must prevail for this process to take place (see also Panebianco, 1988). In a similar vein, Mainwaring and Scully (1995:4-5) introduce the notion of an institutionalized party system which must meet four conditions: stability in the rules and nature of inter-party competition; individual parties with stable roots in society; the granting of legitimacy to the electoral process and to parties by all major actors; and the independent status and value of party organizations.

14. Note, for example, that Hibbings (1988) analysis of institutionalization of the British House of Commons presents data on the membership turnover from 1734 to 1984, data on Speakers from 1735 to 1985, and on the number of questions put to ministers from 1847 to 1946. Similarly, Gerlich (1973) provides an analysis of phases of institutionalization of parliaments in fifteen countries during the last two centuries.

2 The Institutional Origins of the Modern Czech and Slovak Parliaments

Introduction

This chapter begins exploring processes of parliamentary institutionalization and democratic consolidation by asking how the new Czech and Slovak parliaments and institutions were created and how they evolved during the first three years of the post-communist period. What constitutional system was initially adopted in Czechoslovakia? How did it influence the processes that led to the disintegration of the federal state? Why did Czech and Slovak political elites prefer certain institutional options and configurations rather than others in their new states? By exploring these and related questions, the chapter provides an overview of the key problems in the process of constitution-making in Czechoslovakia and the Czech and Slovak Republics between 1989 and 1992. Although still fresh in our memories, this period already constitutes a part of Czechoslovak history. In a sequence of crucial events, it involves the period of *transition*: from the breakdown of the communist regime in November 1989 and the ensuing first round of constitutional bargaining to the first free elections in June 1990. It also covers the beginning of the period of democratic *consolidation*, between 1990 and the end of 1992, which resulted in the split of Czechoslovakia, and thus the subsequent second round of constitutional bargaining - on the constitutions of both the Czech and Slovak Republics.

From Velvet Revolution to Velvet Divorce

Constitutional bargaining between 1989 and 1992

The year 1989 was exceptional in Eastern Europe. A single year saw the implosion of the communist regimes in the whole region. Michael Waller

(1993:219) writes: "if one factor is to be selected as of primary importance in the unfolding of this region-wide drama, it is the withdrawing of Soviet support for these regimes." Indeed, abandoned by the traditional guarantor of their power, the communist leadership in the region found it increasingly difficult to cope with the underlying popular dissatisfaction and organized protest that had surfaced with the sometimes reluctant implementation of Gorbachev's politics of 'glasnost' and 'perestroika' in the preceding years. However, although all the communist regimes in Eastern Europe fell uniformly within one year, the change of the regime in each country was to proceed according to the scenario set by the internal developments of the previous years. Thus, unlike in Hungary and Poland where the changes were negotiated between the reformist communist leadership and the opposition over the period of several months, the orthodox Czechoslovak communist regime clung to power until confronted by a mass protest, which it first attempted to put down and then capitulated to in the space of a few days.[1]

On 17 November 1989, the police brutally repressed a student demonstration on the streets of Prague. The popular reaction was immediate and Prague was flooded with thousands of demonstrators. Within the course of a few days, the protests spread all over the country and on November 24, the Communist Party (KSČ) leadership resigned en bloc. Using existing links between dissident activists, students, actors and critical intellectuals, the opposition was able to organize itself amazingly quickly to direct popular unrest and use the revolutionary momentum to press for the end of the communist regime. The democratizers organized in two umbrella organizations - Civic Forum (OF) in the Czech lands and Public Against Violence (VPN) in Slovakia - which provided shelter for a wide variety of groups, many of which had their roots in the opposition movements that had developed over the preceding decades, and in particular since 1968. Both movements started to negotiate with the government on the surrender of communist monopoly of power, more or less simultaneously, in Prague and Bratislava.

The first problem the opposition had to solve was how to implement the envisaged reforms. The decision was made at the Round Table talks to work with the existing parliament, 'purified' of its most discredited members. The 'purification' was carried out legalistically, using as a precedent a federal law under which the reformers had been forced out of parliament in 1968 (Cigánek, 1992; Jičínský, 1993; Elster, 1995). The key feature of this procedure was to abandon the principle of by-election if there was vacancy in the parliament. Instead of new elections, the new law stipulated that for a limited period of time alternative candidates were to be nominated by political parties and social organizations, together with OF in the Czech Republic and VPN in Slovakia. Accordingly, the Federal Assembly, and somewhat later on also the Czech and Slovak National Council and local councils, engaged in a self-cleansing process, whereby between one-third and one-half of the sitting federal and national councils MPs, as well as local councilors, were replaced by candidates supported by the anti-communist opposition.

Concurrently, the decision was made to form a new government which would reflect the changing balance of forces. The first attempt, under the leadership of Ladislav Adamec - the last chairman of the communist-led Federal government - was unsuccessful. The proposed composition of the government was unacceptable to the opposition which, backed by a massive demonstration in Prague, demanded more changes than the modest ratio of 15 communist ministers to 5 opposition ministers seemed to offer. Adamec resigned on 8 December 1989 and two days later, a new government was installed, under the leadership of Marian Čalfa. This was so-called "Government of National Understanding", which included a majority representation nominated by OF and VPN, which functioned largely unchanged until the 1990 elections. The reconstruction of the Czech and Slovak republican governments followed shortly, under the auspices of OF in the Czech Republic and VPN in Slovakia.

Finally, the decision was made to elect a new president. The incumbent president - Gustav Husák - was for many a symbol of the communist repression which followed the Prague Spring in 1968. In accordance with the Round Table agreements, he abdicated on 10 December 1989, just after he had approved the Čalfa government. The debates within OF and VPN on the likely presidential candidate were numerous, producing two strong candidates: Václav Havel and Alexander Dubček (Jičínský, 1993:66). Both persons obviously enjoyed a major moral authority as the fighters against the old regime, but unlike Havel, Dubček was also a symbol of Czecho-Slovak co-existence. In the end, and in spite of his partial reluctance to accept the post, Havel was chosen as the only common candidate of OF and VPN, especially because of his crucial strategic role during the negotiations following November 1989. Dubček assumed the post of Chairman of the Federal Assembly, which, after the first round of recomposition, supported Havel's election as the president of Czechoslovakia. This was done on 29 December 1989, in a nearly unanimous vote, so that only three days later Havel could deliver his first New Year's address to the country. The much celebrated figure of the Czechoslovak Velvet Revolution became the head of the state, symbolizing the irreversibility of the reforms launched just a few weeks before.

An interesting fact with regard to the election of the president was the proposal to change the existing communist constitution to allow direct election of the head of state (see Jičínský, 1993: 56, 68-69). As in Poland and Hungary, the proposal came from KSČ, which hoped that its candidate, the former federal prime minister Ladislav Adamec, would amass more of the popular vote than the still largely unknown dissident Václav Havel.[2] However, both OF and VPN insisted on the president being elected by the Federal Assembly, partly because it was safer and more consensual to rely on the parliament, partly because there was already a deal between the opposition and KSČ that the president should be a Czech (the federal Prime Minister was a Slovak) and a non-partisan. In other words, the opposition insisted on keeping with the procedure enshrined in the communist constitution. This brings us to the second problem which the opposition had to solve: choosing the strategy of institution-building - in other words, the sequence, timing and nature of constitutional reforms.

All the three newly selected institutional pillars - the president, the Federal Assembly, and the Federal government - together with the prominent opposition leaders of OF and VPN, were in a position to force a number of profound changes to the country's institutional design during the Round Table talks. The KSČ, surprised by the sudden collapse of the regime and subjected to continuous pressures in streets, was in a state of disarray, unable to mount any serious resistance to the opposition. Virtually all proposed changes which originated from within the opposition met with no resistance from the old rulers, and when the Communist Party attempted to force their points onto the agenda, they were defeated by the tenacity of the opposition. Moreover, by 1989, a draft of a new federal constitution had already been worked out by a group of Czech dissident lawyers around Pavel Rychetský. If adopted, it could have served as an interim, if not final, constitutional formula (Stanger, 2000). Instead of a radical change, however, the protagonists of the Velvet Revolution decided to continue with the old communist constitution from 1968, only slightly amended so as to remove its most unacceptable provisions.

In this respect, the strategy chosen by the dissidents was aimed at avoiding any radical steps; and they opted instead for a conciliatory approach. The spirit of unbroken legality and incrementalism became the norm, precluding a swift reform of the existing structure of institutions. There were three principal reasons for this. First, the sudden and total collapse of the communist power was not perceived as such at that time; it was difficult to imagine the comparatively conservative Czechoslovak communist leadership would surrender without resistance - something which encouraged moderation on the part of the opposition.[3] Secondly, regardless of the overall consensus within the opposition, its representatives were constrained by the respect for Slovak sovereignty. The 1968 constitution gave large powers to Slovakia's political representatives, who proved ardent in guarding what was perceived to be an important achievement in the long-standing debates between the Czechs and Slovaks.[4] And since the ultimate goal of the opposition was to avoid any actions that might divide them, no further steps were taken to push through radical constitutional amendments (Elster, 1995). Finally, as Stanger (2000) argues, Havel initially does not seem to have believed that a new constitution belonged at the top of the movement's list of priorities. It was felt that neither the restructured Federal Assembly nor the opposition leaders had enough legitimacy to effect any far-reaching changes. This was enough for the dissidents who, because of their commitments to what many termed as "anti-political politics", tended to underestimate formal rules and institutions and decided to postpone constitutional renewal until after the June 1990 elections.[5]

In the end, therefore, despite the removal of the constitutional articles on the leading role of the Communist party, on the National Front as the official umbrella for all organizations, and on Marxism-Leninism as the official state ideology, the provisions governing both the balance of power between different institutions and the overall federal arrangement remained basically intact. Although nobody inside OF and VPN was exactly keen on the communist constitution (Jičínský, 1993:25), its legal framework was adopted in order to provide rules of the game under which a new constitution would be drafted at a later stage. Moreover, as an integral part of the chosen constitutional reform strategy, it was decided to shorten the term of both the newly elected parliaments and the president. Instead of a regular four-year parliamentary term, and five-year presidential term, the president, the Federal Assembly, and the Czech and Slovak National Councils were to be elected only for two years, the period within which a new constitution was to be promulgated. The driving idea behind the shorter term of the newly elected institutions stemmed from he anticipation about the nature of the coming first elections. As was correctly anticipated, the 1990 elections would be more of a plebiscite against the old regime than a true expression of pluralism. The emerging political forces were expected to develop later, and so it seemed desirable to give the first, *status quo* parliament only a two-year term. It also seems that the idea was strongly endorsed by Havel, since he was, at that time, reluctant to serve for four years.

The desire to bolster pluralism was also behind another crucial decision during the transition period, that relating to electoral law. The decision was to change the majoritarian electoral system then in place to a system based on proportional representation which had been used in the pre-war Republic (1918-1939): indeed this was the first time that a reference to the First Republic was explicitly made, whether with a negative or positive connotation, in re-shaping the institutional structure of the country. On one side, well calculating the advantages it offered to smaller parties, both Slovak representation (VPN), as well as the existing political parties (including the communists) favoured a PR system directly from the beginning. The OF, on the other side, was heavily split on the issue. Havel and some of his associates in particular argued for a majority system allowing for the selection of independent candidates and the marginalization of political parties (Jičínský, 1993:99-101; Elster, 1995). In their view, the First Republic was a clearly negative example, both with regard to the potential effects of PR on the composition of parliament and in the sense that it seemed to magnify dissidents' already negative attitudes towards political parties.[6]

The law was eventually adopted, with all the compromises involved. Havel and his followers were persuaded that PR provided more opportunities for a complete spectrum of parties to be formed - something deemed desirable at a time when new organizations were only beginning to spring up. Under a majority system, it was argued, OF and VPN would very likely exploit their then dominant position by winning all parliamentary seats (Jičínský, 1993, Elster, 1995). Moreover, the new electoral law was considered only temporary (i.e. covering just the first free elections) - a fact which fostered Havel's later attempts to push through an alternative electoral system. As the Federal president, he proposed a new electoral law for the 1992 elections as part of a broader package of constitutional amendments presented to the Federal Assembly in December 1991.[7] However, the proposal, and indeed the whole package of reforms, was turned down by the Federal Assembly, and the electoral law that it had adopted on 27 February 1990 has since been used in Czechoslovakia, and the Czech and Slovak Republics, without any fundamental changes.[8]

Finally, complementary to the electoral law, the Federal Assembly also passed a new law on political parties. Geared to support emerging pluralism, the law first of all legitimized and legalized already existing parties which survived the communist regime (satellite parties and the Communist Party). Secondly, it legitimized *ope iuris* the two major opposition forces, OF and

VPN. Thirdly, it made it relatively easy for new parties to emerge as legal entities: a petition with one thousand signatures was required to register with the Ministry of Interior.[9] Because of the prevailing anti-party sentiments, the document was drafted in a rather vague form, leaving aside, for example, much debated issues of parties' financial resources. However, at the time, the lack of legal provisions on party finances was a deliberate choice of the opposition, in order to extricate newly emerged parties, often dependent on financial aid from abroad, from disadvantages in competition with the materially secured Communist Party.[10] Together with the possibility for parties to credit money from the state to finance the electoral campaign, it was further determined that parties with more than two percent of the vote in either one of the two republics would receive 10 Czechoslovak crowns (then approx. 0.28$) for every vote.[11]

To recap, the decision to carry on with the old communist constitution, the decision to shorten the term of parliaments and president to only two years, and the adoption of a new electoral law were the hallmarks of the hectic period of transition. It should be clear from the above that, in terms of the institutional structure, there was more continuity than change. We can now move on to look in more detail at how the outcomes of the first round of constitutional bargaining were, indeed, extremely important in the events succeeding the first free elections of June 1990. Elster (1995:109), referring particularly to the federal arrangement, notes that the 1968 constitution may be "a unique example of a text that came into life only after death - after the abolition of the regime whose affairs it was supposed to regulate." Furthermore, reflecting on the shorter term of parliaments, he argues that it was also an unfortunate decision, partly because valuable time was lost by campaigning before the next elections, partly because the compression of the time horizon carried a risk of political overheating.

Constitutional Bargaining Between 1990 and 1992

The Federal Assembly, and the Czech and Slovak National Councils, were elected in the first free elections on 8-9 June 1990, with a mandate to adopt a new constitution. The landslide victory of both opposition formations made possible a government coalition of OF and VPN; together with the Slovak Christian Democrats (KDH), they controlled 98 seats in the 150-member Chamber of Peoples, and 102 seats in the 150-member Chamber of Nations. The five percent electoral threshold eliminated 16 parties from entering parliament, so that besides OF and VPN, seven other parties succeeded in gaining representation. The Communist Party (KSČ), which gained 47 seats, was in a clearly secondary position. The situation in the National Councils was not much different, although only four parties gained representation in the Czech Republic, whereas in Slovakia, partly due to a lower threshold applied in 1990, seven parties or coalitions entered the parliament, and the victory of VPN was not as overwhelming as that of OF.

In any event, the constellation of political forces after the 1990 elections was suitable for the formation of three stable governments, one Federal and two republican, and thus for embarking upon the far-reaching political, social and economic reforms. The newly constituted Federal Assembly re-elected Havel as federal president in July 1990. However, while significant advances had been made in the field of social and economic restructuring, political developments in Czechoslovakia became dominated by a shift towards division which culminated in the formation of independent Czech and Slovak Republics at the beginning of 1993. The successful attempts to lay down the basis for a market economy were not repeated when it came to solving protracted disputes about the division of powers between the federation and the two constituent republics, and about the relations between government, parliament, and the president. An examination of Czechoslovak federalism emphasizing the constitutionally-determined parliamentary structure, and an examination of the parties and party system formation, emphasizing the nature of politics underlying such institutional structures should help us to understand the process which led to the end of Czechoslovakia.

The complex institutional structure of Czechoslovakia was set out in the inherited 1968 constitution, and clearly reflected a long-lasting attempt to accommodate national conflict between the Czech and Slovaks via a number of institutional devices. It established Czechoslovakia as a federal state, consisting of two separate republics. The territorially based federation was the institutional embodiment of the geographical position of both nations. The state and linguistic boundaries coincided. Both the Czech and Slovak republics had their own separate unicameral legislative assemblies, the so-called National Councils, and both republics had their own national governments. Each of the two republics acquired a relatively high degree of autonomy to run its own affairs within a given jurisdiction. Education and cultural affairs in particular were the exclusive domains of the republics. The constitutional act on power-sharing which passed in 1990 extended the areas of autonomous jurisdiction even further, including, for example, a provision that the governorship of the Central Bank would alternate annually between a Czech and a Slovak.

At the federal level, the Federal Assembly, on whose support the Federal Government depended, consisted of two chambers, differing in composition. The Chamber of Peoples was elected according to population on a proportional basis, and hence had approximately twice as many Czechs as Slovaks. The Chamber of Nations had an equal representation of 75 MPs elected in the Czech republic and 75 MPs elected in the Slovak republic, thereby over-representing the latter. However, while differing in composition, the chambers were highly symmetric in powers. To become law, legislation had to be passed in both chambers, each of which had their own system of parliamentary committees to report on a bill. According to Article 40 of the Federal Constitution, a quorum of an absolute majority of the members of the Chamber of Peoples, and an absolute majority of both the members of the Chamber of Nations elected in the Czech Republic and in the Slovak Republic was required to take a valid vote.

On the legislation listed in Article 44 of the Constitution (including, for example, budgetary and currency issues, foreign economic relations issues, and issues of citizenship), majority rule was prohibited. This meant that if a vote was taken on any of these issues, each of the two national sections of the Chamber of Nations voted separately. To pass a bill - i.e. not just to provide a quorum - a majority of all elected members had to be obtained in both sections of the Chamber of Nations as well as in the Chamber of People. This voting procedure, known as "ban on majoritization", granted veto power to each national representation in the Federal Assembly on a significant number of legislative acts. Moreover, passing of the Federal Constitution, the adoption of a proposal for referendum, and the decision to declare war, all required a three-fifths majority of all the members of the Chamber of People and a three-fifths majority of all the members in each of the two sections of the Chamber of Nations. This left a rather small number (30) of either Czech or Slovak deputies with effective veto power within the Federal Assembly.

If classified, the constitutional formula in the Czech and Slovak Federal Republic provided for a textbook example of a consociational system (see Lijphart, 1977 for definition, and Lijphart, 1992; Henderson, 1995; Kopecký, 2000 for classification of Czechoslovakia). The government was a grand coalition of political leaders of both national segments, the principle of proportionality was embodied in both the electoral system and in the distribution of important administrative posts, the republics enjoyed a relative autonomy to run their own internal affairs, and there was a strong minority veto in the Federal Assembly. This system was for various and different reasons unacceptable to both the Czech and Slovak political elites, not least because they were simply committed to draft a new constitution. As Table 2.1 demonstrates, a number of key constitutional proposals were brought forth between 1990 and 1992, yet the ones that would fundamentally change the federal arrangements were unsuccessful. We need therefore to understand exactly why under a system of consociational institutions, which is supposed to provide a stable democracy in a segmented society, the Czechs and Slovaks pursued a course of territorial separation over a course of state survival. And, relatedly, we need to understand why almost none of the constitutional proposals to fundamentally change the (consociational) system gained political acceptance.

The structure of institutions features prominently among the explanations for the split of the Federation. Pointing to the supermajority voting requirements and prohibition of majority rule, researchers have argued that such an ill-conceived institutional arrangement produced barriers to compromise and demonstrates how institutions can frustrate peoples' hopes (Mathernova, 1993). Another study argues that the electoral law offered many incentives to organize parties in only one of the two republics, which, in combination with the republic-centered system, made the elections nationalistic contests (Olson, 1993a). This author argued elsewhere in detail that it was not so much the institutional system that was responsible for the break-up of the country, but rather the volatile pattern of post-communist politics that underlined it (see Kopecký, 2000). Echoing Olson's (1994a) later analysis, we could argue that while it was unable to prevent the dissolution of Czechoslovakia at the end of 1992, the complicated structure of institutions (essentially the consociational system) largely accounted for its peaceful character, not least because it had integrated all relevant political forces into the system by the time it was to be dismantled. However, as will be briefly shown, the power-sharing system embodied in the 1968 constitution could hardly survive the rapidly changing landscape of the post-communist Czechoslovak politics.

A characteristic feature of emerging Eastern European democracies has been the high level of voters' volatility (see Rose, 1995; Mair, 1997a).[12] Compared to the early periods of democratization in Europe, only a few potential voters entered the post-communist period of democratization with pre-existing party and social loyalties. The existence of such an open electoral market, it has been argued, is likely to encourage competitive behavior among political elites, and hence potentially destabilize the conduct of democratic politics, since there is something substantial to compete for (Mair, 1991). As Geddes (1995:252) puts it: "In contemporary Eastern Europe almost all votes

Table 2.1: Key constitutional and institutional proposals between June 1990 and June 1992

Date	Proposal	Origin	Content	Result
December 1990	competence law	MPs	amendment to the existing division of power between Republics	accepted
January 1991	new parliamentary standing orders for the Federal Assembly	MPs	change of rules concerning parliamentary parties, parliamentary committees, and the chairmanship of the assembly	accepted
February 1991	constitutional court	president	introduce constitutional court	accepted
July 1991	referendum	president	introduce referendum	accepted
November 1991	voting procedure	MPs	changing of voting procedure in the Federal Assembly - lifting the ban on majority voting	defeated
January 1992	"five points" presidential proposal	president	change of electoral system; increase of presidential powers to rule by decree and to dissolve Federal Assembly; change to the rules on referendum	defeated

are up for grabs...[which]...not only increases the stakes and unpredictability of early electoral contests, it also contributes to the unpredictability and apparent opportunism of party behavior." The Czechoslovak case shows that when it is a relevant issue in a given territory, and when other conflict dimensions (religious, class) are absent, ethnicity offers fertile ground for political exploitation, with potentially destructive effects.[13] The Czechoslovak case also shows that the institutional set-up itself can be politically exploited - for in the absence of class and religious appeals, institutional squabbling is an attractive way for the elite to achieve a distinctive political profile (Zielonka,

1994).

The escalation of national conflict commenced with the disintegration of VPN in 1991, and the subsequent establishment of Mečiar's Movement for Democratic Slovakia (HZDS). The popular success of his evolving nationalist message, as seen in opinion polls, made the panorama of the Slovak political parties dramatically different from what had existed before the 1990 elections, when consensus on the maintenance of the Federation prevailed.[14] The Slovak Christian Democrats, led by Ján Čarnogurský, came in 1991 with the vision of gaining the status of an independent Slovakia within the European Community, a move which shocked not only the Czech political elite, but also the (few) remaining pro-federalists within the VPN dominated Slovak government. Later in the same year, the Party of the Democratic Left (the ex-Communists), another major Slovak party, broke with its Czech counterpart partly because of the support it expressed for the more radical national standpoint of Mečiar in his negotiations within VPN and with Prague.

The new parties that were formed on the remnants of OF and VPN, and other parties around them, continued to model identities primarily on the basis of values: visions of the future, constitutional issues, historical issues, evaluations of the communist past and - crucially for the fate of Czechoslovakia - questions of national identity. With the approach of the second elections in 1992, the Czechoslovak party system became a double party system, in terms of individual parties and patterns of competition. Despite the occasional links, parties in both countries were unable or unwilling to come together in common political action. The electoral system, under which votes for parties were counted separately in each republic, obviously did not generate incentives to forge such links, but the fracture was mainly promoted by divergent political realities in the two republics.[15]

The most salient issues in the Czech lands were the character of the economic reforms and the communist/anti-communist debate on who was responsible for the last 40 years and how to deal with this heritage. Thus, while political discourse in the Czech Republic provided a relatively simple left-right duality - something that continues to shape the party system since the split - the main dividing line in Slovakia was between nationalists and federalists, a divide which continues, albeit in a slightly different form (see chapter 7), to shape the party system in the independent Slovak Republic. By the time the split actually occurred, no Slovak political party could afford to be without a clear policy on Czecho-Slovak co-existence, nor could a Slovak parliamentarian operate without making constant reference to his or her national background.[16] And yet they had to compete, and did so with a vengeance, to differentiate themselves and therefore to gain support within their otherwise undifferentiated and volatile Slovak electoral arena.[17] Across the entire Slovak political spectrum politicians and parties were perpetually shifting positions on the national issue, paving the way for the conflicts with Czech political elite, who often reacted in a purely ad hoc manner to new demands from the Slovak side.[18]

Given the historical salience of the national issue and the fact that the issue essentially involved bargaining over institutions, it came as no surprise that divisions along national lines between Czech and Slovak party leaders - and between Slovak party leaders themselves - gradually assumed a strongly divisive character. Within Slovakia, the mobilization of the population based on new interpretations of the Czecho-Slovak relations led to all-too-frequent impasses over already existing agreements. Most of the Czech political parties, while competing among themselves on other issues, gradually started to see the co-existence of the two nations and the ever-shifting positions of Slovak representatives as obstacles to efficient democratic decision-making, as well as a brake on economic transformation. In the course of three years, a debate which had begun with a rather symbolic discussion about the name of the state (Czechoslovakia or Czecho-Slovakia?) ended in a climate of almost total political immobility, adversity and distrust between the politicians.[19]

Moreover, the failure to reach any meaningful consensus on the shape of institutions can be attributed to the fact that the very political institutions that were to be regulated by a new constitution were participating in the constitution-making process.[20] With regard to the Czechoslovak Federal Assembly and the president in particular, one cannot dismiss the feeling that both invariably promoted the interests of their own institution. Although Federal MPs did not propose complete constitutional change, they nevertheless tried to make their Assembly the most important institution in the whole democratic system, especially when it came down to the establishment of various boards and the subjection of other institutions to a tight parliamentary control.[21] This was perhaps understandable, given the legacy of communist parliaments which were nothing more than rubber-stamp bodies that lacked any effective input in the decision-making process. But the attempts of MPs to create an all-powerful institution by reserving all important functions to the parliament only contributed to the chaos and conflict that dominated the political scene in the period immediately before the split of Czechoslovakia.

Federal president Havel attempted several times to strengthen the presidency (see Table 2.1), adamant in his belief that it would ensure efficiency and prevent chaos in the difficult transition period, while other institutions were weak and fragmented. His ultimate failure to advance most of his proposals lay in his flawed negotiating strategy. Firstly, he relied too much on his moral authority, justifying his proposals as an impartial common good. Such was the case with a package of constitutional amendments presented to the Federal Assembly in 1992, which included increases in presidential powers. Without any prior negotiations in the parliament, Havel submitted his five bills, and when the MPs hesitated to pass them, he called on the public to support him. Threatened by demonstrators and discredited by the media, the Federal Assembly buried them. Second, Havel often invited top representatives of major political institutions for talks, such as the prime ministers and chairmen of parliaments, but tended to ignore representatives of political parties at a time when the parties were not only growing apart from each other but were also becoming the most important actors on the political scene.

The Split of Czechoslovakia and the New Czech and Slovak Constitutions

The increasing importance of political parties was confirmed after the June 1992 elections, when negotiations on the future of the common state moved away from the parliaments and commissions to a series of closed talks between the leaders of the victorious parties - ODS in the Czech Republic and HZDS in Slovakia. Neither Klaus nor Mečiar won a majority within the Federal Assembly or the respective National Councils, but both gained a plurality of votes and seats which gave them an absolute veto power over other parties and over each other.[22] Although they differed in goals, a split really did not seem to be the preference of either of the two bargaining sides: Klaus favored a strong federation and a rapid move to a market economy; Mečiar favored more autonomy for Slovakia (in the form of confederation) and a slow, state-led move towards a market economy. But, given pre-election experiences, the tension of the moment, the personalities of both leaders, and the electoral promises made, the final decisions to split the state became the most logical, although perhaps an ultimately undesirable, outcome.[23] Gordon Wightman (1994:61) writes:

> "The dissolution of Czechoslovakia was.....the result of a confrontation between divergent and incompatible beliefs about what was politically

> attainable, between an illusion on the part of many Slovaks that they could gain the trappings of independence (a declaration of Slovak sovereignty, and recognition of Slovakia in international law) while remaining in a common Czech and Slovak state, and conviction on the part of many Czechs that anything other than a federal system was unworkable and to their disadvantage."

In any case, Klaus and Mečiar's agreements to divide the country had to be approved later by the National Councils and the Federal Assembly. And despite opposition from left-of-center parties and opinion polls indicating that a majority of Czechs and Slovaks wanted to preserve a common state, the process of dismantling culminated on 25 November 1992, when the Federal Assembly voted to abolish the 78-year-old Czechoslovak state.[24]

The declaration of Slovak sovereignty by the Slovak National Council in July 1992, which only the KDH and the coalition of Hungarian parties opposed, was another factor contributing to the defeatist mood on the Czech side and the decision of Klaus and Mečiar to proceed with dismantling of the Czechoslovak Federation.[25] This declaration, more symbolic than formally binding, launched a speedy drafting of the new Slovak constitution, the creation of which was driven more by the question of national prestige than by the deliberations and struggles usually associated with creating constitutions.[26] By the end of July 1992, the Slovak government had already approved the draft of the new Slovak constitution, which was submitted to the Slovak National Council, and which was consequently amended at both parliamentary committees and the floor debate (Malová, 1998). Using both drafts from March 1992 (see footnote 16) and the HZDS's draft as the basis, the proposed Slovak constitution stirred fewer controversies among Slovak parties than did the draft of the Czech constitution among the Czech parties. However, as far as its references to ethno-national issues and articles attempting to institutionalize dominant position of HZDS on political scene were concerned, the debates were no less intriguing than, later on, in the Czech Republic.

On the national front, it soon became clear that unlike the Czech Republic, which emerged from the 'Velvet Divorce' as a more or less homogeneous nation-state, Slovakia was left in a more difficult position. While HZDS and, to a varying degree, other Slovak parties wanted to build a majoritarian nation-state, they faced opposition from a significant Hungarian population on their territory, which were represented in parliament by a coalition of Hungarian minority parties. For the entire period between 1989 and 1992, this political formation had been principally in favor of a common state with the Czechs, since it believed the rights of minorities would be better protected within the Federation than within a new Slovak state. During the negotiations on the Slovak constitution, when a common state became more and more an illusory option, the Hungarian parties made their support conditioned upon a constitutional formula that would recognize Hungarians as a separate nation within the Slovak state. However, the Slovak parties were largely unwilling to compromise on what was, from their electoral point of view, a very delicate issue. Finally, they agreed on a formula that uneasily married national and civic principles. The Preamble of the Constitution states "We, the Slovak Nation...", only later to make reference to "the members of national minorities and ethnic groups living on the territory of the Slovak Republic".[27] As the result of these squabbles, Hungarian deputies, together with KDH, did not support the Slovak constitution in the final vote.

As regard the position of HZDS, a large degree of consensus existed among Slovak political parties on the adoption of a parliamentary system of government with a unicameral parliament. However, the HZDS's proposals aimed at shifting the gravity of power from president and parliament towards government. Empowered by a near majority of seats in the Slovak National Council (to be now renamed by the constitution as the National Council of the Slovak Republic), HZDS attempted to constitutionalize its position in power with a strong cabinet model, one which gave many powers to the Prime Minister. Opposed by the other parties, and pressed by the self-imposed time schedule for preparing the constitution, HZDS enjoyed only moderate success. It succeeded in establishing collective responsibility of the government, whereby the entire cabinet must resign if parliament fails to pass a vote of confidence in the prime minister; it also instituted a governmental veto over laws, forcing the president to return a law to parliament for reconsideration when asked for it by government. The most spectacular outcome, however, was the last-minute striking (in the final floor debate) of the president's power to submit bills, rejected on similar grounds later in the Czech Republic (see below), namely that such a prerogative complicated the legislative process under the Federation.

The appearance of these constitutional arguments as a pure power battle was further exacerbated by the somewhat problematic position of Slovak leaders with regard to the use of tradition as a source of constitutional inspiration. While Czech politicians could and did use the traditions of Czechoslovak statehood as source of inspiration and/or justification for their constitutional proposals - which occasionally made their negotiations sound almost like an idyllic return to where the democratic Czechs naturally came from and belonged to - the Slovak constitutional architects maneuvered themselves out of this possibility in the period of heated symbolic and historical discussions between 1989 and 1992. The Czechoslovak pre-war Republic and its constitutional order came to be seen as a tool of Czech dominance - as an expression of Czechoslovak unitarism and disrespect for state sovereignty of the Slovak nation. The short-lived independent Slovak state during the Second World War, and its authoritarian institutional traditions, were seen by many as similarly delegitimizing and too divisive, which obviously applied even more for the totalitarian traditions of the communist state. Moreover, in a climate similar to that of a national reawakening, one can surmise that should they have been used, the references to foreign examples and models would have caused more problems than solutions. Instead, the new constitution refers in its preamble to a remote past such as the Greater Moravia, "the spiritual bequest of Cyril and Methodius", and "the natural right of a nation for self-determination" - traditions which obviously did not yield a simple usable constitutional formula.

Therefore, the final constitution was a rather lengthy document largely adopting provisions from the old federal constitution, such as parts of the Charter of Fundamental Rights and Freedoms and provisions for a Constitutional Court, and partially rewriting and adding other provisions in the heat of uneasily reached compromises (such as the ones concerning executive-legislative relations; see Malová, 1998). Time pressure was clearly responsible for what some observers deemed a hasty and contradictory formulation of numerous constitutional provisions. As a result, the final document was more of an "expedient bargain", to borrow Geddes's wording, rather than a solid constitutional compromise between seriously deliberating parties.[28] Moreover, the tensions between the HZDS government, selectively supported by SNS and SDL, and the opposition, consisting of KDH and Hungarian parties, were apparent not only during the negotiations, but also during the ratification of the constitution on the 1st September 1992.[29] While the MPs of the government parties supported the constitution, many of them more because of its symbolic value than as a genuine endorsement of its provisions, MPs of the opposition parties either voted against or abstained.

Unlike in Slovakia, the process of drafting the Czech Republic's new constitution started only after it was clear that the common state was no longer a viable option, and hence the final version was drafted without any reference to the federal state. The work on the constitution was dominated by proposals from the government commission established in mid-June 1992 (see Jičínský and Škaloud, 1996). This commission included many MPs from the Federal Assembly, who were involved in constitution-making under the Federation. The Czech Parliament established its own commission, which included representatives of all parliamentary parties, and was supposed to set forth alternative proposals to those of the government commission. However, in practice, the government commission played a leading role, acting in some ways almost as a de facto constituent assembly. The MPs in the parliamentary commission concentrated on commenting and on amending government drafts. Compared to the process of constitution-making under the Federation, which was characterized by competing proposals produced from multiple sources, this mechanism contributed to a degree of cohesion and consistency, as few serious alternatives were put forth. Furthermore, compared to Slovakia, Czech constitutional architects had also relatively more time to discuss various issues that proved to be stumbling blocks in reaching the consensus.

The key issues of the debate were the quorum for passing constitutional laws, the scope of the president's powers, the structure of parliament, the territorial division of the republic, and whether the Charter of Fundamental Rights and Freedoms, passed by the Federal Assembly in January 1991, should be an integral part of the constitution. History played an especially powerful part in shaping the Czech constitution. Whether as a result of experience from the previous three years, or because of the democratic traditions and institutions of the First Republic, the past seemed more influential than, for example, models from other countries.[30] However, the past references were made in a different context than that of in the previous three years. Particularly important in this respect were the following: the existence of a crystallized division between the right-of-center coalition and the left-of-center opposition, which provided for two relatively cohesive ideological blocs; and the legal and political problems accompanying the dissolution of the Federation, which presented negotiators with specific problems to solve.

The negotiations on the presidency are a primary example of how the constitution was influenced by recent political developments. Knowing who the likely candidate for the first Czech president was, the coalition parties, and in particular Klaus' ODS, aimed at creating as weak a presidency as possible. The critical attitudes of the right-of-center politicians, which stemmed from the period when Havel tried to push through his constitutional measures under the federation, prompted the coalition to restrict his charisma by institutional means. Moreover, the government, which made its amendments to the commission proposal, feared the creation of a strong executive duality and Klaus personally was, in turn, accused of deleting provisions of the draft. In the end, it was the opposition Social Democrat party that looked favorable to Havel as a person, as well as on the concept of a stronger presidency, and that secured the future Czech presidents at least the right of suspensive veto on legislation. However, the largely ceremonial presidential powers finally embodied in the constitution (see Table 2.2 and also Chapter 5) are a far cry from the strong presidency advocated by Havel, during both his term as federal president, and his attempts to influence negotiations on the Czech constitution in the press and backroom meetings with the framers.

The controversies and discussions around the territorial division of the country ran in a similar vein. Views differed widely from party to party. For example, the representatives of the Movement for Self- Governing Democracy - Association for Moravia and Silesia (HSD-SMS) demanded the establishment of a small number of self-governing units (Moravia and Silesia being one of them) and linked their support for the entire constitution with this question. The coalition parties in general, and again ODS in particular, argued strongly against it, motivated by the negative experience of the federal arrangement of Czechoslovakia. Their preference was for a centralized unitary state, so as to avoid clashes and squabbles between territorial units and the center. No robust compromise could be reached on this issue and the constitution left the issue to be solved at a later debate.[31] As a result, the MPs from Moravian parties were among those voting against the constitution, insisting that Moravians constituted a separate nation with the right to constitute their own assembly and government.

The question of the upper house, perhaps the most controversial issue, bears the hallmarks of political problems associated with the dissolution of Czechoslovakia and their influence on the constitution. The heated debate revolved around two intertwined issues. The most general issue was whether to make a provision for a Senate at all, and if so, what powers the institution should have. The second issue involved the method by which the proposed Senate should be constituted and, in particular, whether the MPs from the dissolved Federal Assembly should automatically become the first senators. While the first question was solved in favor of the upper house, which senators should fill the first Senate remained a largely unsolved question until 1996. The transfer of federal deputies, originally agreed upon by the party leaders in exchange of the federal MPs' vote for the dissolution, was rejected by the deputies of the Czech parliament only few days after the vote that had ended Federation.

At a time when comparable institutions in the world are abolished (Denmark in 1953 and Sweden in 1970), or are subjected to regular discussion of their existence or reform,[32] the question that must be addressed is what were the main conceptions behind the introduction of the Senate in the Czech Republic. The above suggests that the *raison d'être* for establishing the upper house was to accommodate the Federal MPs who, by voting on the bill to dissolve the Czechoslovak Federation, were going to lose their political role. Pehe (*RFE*, 12.11.1993) notes that the parliament's decision to create the Senate was widely seen - particularly by media - as an incentive offered to Federal Assembly deputies to pass the constitutional law abolishing the federation. The federal MPs vociferously argued that their mandates, won in the same elections as those of the deputies in the Czech parliament, had the same value. In turn, the Czech leaders bargaining with the Slovak side on the dissolution of the country feared that their attempts to settle the split peacefully and quickly could be jeopardized by the anxiety of federal MPs. Even after the successful vote on dissolution, when the Czech parliament MPs changed their minds, the federal deputies sent a letter, advising them mildly to avoid rivalry and to accept transfer of MPs from the Federal Assembly to the newly established Senate.[33] Moreover, a situation in which former MPs were made redundant was also uncomfortable for most political parties, since many of their first rank candidates were seated in what was until then the main legislative body in the country. A feeling that they could constitute powerful factions inside the parties prompted party politicians to seek institutional solutions.

Although one would probably not find a strictly comparable example in the legislatures of other countries, this reasoning suggests parallels with the design of bicameral parliaments during the period of extension of universal suffrage and principles of liberal democracy. The European upper houses were said to be "defended as bulwarks against the rapidly encroaching democracy, an essential limitation upon the power of majority" (Bogdanor, 1992:411). The similarity here is that institutional design closely reflected the private interests of its engineers. While the upper houses in Europe protected the interests of aristocracy, the Czech Senate was designed to protect interests of a small group within the political elite. As Elster (1995:123) argues, subscribing to this view, "the making and implementation of the Czech constitution stands out in this respect, as an example of blatantly self-serving constitutional design".

On balance, however, one should not overlook other conceptions and considerations, which were equally important in the inclusion of a Senate in the new constitution. The original idea of Senate came from ODA, a small conservative party, which argued in summer 1992 for institutionalizing a division between public and private law. Inspired by the work of F.A. Hayek, the party argued that the lower chamber should deal with short-term legislation, such as the budget, whereas the upper chamber should consider laws of long-term and structural importance, such as property rights. Both chambers should be elected at different times and by different methods, so as to prevent them from being too similar in composition.[34] The ODA subsequently became the strongest defender of the Senate, even though its rather radical conception was remolded by more functional and political considerations. According to constitutional architects, the main functions that the Senate is supposed to perform are the revision and examination of legislation from the lower house, and the provision of a measure of continuity against sudden electoral swings. The latter was especially important for many coalition politicians who, at that time, could not conceive an alternative to their right-of-center government. A fear that a sudden swing of electoral mood could produce leftist government made them convinced that the Senate could be useful as an eventual counterbalance to it.[35] Therefore, the Senate had different appeals to different groups of politicians and its creation was as much pragmatic and cynical as it was motivated by specific conceptual or political considerations.[36]

Finally, the debate on the inclusion of the Charter of Fundamental Rights and Freedoms testifies to the ideological division between the coalition and opposition. The coalition parties argued that the Charter, in the form in which it was adopted by the Federal Assembly in 1991, was too ambitious and that many of the rights listed could not be guaranteed. Adamant in their liberal-conservative views, the government parties argued that it should contain only the most fundamental political rights, and not specify any social rights. On the other side, the left-of-center opposition parties, many of whose representatives were the drafters of the charter in 1991, argued for the inclusion of the full text of the charter in the constitution. As with the Directive Principles of Social Policy in the Irish constitution (Article 45), though without any explicit reference to it, the compromise that was reached refers to the charter as part of the constitutional order, but does not make it an integral part of the constitution.

Clearly then, the Czech constitution was the product of a political deal made under pressing conditions and within a specific context. It was a deal among parties with competing views which were informed as much by rational calculations as by the exigencies of the moment. Nevertheless, the constitution was adopted (by a vote in the parliament on 16 December 1992) by a remarkably consensual vote of 172 to 6 (with 10 abstentions), and with less of an ambivalence concerning its content and symbolic value, unlike in Slovakia. In his New Year address to parliament, prime minister Klaus said:

> "We reached a comprise tolerable for all sides, and this is why the Constitution was approved in the Czech National Council by a convincing majority. We reached an important consensus among political parties, and this gives hopes for the future that the newly born Czech Republic will carry a minimum of scars and scratches from the initial difficult period of her existence" (Klaus, 1994).

A decision was made to include a provision to the constitution by which any constitutional amendment would require three-fifths of all deputies of the Chamber of Deputies and three-fifths of those senators present - a provision that initially was not favored by the coalition. This meant that in the absence of sufficient political will, dramatic constitutional changes were unlikely in the period to come. Slovakia too adopted a similarly high barrier to change its constitution: the support of at least three-fifths of all deputies of the National Council is required to adopt or amend the constitution or any constitutional law.

However, despite the important differences in the way they were agreed upon, Table 2.2 shows that the Czech and Slovak constitutions produced very similar institutional regimes. Both new republics were established as parliamentary systems of government in which government depends on the support of a parliamentary majority and can be removed from office by a legislative vote of no confidence. Presidents in both countries are indirectly elected and enjoy, at least on paper, largely ceremonial functions. Both judiciary systems include a Constitutional Court. The major differences are in the structure of parliament, in that the Czech Republic opted for a bicameral legislature; and in the plebiscitary elements of the constitution, in that the Slovak constitution provides for referenda (which are possible on all questions except basic human rights and freedoms, taxes, and the budget).[37] Another important difference concerns electoral laws: while the principles (not the laws) of election to both chambers of the Czech parliament are anchored in the constitution, the Slovak constitution leaves both to be specified by law, making them easier to alter.

The comparison with the constitution of the First Republic is telling for the Czech constitution in particular, not only because references to the First Republic were often used in the debates, but also because the new constitution explicitly refers to the traditions of both Czech and Czechoslovak statehood.

Table 2.2: Structure of institutions as embodied in the 1992 Czech and Slovak constitutions: Compared with the First Republic

Institution	First Republic	Czech Republic	Slovak Republic
Parliament	National Assembly; supreme organ of legislative authority; bicameral: Chamber of Deputies, consisting of 300 members elected for 6 years and Senate consisting of 150 members elected for 8 years; Chamber of Deputies supreme powers vis-à-vis Senate	Parliament of the Czech Republic; supreme organ of legislative authority; bicameral: Chamber of Deputies, consisting of 200 members elected for 4 years, and Senate, consisting of 81 members elected for 6 years; one third of senators to stand for re-election every two years; Chamber of Deputies supreme powers vis-à-vis Senate	National Council of the Slovak Republic; supreme organ of legislative authority; unicameral: consisting of 150 members elected for 4 years
Government	supreme organ of executive authority; responsible to Chamber of Deputies	supreme organ of executive authority; responsible to Chamber of Deputies	supreme organ of executive authority; responsible to the National Council
President	Head of State; elected in joint session of Chamber of Deputies and Senate for 6 years; limited formal powers include suspensive veto on legislation	Head of State; elected in joint session of Chamber of Deputies and Senate for 5 years; limited formal powers include suspensive veto on legislation	Head of State; elected in a session of the National Council for 5 years; limited formal powers include suspensive veto on legislation
Judiciary	independent judiciary includes Constitutional Court	independent judiciary includes Constitutional Court	independent judiciary includes Constitutional Court
Referendum	yes: could be proposed by the Government if National Assembly defeated its bill	no	yes: called by the president when petitioned to do so by 350,000 citizens or whenever the National Council resolves to call it
Electoral system	PR for the election of both houses of the National Assembly; PR principle of the law anchored in the Constitution	PR for the election of Chamber of Deputies; majoritarian system for election of Senate; principles of both laws anchored in the Constitution	PR for the election of the National Council; neither principles nor law anchored in the Constitution

The new constitution, however, departs significantly from the old one, for example, on matters such as referenda and the Senate. The idea that the First Republic's constitution be adopted *en bloc* (an idea which was advocated especially by a handful of Czech politicians shortly after 1989), gave way to options based on totally different goals and motivations. In fact, it is hard not to conclude that the reference to the First Republic was nothing more than an instrumental search to legitimize particular party proposals, which had precious little to do with the conceptions advocated more than 70 years ago. The debate on the Senate is a good example of this pragmatic use of history. Thus, while there is no doubt that home-grown traditions played a more important role in the Czech (and to some extent also Slovak) constitution-making process than imported inspirations and models, the influence exerted by both exigencies of the moment and the experiences of the previous three years under the federation should put this legacy into a more balanced perspective.

Conclusions

The national issue dominated constitutional bargaining between 1989 and 1992 and culminated in the establishment of the independent Czech and Slovak Republics. This first phase of constitution-making highlights the importance of decisions made during the period of transition. The Czechs and Slovaks decided, for the reasons discussed above, to continue with the old communist constitution and, in the eyes of many, paid a heavy price for it. However, to subscribe unquestionably to the arguments that see this particular legacy as the crucial factor behind the split of the federation is problematic. The truth is that some kind of quick constitutional bargain involving a new constitution, perhaps drafted by a special constitutional assembly, could have eliminated the constitutional bargaining from the volatile process of post-communist politics. Yet, it is by no means sure that this process would not somewhere down the line have created pressures to amend such a constitution in accordance with changes in the political scene. Equally, it is very unlikely that a new constitution could have escaped the national problem that had always necessitated compromises in the past. And one wonders how different it would have been from the 1968 constitution, which provided the power-sharing framework for the Czechoslovak federation.

In this light, the decision to shorten the term of the Federal Assembly to only two years was a blessing rather than a hindrance, for it is not too difficult to imagine what would have happened if the political stalemate which characterized the Czechoslovak political scene before the 1992 elections had continued for another two years. At the very least, the dissolution of Czechoslovakia indicates that without a minimum prior level of consensus on the maintenance of the system, the institutions themselves will not produce it (Kopecký, 2000). Even consociational system of institutions must be an embodiment of the existing will of the elite to compromise and to arrive at an acceptable solution - at least in order to secure a stable democracy in a segmented society. If the institutions are enforced or, as in the case of the Czechoslovak Federation, inherited, they are more likely to frustrate actors and exacerbate the conflict by providing opportunities for the misconduct of politics.

Although the debates on the new Czech and Slovak constitutions in 1992 were far less loaded and explosive than in the years immediately preceding, this did not mean either legacies that the past were any less influential nor that the particular context in which the constitution was drafted was any less important in shaping the final outcome. The Slovak constitution was adopted in a very short period of time, as a matter of prestige and symbolism, leaving too many ambiguities and too much imprint from the institutional conceptions of one dominant party. Needless to say, time pressure was an equally important concern for the Czech designers. However, the fact that, at the time the constitution was debated, the Czech political scene was already reasonably stabilized made a crucial difference. It provided for a relatively stable set of opinions and ideological motivations, conveniently structured into two blocs of political parties, which were interested above all in forging a compromise under which they were to operate in the future. The fact that some issues were simply left unresolved for the period to come should not obscure the comparatively more solid level of consensus and constitutional consistency reached in the Czech Republic. Thus, while Czech and Slovak constitutions erected essentially a very similar structure of government, the process and circumstances surrounding the bargaining in Slovakia left more question marks as to whether in the future the constitution will command sufficient respect and support from all political actors.

Notes

1. For a fuller discussion of the events that led to the collapse of the communist regime in Czechoslovakia see Wolchik (1991) and, in a comparative perspective, Waller (1993).

2. Outside of Prague, public popularity of Václav Havel grew steadily only thanks to a promotion campaign of OF and VPN. On December 12, for example, the whole country had the first opportunity to meet Havel, as the presidential candidate of OF and VPN, on the TV screen. At the end of 1989, a few days before the presidential election, his candidacy was supported by 89 percent of the population (Herzmann, 1992).

3. Jičínský (1993:22), a participant in the Round Table talks, writes: ".. at the time changes were taking place, the large Soviet army was still on the territory of Czechoslovakia. The old structure, with its frightening police and army apparatus, which the Minister of Defence Václavík called upon as late as 29 November to protect the state and its internal security, was feared for its potential use against those who represented emerging democratic forces". In a similar vein, Calda (1996:166) concludes his detailed account of the Round Table talks: "The OF and VPN side in particular lacked reliable information about the weakness of the establishment's position, and so the compromise reached left more power to the Communists than was necessary".

4. Federalization of Czechoslovakia in 1968 was an integral part of the package of reforms associated with the Prague Spring movement. Slovaks in particular considered decentralization of the socialist system crucial: some argue that " Slovak demands for autonomy relegated the cardinal problem of liberalization to a lesser order of urgency, allowing Stalinist elites in Slovakia to survive behind patriotic rhetoric" (Ulč, 1974; see also Skalnik-Leff, 1988). Be that as it may, it is important to note that the Rychetský's draft of the constitution in 1989 did not contain provisions on the Slovak veto in the voting inside the Federal Assembly (Stanger, 2000), which is precisely what the 1968 constitutional reforms established (see also below).

5. For an excellent discussion on the concept of anti-politics in dissidents' thinking see Jørgensen (1992) and, in the context of Czechoslovak politics, Brokl (1992).

6. Note that the pre-war Czechoslovak Republic was primarily a party democracy, or, as some have it, "the dictatorship of political parties" (Broklová, 1992:74 see also Rothschild, 1992 and Skalnik-Leff, 1988). Party system stability descended from the mutually reinforcing blend of institutional factors and the fabric of Czechoslovak society. In addition to a very stable, albeit numerically restricted electoral base (no party was able to master more than a fourth of the popular vote), the rules of the game actively aided the emergence of strong party politics too. The centrality of parties, especially the traditional Czech parties, was already apparent during the constitutional bargaining in 1918, and it is thus no surprise that a number of constitutional provisions provided for both strengthening parties' position within the polity as well as for the position of leadership within parties. Among these was, first of all, the PR based electoral system, providing for compulsory voting and closed party-ordered lists of candidates. Together with the rules that a deputy or senator must give up his seat should he leave the party during the legislative term, and the deputies' and senators' compulsory membership in a parliamentary party (club), this endowed party leaderships with a formidable system of discipline to ensure unity within their respective party organizations.

7. Havel's electoral bill aimed at dividing the country into small electoral districts in which voters would cast their votes for individual candidates rather than for political parties. The president defended his proposal in the 1992 New Year's speech, arguing that the new electoral law provides for "deepening the link between voters and MPs, and for providing stability and cooperation to the future parliament, government, and the whole political system" (Havel, 1992:139).

8. Note that the law was accepted nearly unanimously by the Federal Assembly, with only Hungarian minority MPs abstaining, due to the failure to include special legal provisions on minority representations. Shortly afterwards, the Czech and Slovak National Councils approved their own electoral laws, which nevertheless reflected the basis conception of the federal one. For more details see Chapter 3.

9. However, the similar Polish law required 15 signatures only, making registration of political party in comparative terms a mere formality.

10. Note, for example, that this was precisely the other way around in Poland in 1990, where the still-strong Communist Party was able to block provisions allowing parties to obtain financial support from abroad, clearly in the hope that it would disadvantage Solidarity and the other newly emerging parties.

11. For more details on party financing in Czechoslovakia and the Czech and Slovak Republics see chapter 3.

12. As more recent studies show (see Kitschelt, 1994; Tóka, 1996), electoral volatility may be slowly decreasing, partly as a result of the emergence of a more stable pattern of linkages between parties and electorates. But during the critical period of Czechoslovak history, i.e. 1990-1992, the parties and party system were in considerable flux.

13. In a very stimulating essay Frye (1992) pinpoints a number of reasons why class and religion, as opposed to ethnicity, could not easily become sources of popular mobilization in the Soviet Union, Czechoslovakia and Yugoslavia.

14. Vladimír Mečiar, nominated by the Public Against Violence movement, became prime minister of the Slovak government in the end of 1990. At that time, he was in favour of a federal Czechoslovakia. Half a year later he began to emphasize national principles and the importance of Slovakia's individuality. In 1991, when he was dismissed from the government and formed his Movement for Democratic Slovakia, the principle of federation was largely abandoned by him. In 1992, Mečiar's party won the elections with a program to declare Slovakia's own sovereignty and full international subjectivity (whilst remaining within the Czechoslovak federation), drifting from his previous federalist conviction toward a sort of confederation. For further details see Flores Juberías (1992), who provides a comprehensive account of the events leading to the split of the Federation, with a particularly emphasis on political parties.

15. A number of social science studies pertaining to sociocultural and historical differences point, for example, to an increasingly different social climate in Slovakia (Bútorová, 1993; Machonin, 1992); to the existence of a variety of cultural stereotypes that inflamed the relationship between the Czechs and the Slovaks (Malová, 1993); and increasingly divergent and paradoxical mass attitudes towards the institutional form of Czecho-Slovak co-existence (Krivý, 1993). For a review of this literature see Wolchik (1994).

16. As the Czech-Slovak conflict became more and more politicized almost all Slovak parties submitted their own drafts of the constitution. In June 1991 the Slovak National Council decided to form a special commission, which consisted of one MP from each parliamentary party and which worked on drafts of the new constitution. As a result, several versions of the draft of the Slovak constitution were submitted for public debate in March 1992, and these served, later on, as the basis for the new Slovak constitution (see Tatár, 1994; Valko, 1994).

17. Note that those Slovak parties which tried to maintain the status quo within the Federation (Public Against Violence after its split in 1991, the Greens, and the Democratic Party) performed very badly in measures of popular support before and during the 1992 elections.

18. The only party with a relatively stable position was the Slovak National Party, which was pursuing a program of full national independence, but even this party had favored a confederal model for the Czecho-Slovak relations before the 1990 elections.

19. The so-called hyphen erupted shortly before the 1990 elections, when Slovak politicians demanded to use the spelling "Czecho-Slovakia" instead of "Czechoslovakia". This alternative, with the hyphen and capital S, was opposed by many Czech leaders. The compromise that was reached included the acceptance of two different names: the hyphen was used in the Slovak language, while the Czechs used "Czech And Slovak Federal Republic".

20. After the June 1990 elections, Federal Assembly formed two commissions to work on the draft of a new constitution. The Federal Commission, responsible for drafting proposals and coordinating the constitution making process, was composed of the MPs from all three parliaments and was chaired by Speakers of three parliaments. The deputies' commission, composed of experts and MPs nominated by parliamentary parties, was supposed to discuss drafts from the Federal Commission. However, in June 1995 after an abortive meeting between political leaders on a new federal constitution at Kroměříž, the members of the Federal Commission agreed that the National Councils should make the decision on the structure of the state. The commission lost its integrative role towards the Commissions of the National Councils (see Jičínský and Škaloud, 1996), and even though it prepared a new constitution to put before the Federal Assembly in Spring 1992, it was clear that it would be opposed by Slovak leaders. Most politicians and commentators were waiting for the results of forthcoming 1992 elections.

21. See Jičínský (1995) and Cigánek (1992), both providing a valuable analysis of the functioning and the role of the Federal Assembly between 1990 and 1992 with a particular emphasis on constitutional and institutional changes.

22. For more details see Linz and Stepan (1996), who provide a comparison of the actual results (seats and votes) with votes needed to veto any significant federal related legislation in the Federal Assembly.

23. The decision to split the country was made during a meeting of the political leadership of ODS and HZDS in Bratislava on 22 July, where both sides agreed to push the Federal Assembly to pass a law to end the Federation by September 1992. They also adopted an outline of how the two independent states would cooperate within the spheres of the economy, citizenship, foreign policy and defense. This decision came after the important vote in the Federal Assembly on 3 July 1992, in which Havel was not reelected as federal president in the two rounds of presidential elections, thanks entirely to Slovak MPs' opposition. President Havel resigned from his post on 17 July, even though he could have remained in office constitutionally until 4 October 1992. One of the common state's strongest advocates was thereby seen to have given up on it. For more details on the process of dissolution, see Pehe (1992a; 1992b).

24. The bill on methods of dissolving the Czechoslovak Federation, which was finally agreed upon by the Federal Government in August 1992, had first been defeated by MPs of both chambers of the Federal Assembly in October 1992. Both HZDS and ODS then embarked on a concerted campaign, trying to persuade opposing parties to vote on the dissolution without calling for a referendum. They finally narrowly succeeded in pushing it through the Federal Assembly with the help of the Slovak Social Democrats.

25. Similar proposal from the Slovak National Council to proclaim Slovak sovereignty was marginally defeated shortly before the June 1992 elections, this time due to the opposition of the Slovak Party of the Democratic Left (SDL). As a result, HZDS made a firm electoral commitments to both declare Slovakia's sovereignty after the 1992 elections and to enact a new Slovak constitution.

26. Note that the Slovak constitution was initially prepared as the constitution of Slovakia within the federal state. This was possible according to the 1968 federal constitution which allowed, in addition to the constitution of the common state, constitutions of the constituent republics (under the communist regime, these had not been written). Some argue, however, that the Slovak constitution that was drafted after the 1992 elections was not anymore formulated as the constitution of Slovakia within the federal state, though still referring to some federal laws, but as the constitution for an independent Slovak state (see Valko, 1994).

27. The draft presented to the parliament in August 1992 began with the words "We citizens of the Slovak Republic", but it was changed in the final version, after discussions in the parliament.

28. For critical views on the Slovak constitution see Tatár (1994) and Kresák (1994). See also the analysis of Malová (1994a) who, using the work of Przeworski, argues that the Slovak constitution was written under conditions which meant it was largely custom-made for one party, i.e. HZDS, and hence possibly unstable in the future.

29. The 1st September has since been a national holiday in Slovakia - the so-called 'Constitution Day' - which is another indication of the symbolic importance ascribed to the adoption of the Slovak constitution.

30. Note that the constitutional model of the French Third Republic provided the primary source of inspiration in drafting the constitution of the First Republic. The scholars agree that the final document also displayed features of the American, Weimar Republic, British, and Austrian constitutions (Beneš, 1973; Broklová, 1992; Rothschild, 1992). The French model contributed provisions concerning the organization of parliament; the American model inspired the preamble of the constitution, as well as provisions concerning the judiciary system and, in combination with the Weimar model, the institution of president; the Austrian constitution was the model for provisions on political parties and civic rights; the British model helped to justify curbing elements of direct and plebiscitary democracy.

31. The constitution states that the Czech republic is to be divided into municipalities and larger self-governing units - regions or lands. However, it leaves this to be specified by a separate law. With regard to the issue of Moravian nationalism, it is important to note that the constitution emphasises a civic rather than a national concept of citizenship, even though it notes that the document was adopted by Czech citizens in Bohemia, Moravia and Silesia. Therefore, the constitution recognizes separate, historically determined regional identities, rather than a national principle.

32. It is important to note here that, regardless of attempts to dismantle or reform upper chambers, bicameralism is still widespread. According to Tsebelis and Money (1997), approximately one-third of the world's legislatures is bicameral, and so are about 40 percent of European legislatures (excluding some Eastern European countries).

33. The letter was reported in the daily *Dnes*, December 5, 1992.

34. The First Czechoslovak Republic (1918-1938) was in this respect considered a negative example, as it had two chambers composed in an identical manner.

35. Note that when left-of-center opposition parties set forth their proposals to eliminate the Senate from the constitution (ČSSD in November 1993 and KSČM in July 1996), a leading ODA politician remarked that "attempts at such revisions originate from the representatives of those political forces against which the Senate was originally devised".

36. This balanced account helps to explain why a relative consensus on the existence of the Senate disappeared quickly after the promulgation of the constitution. For many of the Senate's original advocates, particularly the pragmatists, the institution lost its value once it could not serve their short-sighted aims. The difficulty arising from this was that the u-turn not only polarized the elite, but also gave rise to the widespread public unpopularity

of the upper chamber. Some parties, such as the far-right Republicans and far-left Communists, tried to capitalize on it and used the issue as a tool for strengthening their popular appeal. As a result, four proposals to eliminate the Senate from the constitution were tabled between 1993 and 1996, all arising from the opposition parties. However, the governing coalition did not support constitutional changes, despite sceptical comments from prime minister Klaus, who in January 1993 remarked that he could imagine parliament without the Senate and, in 1994, openly admitted that he would not have allowed the Senate into the Czech constitution if he had not been so preoccupied with negotiations with Slovak Prime Minister on Czechoslovakia's dissolution. Instead, the real political battle between 1992 and 1996 focused on the electoral formula for the upper chamber which, although conceived by the constitution as a majoritarian system, proved to be an inter-party, rather than coalition-opposition issue

37. Note that the Czech constitution does mention, if somewhat vaguely, the possibility of direct democracy. The constitution states in Article 2 that "a constitutional law may stipulate cases where the people may exercise state power directly". However, such a law is not included in the text, and it is therefore argued here that referenda have not been instituted by the Czech constitution.

3 Parliaments, Parties and Electorate: Organizing Representation

Introduction

Under the broad theme of *representation*, this chapter explores the first major aspect of parliamentary institutionalization considered in this study - the relationships between the Czech and Slovak parliaments and the electorate. The particular form in which these relationships become institutionalized in any political system depends on many formal and informal practices and is therefore difficult to depict precisely. Parliamentarians may see themselves as representatives of a nation or of local communities, as policy-makers or as representatives of organized groups. They may see themselves as trustees or delegates. These perceptions or role models can overlap in practice and, moreover, cannot be understood without examining a range of political institutions involved, be that the electoral system or the nature of parties and party systems.

However, given the historical, social and political context in which the system of representation developed in the Czech and Slovak Republics, we can formulate some preliminary expectations about the form institutionalization may take. Electoral systems based on party lists, combined with relatively large electoral districts, are two factors which are likely to strengthen the party machines and prevent MPs from forming links with their constituencies.[1] Rather than being primarily individual representatives of a particular district or geographical area in which they contest elections, MPs may feel more like members of their collective party organizations, with voters conceiving of parties as the principal representative actors. Moreover, even if Czech and Slovak MPs profess strong direct links with their particular constituencies, it is clear that they must also take into account their roles as 'controllers' and/or 'supporters' of (party) government. Both countries opted for a parliamentary system of government and in both countries political parties grew in importance as the players involved in constitution-making, as well as in policy-making. Therefore, the Czech and Slovak MPs interact not only with the electorate, but also with the government and the political parties that form it - a political context which is likely to influence their conceptions and activities in the sphere of representation.[2]

The chapter will check these preliminary expectations by exploring relationships between Czech and Slovak parliaments and their electorate from a number of different perspectives. In the first section, we will deal with the properties of electoral laws, addressing in detail the mechanism by which representatives are selected by the represented, and the historical and political context which determines their current shape. We will be primarily interested in the extent to which electoral systems are indeed geared towards either party or individual forms of representation. This section will also include a brief summary of MPs' attitudes to the electoral system in both polities. The second section will concentrate on a closely related aspect of the relationship between parliaments and the electorate: the role of individual MPs in representation. We will be primarily interested in the focus of representation, i.e. how Czech and Slovak MPs see their official duties as representatives. Finally, through the analysis of their organizational development at the grass-roots, the third part will explore the role played by major collective organizations involved in representation - political parties.

Electoral Systems

In the more than nine years since the beginning of democratization, from November 1989 till December 1998, there were six parliamentary elections held on the territory of the former Czechoslovakia. The first free elections - to the Federal Assembly and the Czech and Slovak National Councils - were held simultaneously in June 1990. The same set of parliamentary elections was repeated in June 1992. Since the split of the Czechoslovak Federation in 1993, parliamentary elections were held in each of the two successor Republics. Early elections to the unicameral Slovak National Council were conducted in September 1994 and regular elections were held in September 1998. In the Czech Republic, regular elections to the Chamber of Deputies (the Lower House of the Czech Parliament) were conducted at the end of May 1996, and early elections were conducted in June 1998.[3] Common to all these post-communist elections is the fact that they were conducted under very similar PR list systems.

Table 3.1 presents the developments and main features of the Czech and

Slovak and Czechoslovak electoral systems from 1918 to 1996. In this period, three fundamental changes in electoral laws were made. The beginning of Czechoslovakia's existence as a sovereign republic in 1918 was marked by the introduction of the PR list system, using closed party lists. The main idea behind the choice of a PR list system was to protect the political rights of national minorities and to safeguard the newly emerging democratic system against an eventual takeover by the radical left's political groupings (Krejčí, 1994). With only minor changes, the system was used for national elections until the end of the Czechoslovak First Republic in 1939, and also during country's brief return to democracy after the Second World War (1945-1948).

For the first elections under the communist regime, held in 1954, the electoral system was fundamentally changed: from a PR list system to a majoritarian system, very similar to the one used in the French Fifth Republic. However, the nomination of candidates, and hence the degree of choice, was limited to the bureaucratic apparatus of the regime, which made elections almost a pure formality. Issued with formal guidelines according to which candidates should be selected, Party committees at district and local levels had little discretion over the choice of candidates, even though the real selection was often accompanied by a good deal of consultation and bargaining (see Pravda, 1978).[4] After the selection, nominees were presented to the pre-election voters' meetings, which were used as a method of campaigning, as well as a means of legitimation for the actual lack of choice on the ballot. Combined with coercive measures to make sure that all citizens would vote, the officially chosen candidates (the so-called list of National Front candidates) were always approved by nearly 100 percent of the electorate, which obviously made the eventual second round embodied in the Czechoslovak electoral law an obsolete formality.[5]

The origins of the current Czech and Slovak electoral systems date back to the early days of 1990, when several Round Table meetings between the Communist Party, Civic Forum, Public Against Violence and some smaller parties put the topic of future electoral system at the top of the agenda. As we saw in the previous chapter, the key issue was a choice between some form of PR system (which the negotiators associated with the power of political parties), and some form of a majoritarian system (associated with the selection of independent and strong personalities). While there was a relatively high consensus among most actors on the adoption of a proportional system, particularly Václav Havel and some of his associates favoured a system that would allow for the selection of independent candidates. As we

Table 3.1: Features of Czechoslovak, Czech and Slovak electoral systems (1918-1996)

Parliament	Year	# of mandates	# of districts	District magnitude	Formula for seat allocation
National Assembly	1918 - 1938	450 - Chamber of Deputies: 300 - Senate: 150	- Chamber of Deputies: 23 - Senate: 13	6-24	Hare quota in districts; redistribution on national level (Droop quota + largest remainders)
National Assembly (from 1968: Federal Assembly)	1954 - 1989	368 from 1968: - Chamber of Nations: 150 (75 Cz/75 Sk) - Chamber of People: 150 (100 Cz/50 Sk)	368 from 1968: 300	1	majority in single-member districts; two best candidates in second round: majority
Federal Assembly	1990	- Chamber of Nations: 150 (75 Cz/75 Sk) - Chamber of People: 150 (101 Cz/49 Sk)	12 (8 ČR; 4 SR)	36640	Droop quota in districts; redistribution at republic level (Droop quota + d'Hondt for remaining seats)
	1992	- Chamber of Nations: 150 (75 Cz/75 Sk) - Chamber of People: 150 (99 Cz/51 Sk)	see 1990	see 1990	see 1990
Czech National Council	1990	200	8	13-40	Droop quota in districts; redistribution at republic level (Droop quota + d'Hondt for remaining seats)
	1992	200	8	13-41	see 1990
Chamber of Deputies of the Parliament of the Czech Republic	1996	200	8	14-41	see 1990
Slovak National Council	1990	150	4	12-50	Hare quota in district; redistribution at republic level (Droop quota + d'Hondt for remaining seats)
	1992	150	4	12-50	see Federal Assembly 1990
National Council of Slovak Republic	1994	150	4	12-50	see 1992

Parliament	Year	Legal threshold	Ballot structure	Submission of electoral lists
National Assembly	1918 - 1938	only for national redistribution: 1 mandate or 20,000 votes in any district	closed party lists	registered political parties
National Assembly (from 1968: Federal Assembly)	1954 - 1989	-	effectively only one candidate per district	bureaucratic power apparatus of the regime
Federal Assembly	1990	5% in either republic	ordered party lists; max. of 4 preferential votes; majority of those who used preferential votes needed to move up on the list	parties, movements or coalitions of 10,000 members or 10,000 signatures or combination of both
	1992	5% for individual party; 7% and 10% for coalitions of 2-3 or more parties respectively in either republic	ordered party lists; max. 4 preferential votes; 3% of party vote in district needed to move on the list	see 1990, except for parties already represented or parties polling 10,000+ votes for Chamber of People in 1990
Czech National Council	1990	5% nationally	see Federal Assembly 1990	see Federal Assembly 1990
	1992	5% for individual party; 7%, 9% and 11% for coalition of 2, 3 or more parties respectively	ordered party lists; max. 4 preferential votes; 15% of party vote in district needed to move on the list	see Federal Assembly 1990, except parties already represented or polling 10,000>votes for the Czech National Council in 1990
Chamber of Deputies of the Parliament of the Czech Republic	1996	see 1992	ordered party lists; max. 4 preferential votes; 10% of party vote in district needed to move on the list	registered parties or coalitions
Slovak National Council	1990	3% nationally	see Federal Assembly 1990	parties, movements or coalitions of 1,000 members or 1,000 signatures or combination of both
	1992	5% for individual party; 7% and 10% for coalition sof 2-3 or more parties respectively	see Chamber of Deputies of the Parliament of the Czech Republic 1996	parties, movements or coalitions of 10,000 members or 10,000 signatures or combination of both, except of parties already represented in the Slovak National Council
National Council of Slovak Republic	1994	see 1992	see 1992	see 1992

Sources: electoral laws; Broklová (1992); Krejčí (1994)

Notes: despite similar numbers, district magnitude in all elections since 1990 has not been pre-fixed, but is calculated according to the actual participation of voters in the elections.

also saw, for several reasons the final decision was to adopt a list PR system, which marked not only the return to free democratic elections, but also to the PR list system of the pre-war republic. However, the reference to the previous democratic tradition, which was present throughout the debates, was not strong enough to lead to an identical electoral system. In fact, the First Republic was often used as a negative example of the political consequences of the list PR systems by those politicians and academics arguing for a majoritarian electoral system. Therefore, once the few proponents of a majoritarian system lost to those favouring a PR system, the designers of the new electoral law remained under pressure to take into account some of the grievances against PR list systems, including those used in the First Republic. This can be seen most clearly in three key aspects of the new electoral system: the formula for seat allocation, the legal threshold, and the ballot structure.

Compared to the electoral system of the pre-war republic, which used the Hare quota in districts for the first-tier distribution of seats, the new federal electoral system introduced the Droop quota. The reason for this change was to minimalize the number of seats going to the second tier for redistribution on the national level, and hence to decrease the role of party organizations in influencing candidate selection at the latter stage of the electoral process.[6] The same formula was adopted in the 1990 Czech National Council elections, and it has remained for both the 1992 and 1996 elections. The Slovak National Council still used the Hare quota in the districts for the first free elections in 1990, but introduced the Droop quota for the 1992 elections and the early elections in 1994. In practice, the number of mandates redistributed through the second tier has indeed decreased. In the 1992 elections to the Chamber of Deputies of the Federal Assembly, 15 mandates for the parties in the Czech Republic, and seven mandates for the parties in the Slovak Republic were left undistributed after the first scrutiny. Our own recalculation of the electoral results, using the Hare quota instead of the Droop quota, shows that the number of mandates allocated in the second-tier would have risen to 26 and 12 respectively. Thus, while distribution with the Droop quota left 22 unallocated seats after first scrutiny for the whole 150-members Chamber of Deputies, the Hare quota would have left a total of 38 seats.

The second innovation to the electoral system concerned the legal threshold.[7] While the legal threshold in the First Republic was negligible (see Table 3.1), fostering a fragmented multi-party system, it was set at five percent of the votes for the 1990 elections to both the Federal Assembly and the Czech National Council. Behind the introduction of the threshold was obviously an attempt to avoid excessive fragmentation of parliaments. The actual percentages were probably influenced by foreign examples, specifically that of neighboring Germany. Furthermore, four or five percent is now widely seen as a judicious level at which the smallest parties are eliminated, while the PR principle remains basically intact (Lijphart, 1992). However, in 1990 the hurdle for parties to enter the Slovak National Council was only three percent, which was determined as a result of two internal political considerations rather than by external models. The three percent requirement was seen as a safety measure to securing representation of the Hungarian minority, whose representatives were in fact the strongest opponents of the use of the five percent threshold for the elections to the Federal Assembly at the time the new law was discussed. In the same vein, the three percent hurdle was supposed to provide for the representation of the pre-war Democratic Party, which was trying to re-establish itself on the Slovak political scene, and which had at that time some support among new Slovak political elite.

With regard to the fragmentation of parliament, practice only partly confirmed the expectations of the designers of the electoral system. In terms of electoral results in 1990, the number of parties gaining representation in the Federal Assembly and both National Councils was indeed low: eight parties in the Federal Assembly, four and seven parties in the National Councils respectively. In addition to the effect of the legal threshold, the results were also highly influenced by the character of the 1990 elections itself. They assumed the character of referenda on the rejection of the old regime, and voters, instead of splitting their votes among a number of competing parties, voted for the OF and the VPN or one of the traditional parties. It was solely due to the lower threshold that more small parties gained representation in the Slovak National Council, including the Democratic Party and the Hungarian minority parties. However, the picture changed quickly. Instability on the level of individual parties, movements, and coalitions elected in 1990 and their subsequent splits and mergers, produced highly fragmented parliaments. As against the initial eight parliamentary parties in the Federal Assembly in 1990, for example, MPs were organized in no less than 16 parliamentary parties at the end of 1991.

The way in which the three parliaments functioned during the period 1990-1992, in particular the process of parties' splits and mergers, led to important changes in legal thresholds for subsequent elections. As can be seen from Table 3.1, the basic five percent requirement has not been changed, neither for elections to the Federal Assembly in 1992, nor for the National Council or the Chamber of Deputies in the Czech Republic in 1992, or 1996 respectively. This said, we can see that the Slovak National Council increased the threshold for individual parties to the level of five percent, making the threshold comparable, and legal thresholds for coalitions of parties were introduced for elections to all three parliaments. This measure of electoral engineering was taken to increase the price of tricky pre-electoral calculations, whereby small parties joined to form electoral coalitions, passed the five percent threshold, and once in the parliament split again into a number of small parties, thus producing a fragmented parliament through the backdoor.

Although this has arguably changed the strategies of individual parties, at least in that the party leaders have been more conscious of the eventual pay-offs of opting for an electoral coalition, the outcomes with respect to the fragmentation of parliamentary representation have not been as straightforward as was hoped. Prior to the 1992 elections, there were already numerous debates on the status of the Liberal Social Union in the Czech Republic, in particular whether it should stand as an electoral coalition of three parties (where it would face a nine percent threshold), or a new unified party (five percent threshold). And while the decision was taken by the Electoral Commission to allow the LSU to contest elections as a single party, shortly after it was elected, the Union broke down precisely into those three smaller parties.[8] Moreover, the Slovak elections in 1994 showed that, where bigger parties are willing, small parties can avoid costly electoral coalitions by placing their candidates on the lists of electorally safe parties (without forming official coalitions). The 18 parties and electoral coalitions which registered for the 1994 elections in fact represented 31 parties and movements. The seven political groups which gained seats in the Slovak parliament represented as many as 16 political parties and movements (Zemko, 1995; Malová, 1995b).[9]

The third important innovation of the electoral system concerned the ballot structure. Compared to the system used in the First Republic, which utilized closed lists of candidates ordered by political parties, the new Czech and Slovak electoral laws provided voters with the possibility of altering the proposed lists by casting preferential votes. This change has been a clear concession to those arguing for a more personalized act of voting. As can be seen from Table 3.1, the rules concerning preferential votes have been subject to changes and variations between the three parliaments. The basic provision that voters can use a maximum of 4 preferential votes has remained intact for elections for all parliaments since 1990. However, there were changes in the number of votes needed for the candidate to move up on the list. In the three parliaments in 1990, the requirement was as follows: a minimum of 10 percent of voters for a party in a district must use their preferential vote in order for these votes to be taken into account (first threshold). If this condition was satisfied, the candidate who obtained preferential votes from a *majority of voters for his/her party who used them* secured the first seat (second threshold). Given that voters could cast four preferential votes, this means that four candidates could theoretically move up on the list. While the first condition (threshold) remained intact in all electoral laws ever since, the second threshold condition was changed in the subsequent elections in 1992, and the current electoral laws in both the Czech and Slovak Republics are stricter, stipulating that at least *10 percent of his/her party's total vote* in the district are needed for a candidate to move up on the proposed list.

The experience from all elections indicates that the use of preferential votes has so far been relatively positive for those who hoped it would personalize the voters' selection of candidates. Firstly, there has been an increase in the use of preferential votes between elections: Krejčí (1994) reports that Czech and Slovak voters in the 1992 elections used them more than in 1990, and the Slovak voters more so than the Czech voters. Secondly, and as the available evidence shows, there were numerous cases in the Czech and Slovak parliaments (National Councils) when preferential votes altered original ranking of candidates and this was again, in relative terms, more so in Slovakia than in the Czech Republic. In Slovakia, the 1990 elections saw 13 (out of 150) MPs elected thanks to preferential votes, 9 MPs in 1992, and in 1994 it was 10 deputies. In the Czech Republic, 17 (out of 200) MPs were carried in by preferential votes in 1990, 13 in 1992, and only one in 1996.

At times, the results of preferential voting were upsetting for some candidates and political parties. In the 1990 election, for example, voters were largely unaware of the candidates of the democratic opposition. In order to promote their campaign, both OF and VPN placed a number of well-known popular artists and actors on their lists but, because of their unwillingness to serve as MPs, located them low on the list. To the surprise of many, voters allocated them sufficient preferential votes so as to guarantee them seats in parliament. Very shortly after the election, a number of such "accidentally" elected MPs resigned their mandate and were replaced by those more willing to serve, but less popular. Similarly, the 1994 elections in Slovakia caused a small embarrassment for the coalition Common Choice (SDL and two other parties). The pre-electoral arrangement between participating parties guaranteed places high on the list for the leaders of smaller partners of SDL. To their surprise, some of these 'safe' candidates were eliminated by preferential votes, which were largely allocated to the better-known and established candidates of SDL placed lower on the list.

However, the evidence also shows that while the voters' more active use of preferential votes may have increased the likelihood of candidates being elected in a different order from that on the list, the number of candidates actually jumping the list has not increased at all. The fact that voters cast preferential votes more frequently than in 1990 is not surprising. It follows from their increasing experience with, and the knowledge of, both the electoral system and the candidates. Nevertheless, the preferences seem to be allocated in such a way that they fail to favour particular candidates from lower on the list. The change in the (second) threshold mathematically means that more candidates can jump on the list, but to do so, they need more preferential votes than before. But whether a lack of increase in the number of promoted candidates has been a matter of coincidence or, more likely, the conscious strategies of selection procedure within parties (whereby candidates with the most appeal to the voters are placed at the top of the list and voters thus only confirm a well ordered list) remains open to further investigation.[10]

On the whole, therefore, the new electoral systems devised in 1990 differ in many important respects from the system used in the First Republic. From our relatively short historical perspective, the new electoral system has nevertheless been similar to that of the pre-war period in its relative stability: from the moment it was conceived there have been no changes in its basic structure. Both the Czech and Slovak Republic retained the PR list system, notwithstanding earlier alternative proposals, as well as the division of the country, and the subsequent second round of constitutional bargaining. The changes made to the 1990 electoral systems have not fundamentally altered the basic idea of the law, but more the important details, favouring bigger and already established parties over small and newcomer parties. This has been most clearly demonstrated in the increasing legal thresholds, but also in provisions related to state financial support for political parties. In both countries, the percentage of votes cast needed to qualify for reimbursement of campaign cost has been increased (see part 3.3 in this chapter). Moreover, according to the 1996 election law, parties in the Czech Republic are obliged to pay a deposit of 200,000 CK (about $7,800) in every electoral district where they wish to present candidates, which is returnable only if they pass the nationwide legal threshold.

The direction of electoral engineering seems, so far, merely to maintain the status quo of current political parties which are, understandably, not eager to abandon advantages the system gives to them. It is instructive to see that the threshold requirements, and their changes, have not generated much debate about their effects on the proportionality of electoral results. Without a doubt, the big percentage of total votes which were lost by being cast for parties unable to pass the threshold clause in the 1990 and 1992 elections (to both the Federal Assembly and the National Councils) produced highly skewed electoral results. In 1990, for example, 17 percent of the votes to the Chamber of People in the Czech Republic, and about 15 percent in the Slovak Republic were 'lost'. A similar situation appeared in the elections to the National Councils. In the Czech National Council elections, almost 19 percent of the active voters in 1990, and even more in 1992, gave their vote to parties which did not pass the legal threshold. Clearly, it is not the electoral system *per se* which is to be blamed for lack of proportionality, but the lack of debates on the topic only underlines the expectations which the Czechs and Slovaks have of their electoral system: in theory it should not only provide for the adequate representation of a wider spectrum of interest (i.e. PR principle), but it should also help to rationalize the party system by countering proliferation of small parties (i.e. thresholds).

In the long term, these two desired effects are very likely to occur *if* the Czech and Slovak electoral systems continue in force over time. Voters will then become aware of the full repercussions of the system so that fewer votes are lost and electoral results become more proportional. Indeed, it is striking to see that compared to the 1990 and 1992 elections, voters in the 1994 elections in Slovakia and in the 1996 elections in the Czech Republic, were less willing to give their vote to parties with little or no chance of passing the threshold requirements. In Slovakia just under 13 percent of votes were wasted in 1994, while in the Czech Republic, in 1996, it was slightly more than 11 percent. Moreover, and as said above, the electoral system has produced an observable effect on the parties' strategies, in that small parties merge together or form electoral blocks in order to pass the threshold. And although the thresholds alone can not assure the stability of individual parties after the elections, their existence has nevertheless fostered a climate in which bigger and stable parties are valued, both by voters and politicians.

This all said, it is interesting to see that many of the controversial issues which occurred during the debates on the choice of the electoral system, namely that of the role of political parties as opposed to the role of independent candidates, are still echoed in the views of the political elites in both countries. Survey data in Table 3.2. indicate that, in general, the Czech MPs were satisfied with their country's electoral system (86 percent). The majority of the Slovak MPs were satisfied too, but comparatively less than their Czech counterparts. The cross-tabulation of the Slovak survey population by party revealed a higher dissatisfaction among the KDH and Coexistence MPs. The most frequently mentioned negative aspect of the electoral system by the 'dissatisfied' KDH MPs was that it gives too much power to political parties. The Coexistence MPs saw the legal threshold as too high, which is exactly the aspect of electoral system mostly contested by the representatives of the Hungarian minority since 1990.

Table 3.2: Satisfaction with the electoral system

	Czech Republic		Slovak Republic	
	#	%	#	%
Yes	144	85.7	66	68.0
No	20	11.9	27	27.8
Does not know	3	1.8	2	2.1
No answer	1	0.6	2	2.1
Total	168	100.0	97	100.0

From Table 3.3. we can see that about a fifth of both Slovak and Czech MPs mentioned 'too much party orientation' as one of the most negative aspects of the 1992 electoral system. In Slovakia, this was the most frequently mentioned shortcoming of the system from all arrangeable answers. The same category featured frequently in the answers of Czech MPs but, compared to the Slovak MPs, they were more concerned about the legal threshold. The analysis of open-ended answers shows that this was largely a reflection on the problems of applying thresholds to coalitions of parties, and (as mentioned above) a reflection on the debates and the decision on the case of LSU in the run up to the 1992 elections. Furthermore, a fairly high percentage of Czech MPs (11 percent) mentioned the electoral campaign - as a precursory to the amendments of the electoral system made in the run-up to the 1996 elections. At that time, regulations concerning the length of the campaign and the access of political parties to the media were both hotly contested issues when the parliament discussed small amendments to the electoral law. The changes included rules on the fair allocation of TV time for all contesting parties, as well as stricter rules against campaigning and polling during the last few days before votes are cast.

Table 3.3: Most negative aspects of the electoral system (% of MPs)

	Czech Republic (N=168)	Slovak Republic (N=97)
Proportionality (lack of majoritarian principle)	1.8	2.1
Too party-oriented	19.6	20.6
Preferential votes	6.5	2.1
Legal threshold	22.6	6.2
Electoral campaign	11.3	0.0
Electoral districts	5.4	11.3
Unarrangeable answers	20.8	37.1
No negative aspects	14.9	6.2
DK/NA	7.1	23.7

Note: the survey question was: "What are the most negative aspects of the electoral system under which you were elected in 1992?". Respondents could give up to three answers. Listed are the percentages of MPs who mentioned one or more aspects within the given category.

Table 3.4. shows that in both countries, the principle of proportionality was the most frequently mentioned positive aspect of the electoral system. Yet, while in the Czech Republic this represented by far the biggest category from all answers, in Slovakia the existence of preferential votes was mentioned almost as often. This seems indicative of the general impression given by the data in both tables: the issue of the influence of parties as opposed to the influence of personalities remains present in the views of political elites in both countries, but this tension seems to be more pronounced in Slovakia than in the Czech Republic. In other words, if we combine answers on positive and negative aspects, the Czech MPs display more of a positive commitment to the party influence variables, whereas the Slovak MPs appear inclined to emphasize those aspects of the electoral system favouring its personification. On the surface, this meshes with the proposed changes of the electoral system which have repeatedly been raised in Slovakia since March 1996, and which have been driven by the governing HZDS. The party publicly announced its commitment to replace the existing PR system with either a combination of PR and majoritarian system or, as is the personal preference of the party leader Mečiar, a British-style first-past-the-post.[11] In line with the electoral reform proposal, HZDS undertook the reorganization of the regional structure of the country. The territorial reform, the law of which was passed in the Slovak parliament on 3 July 1996, divides Slovakia into 8 regions and 79 districts - a structure highly suitable for the introduction of single member constituencies.

Table 3.4: Most positive aspects of the electoral system (% of MPs)

	Czech Republic (N=168)	Slovak Republic (N=97)
Fairness	18.5	17.5
Proportionality	44.0	19.6
Party-oriented	5.4	5.2
(Existence of) preferential votes	7.1	15.5
Positive influence on party system	16.1	6.2
Unarrangeable answers	26.8	26.8
No positive aspects	3.0	4.1
DK/NA	6.0	15.5

Note: the survey question was: "What are the most positive aspects of the electoral system under which you were elected in 1992?". Respondents could give up to three answers. Listed are the percentages of MPs who mentioned one or more aspects within the given category.

However, the proposed personification of the electoral system in Slovakia must be seen in perspective. In fact, Mečiar announced his plans for electoral reform at a party conference in March 1996, also noting that HZDS will transform within two years from a less organized movement to a strong and organized party. In seeking to change the current party-list-style voting, HZDS is merely intending to introduce perhaps an extreme measure that will ensure the emergence of two main political forces in the country, one of which would be HZDS. In other words, the proposed electoral reform must be seen in the context of power struggles associated with the polarized Slovak political scene, an issue that will surface in other parts of this study, rather than in the context of differing conceptions of democracy and the roles of individual MPs exhibited by the answers in our survey. In this respect, it is instructive to note that the law on territorial reform was almost unanimously opposed by the opposition, even by parties like KDH which has long been inclined strongly in favor of a majoritarian electoral system. If the 79 administrative districts were to be used in a new electoral law, the way in which they were drawn ensures that HZDS will benefit electorally, with primarily Hungarian minority parties being on the losing end. In addition, despite the existing cooperation agreement between KDH, SDL and DU, their leaders know that a much closer unity between their parties would be required if a credible alternative to HZDS is to be presented under first-past-the-post.

Neither is the Czech Republic by any means immune to further electoral engineering. Although the existing balance of political parties is far more favorable to the maintenance of the current PR system, the results of the 1996 elections produced a constellation of parties that once again made it difficult to establish a majority controlling government coalition.[12] The resulting minority coalition cabinet might of course become an acceptable form of governing, such as during the First Republic. Nevertheless, many politicians and commentators quickly jumped on the relatively easiest (though by no means most predictable) of plans - manufacturing majorities by juggling with the electoral law. And it is likely that debates on a new electoral system will resurface in the post-1998 elections period. However, unlike in Slovakia, the task of electoral engineers in the Czech Republic is more complicated. Chapter 2 showed that the principle of PR for the election of the lower house is anchored in the constitution which, given the existence of many smaller parties in and out of the parliament, makes it more difficult to undermine proportionality. As a result, the more serious debates have so far focused on rehearsing the various measures, such as the further raising of thresholds or decreasing the number and size of electoral districts, which would create the desired effect without a major constitutional overhaul.

Representation and the Role of Individual MPs

The previous section showed that regardless of later changes, current PR electoral designs based on party lists, combined with relatively large electoral districts, are clearly favorable to party-oriented forms of representation. Our analysis of electoral systems suggests that Czech and Slovak MPs are more likely to feel themselves to be members of party organizations, rather than representatives of a particular district or geographical area in which they contest elections. The data on the decreasing tendency of candidates in both countries to be elected on the basis of preferential voting partly underscores a move in this direction, at least from the perspective of voters. However, our evidence also suggested that partially personalized voting continues to be popular among the political elites, and that many MPs in both countries, and in Slovakia in particular, are amenable to extending it. Therefore, what we need to know now is whether these concerns for the personification of the electoral system are also reflected in individual MPs' conceptions of representation.

Table 3.5. summarizes the answers Czech and Slovak MPs gave to an open-ended question: "What do you consider to be the most important task you have to perform as an MP?". It divides answers according to the most frequently mentioned and definable categories. In addition, to give an impression of the focus of representation, the table also provides the

Table 3.5: The most important task of an MP

	Czech Republic		Slovak Republic	
	N	%	N	%
Representation	*25*	*14.9*	*23*	*23.7*
- electorate	17	10.1	22	22.7
- region, district, city	8	4.8	1	1
Democracy, transformation	*70*	*41.7*	*26*	*26.8*
- contribute to transformation of society and economy, building of democracy	22	13.1	4	4.1
- contribute to good lawmaking (in general)	14	8.3	14	14.4
- contribute to a particular policy field	34	20.2	8	8.2
Government	*5*	*3.0*	*1*	*1.0*
- to check on government	4	2.4	1	1.0
- to support government	1	0.6	–	–
Party	59	35.1	40	41.2
- to fulfill the party program	59	35.1	40	41.2
Other	*6*	*3.6*	5	*5.2*
Do not know/no answer	*3*	*1.8*	*2*	*2.1*
Total	*168*	*100.0*	*97*	*100*

distribution of representative tasks that were mentioned according to the question of *who is represented*.[13]

The first striking feature of this evidence is that representative tasks as such were not the most prominent category featuring in the answers from both countries. While fulfilling the party program was the largest category in Slovakia (41 percent of MPs), and second largest in the Czech Republic (35 percent of MPs), "to represent" was in fact the second lowest category in both countries: if we discount the small percentages of 'other' and 'does not know/no answers', only tasks related to the government scored lower. Although MPs could give one answer only, which might obscure the likely finding that representation is *also* important, we nevertheless obtain a clear picture of perceived priorities. Rather than representing their constituencies, the activities MPs prioritize appear to be various forms of law- and policy-making activities (e.g. democracy, transformation), which are especially prominent in the Czech Republic, and 'party programs', which are especially prominent in Slovakia.

If we bear in mind the low priority attributed to representation in general, further evidence on the questions (of focus) of representation can be gleaned from data in Table 3.6. These figures are derived from answers of MPs who were presented with six groups which they could represent and, using a 1 (not important) to 7 (very important) scale, were asked how important it was for them to represent each of these groups. As we can see, the scores were relatively high for each category, perhaps indicating ambiguous perceptions

Table 3.6: Focus of Representation

	Czech Republic (N=162)		Slovak Republic (N=95)	
Group	Mean	Std. dev.	Mean	Std. dev.
Voters in your constituency who voted for your party	6.06	1.26	5.82	1.61
All voters in your constituency	4.68	1.76	5.15	1.65
All voters who voted for your party nationwide	6.03	1.21	5.77	1.53
Nation as a whole	5.15	1.58	5.41	1.70
Specific social or professional groups	3.75	1.95	4.58	1.75
Members and activists of your party	4.98	1.69	5.33	1.73

of what a precise focus on the side of MPs is, with differences somewhat more clearly pronounced in the Czech Republic than in Slovakia. Nevertheless, even these patterns confirm a trend indicated in Table 3.6: parties in both countries are clearly important in terms of representation, whether it is in shaping the most important task the MPs feel they must fulfill (e.g. party programs), or whether it is in their actual focus of representation. While the only constitutionally correct answer to the question of focus is to represent all citizens[14] (in the case of our survey 'the nation as a whole'), we can see that two other categories referring to party voters (in their constituencies and nationwide) were ranked more important.[15]

Referring back to data in Table 3.5., the second interesting finding is that among those few respondents who mentioned representative tasks, less than half in the Czech Republic and only one MP in Slovakia considered the most important task some form of geographical (e.g. city, region, district) representation. At first sight, this sits somewhat uneasily with the findings in Table 3.6., which indicate that voters for the party in MPs' constituency are as important foci of representation, actually with the highest score for importance in both countries. The explanation for this apparent discrepancy, and a further piece of evidence on the role of individual MPs in representation, can be found if we look at the complex relationship between Czech and Slovak electoral laws and the developments in the processes of parliamentary recruitment.

On the most general level, our data confirm what one would expect given the shape of electoral systems: the way to parliament in both countries derives exclusively from membership and activity in a political party. A full 80 percent of MPs in the Czech Republic and 72 percent in Slovakia said they were active in their party before being nominated to the parliament.[16] If we add to this that over 10 percent of MPs in both countries who were not active prior to elections, but had been asked by a party, the picture that emerges is one of clear dominance of the party as a way of recruitment to the parliament. Open nominations or nominations by social groups account for only a marginal number of MPs - a finding which can partly be explained by the fact that only parties are allowed to field candidates in national elections. Therefore, these findings provide us with yet more evidence on both the likely dependency of MPs on their respective party organizations, as well as the increasing difficulty individuals face in obtaining a seat in the parliament without active involvement in a particular party.[17] Therefore, given the hitherto relative unimportance of preferential voting, the composition and ordering of candidates on the list is, from the view point of MPs, clearly a decisive stage in the electoral process and the question of how such nominations are conducted within Czech and Slovak parties is of crucial importance.

From a formal perspective, in neither of the two countries is the compilation of lists subjected to legal control. It is solely a matter of the decision-making procedure inside each political party. Their top-down organizational structure (see below) can probably also best explain the internal party rules that provide, at least on paper, for a centralized selection of candidates for public office. Provisions of this sort are contained in the party statutes of ODS, KDU-ČSL and KSČM in the Czech Republic, and the KDH and HZDS in Slovakia. For example, the party executive of ODS decides by simple majority on the lists of candidates proposed by the regional organizations. The party executive of KSČM decides on the deputies for party organs and other institutions, and on proposed candidates for parliament. The leadership of KDU-ČSL is entitled to prepare the lists of candidates for parliament from nominations made by lower party sub-units, and is allowed to challenge up to one-third of these original nominations. The leadership of KDH in Slovakia proposes candidates for parliamentary elections, thus adding to proposals made by the regional leaders.

In practice, however, the selection pattern in both countries seems to confirm the general observation made in a study of 8 European countries and Japan, edited by Gallagher and Marsh (1988). The authors conclude that while the electoral system does not have a direct impact upon the degree of centralization of candidate selection within parties, it influences the mechanics of the selection process in every country; and that the PR list systems tend to carry with them the need for a balanced ticket. This balancing in the Czech and Slovak Republics has so far ensured that top party leaders, together with the most prominent MPs, are nominated with a clear priority, and often after the significant intervention of the national party. In many cases, top candidates were even parachuted into local constituencies in which they do not live. Thus, apart from the important issue of party centralization to which we return later in this chapter, the main implication with regard to MPs' constituency links is that a significant number of Czech and Slovak MPs contested elections in constituencies with which they have few natural ties and to which they showed little willingness to pay attention once elected.

There seems to be a slight difference among parties, or individual MPs, in one respect, however. Those parties which have a strong territorial base, such as the rural communities that dominate KDU-ČSL in the Czech Republic or the Hungarian parties in Slovakia, do have more pronounced links with localities, which are helped by their established local party organizations.[18] Equally, there is an indication that some of the MPs from KSČM in the Czech Republic and SDL in Slovakia were active in constituency services on an individual basis. The explanation is an historical one, since many of the (ex-) communist MPs acquired their behavioral patterns under the previous regime, where servicing a clearly defined single-member constituency was seen as an important part of a deputy's job. Referring to this transfer of constituency bound mentality to the post-communist period, Jičínský (1995:6) writes that "while being elected on the list of a party, many MPs felt more like independent individuals...rather than representatives of certain political ideologies, bearing responsibility for their execution". Thus, even if these cases are an exception, and even if constituency services do not necessarily exclude other role models or priorities, there are grounds to suggest that some form of territorial representation exists in both countries.

Moreover, a tendency to divorce representatives from their localities is increasingly offset by the nomination process that proceeds once the leaders are safely and often tactically placed in constituencies. The regional and local party offices are generally responsible for constructing the lists in both countries. And the last elections, in the Czech Republic at least, showed that the battle for high places between the sitting MPs and the new candidates can be fierce, often prompting deputies to rush back to their local party before elections and engage in a process of bargaining to secure nomination. In other words, because local party organizations developed with the passage of time, the generally prevailing lack of territorial representation in both countries, with MPs largely selected and active only in the capital cities, may become an idiosyncrasy of the past. This is not to say that the Czech, and perhaps Slovak MPs, will become local case workers, vitally concerned with the promotion of territorial constituency. But a partial decentralization of nominations (the national party veto remains in the rules), which some parties (ODS) granted with the explicit purpose of promoting MPs' communication with their constituencies, may well lead towards more pronounced foci of representation on constituency in the future.

In fact, referring again to the Czech Republic, a shift towards a more active constituency representation can also be prompted by the recent (1995) introduction of generous constituency allowances, which enable and oblige MPs to rent an office in their constituency. The proposal was defended in parliament on the basis of a need to create the conditions for, citing from one personal interview, "a confrontation of a mandate from electors with that from the party". Until this allowance was introduced, Czech MPs spent their constituency week either in an office paid for privately or, in the majority of cases, used the offices of local party organizations. This is something the Slovak MPs must continue to rely on during their constituency week. Although agreed upon in principle and provided for by law, a comparable allowance will not be introduced in Slovakia until the year 2001. However, the question of whether the Czech (and Slovak) MPs will become more active in their electoral district and how they will do so remains open. Judging from the relatively short experience of the Czech Republic, it seems that their constituency role will be of more importance, but only if it can be fitted with the interstices of party: a number of Czech deputies effectively support their own local party with constituency money (for example all the MPs of KSČM), and hence use these resources as an opportunity to develop a personal reputation before the next round of nominations.

Therefore, despite attempts to at least partly support a more active involvement of MPs in regional and geographical representation, it is apparent that the party still holds a dominant position in both countries, and that MPs themselves are not particularly opposed to this form of representation. As a way of concluding this section, let us emphasize that the question of MPs-electoral constituency links in both countries cannot be seen outside the more general tendency towards political professionalization. In our survey, an overwhelming majority of 88 percent of Czech MPs and 81 percent of their Slovak colleagues either agreed or agreed completely with the statement that "being an MP should be a full-time job". Similarly large majorities of Czech and Slovak respondents also stated that they did not have any occupation other than that of being an MP (71 percent and 75 percent respectively).[19] Although other sources of income for MPs are not strictly forbidden (but compulsory to declare), the tendency toward professional deputies and politicians has been promoted in both countries by significant increases in deputies' salaries, introduction of travel and accommodation allowances, and by general improvements in MPs' working conditions, for instance, the new parliamentary buildings. On one hand, the fact that membership in parliament has become a full-time and financially lucrative profession means that Czech and Slovak MPs are dependent on their party organizations. This may well reinforce the tendency shown in Tables 3.5 and 3.6: parliamentarians will see themselves primarily as partisans or (specialized) lawmakers, rather than representatives of a constituency or, in fact, representatives at all.

On the other hand, increasing professionalization also empowers Czech, and to a lesser extent Slovak MPs to perform their representative duties on a more consistent and solid basis. Apart from the territorial constituency link, it also improves conditions for serving the non-geographical interests of various social, religious, professional and sectoral organizations that are increasingly approaching parliamentarians at their principal workplace. Therefore, professionalization can, in this way, enable MPs to look beyond the confines of their party, and to develop an independent source of expertise, information and even popularity. Data in Table 3.5 does not strongly indicate that such an activity features on the list of MPs priorities. But one should bear in mind that, at the time of our survey, lobbying in parliament was a relatively rare occurrence, which increased in fashion and practice only as the associative system in both countries developed at least some organizational potential to challenge or circumvent the still-dominant party mode of representation.

Representation and the Role of Political Parties

The previous two sections showed that Czech and Slovak voters vote (at least in the national elections) for political parties. The focus of MPs' representation are voters of their own parties. The parties and their programs are crucial for shaping the task of most of the Czech and Slovak MPs in their work in parliament. Inevitably, then, we must now turn to focus on political parties in more detail, by analyzing their organizational features. Parties as organizations comprise different elements, each of which interacts with all of the others (see Katz and Mair, 1994). Our discussion will be primarily focused on the organization of Czech and Slovak parties 'on the ground' as this is the aspect most obviously relevant to the question of representational links between parliaments and electorate. The party 'on the ground' will be taken to include the members - both direct members as well as indirect members.

Furthermore, we shall distinguish between three categories of parties: continuous parties; revived parties; and newly emerged parties. These three categories, as we shall see, are relevant to the party organizational development on the ground. The classification is based on one criterion - the parties' source of organization.[20] The category *continuous parties* includes organizations whose history goes back to the pre-communist period and, most importantly, parties whose organizational continuity was not disrupted by the communist regime (examples include KSČM and KDU-ČSL in the Czech Republic and SDL in Slovakia). The category *revived parties* stands somewhere between the continuous parties and the newly emerged parties. If we apply the organizational criterion strictly, they would appear in the category of newly emerged parties, since their organizational existence was inhibited by the communist regime. The term 'inhibited' is, however, more accurate than totally disband. The current activities of such parties are based on the symbols and traditions of the often identically named predecessors from the pre-1948, and that leaves a mark on their organizational style (examples include ČSSD).[21] Finally, the parties in the category *newly emerged parties* represent the bulk of the current Czech and Slovak party spectrum. Their organizations were built from scratch and, from the party organizational point of view, such parties provide a laboratory example of the complex process of party building and party institutionalization (examples include ODS and SPR-RSČ, HZDS and KDH). Tables 3.7 and 3.8, providing a chart of the organizational history and electoral fortunes of all Czech and Slovak parties dealt with in this study, are included here for general orientation of the reader.

Party organization on the ground, or the party as a membership organization, has come to feature frequently in the writings on parties in post-communist Europe. So far, general theoretical arguments, often derived from earlier experiences with parties and processes of democratization, and supported by the preliminary tests and data sets from Eastern Europe, suggest a relatively underdeveloped party membership organization. There are a few factors which obstruct the firm establishment of parties in post-communist societies on the ground. The first relates to the fact that party membership is first and foremost a function of individual motivations to join. The primary incentives for grass-roots members to join are public purposive, symbolic and solidaristic (Katz and Mair, 1994). This is exactly where the problem of new post-communist parties lies. Forty years of communist rule created a highly atomized society, in which party is a dirty word, and people show little willingness to actively participate in political organizations or closely identify with partisan symbols and all-encompassing ideologies. The extent to which today's Czech and Slovak citizens are thus demobilized against taking genuine collective action turns out to be the crucial determinant for individual motivations to opt for party membership. Even the recruitment-oriented parties face enormous difficulties in mobilizing new members.

Table 3.7: Main Czech parties between 1990 and 1996 (results of elections to the Czech National Council/Chamber of Deputies)

Name of the party	Period / Election				
	June 1990	Between elections	June 1992	Between elections	May 1996
OF - Civic Forum	49 5	Splits into a number of parties	-	-	-
ODS - Civic Democratic Party	-	ODS splits from OF and forms electoral coalition with KDS	29 73	(Part of) KDS merges with ODS	29 62
ODA - Civic Democratic Alliance	-	ODA splits from OF	5 93	No major developments	6 36
KDU - Christian Dem Union	8 42	Electoral coalition KDU splits into KDS and KDU- ČSL	-	-	-
KDU- ČSL	-	Emerges as a splinter from KDU	6 28	(Part of) of KDS merges with KDU- ČSL	8 08
KDS - Christian Democratic Party	-	Emerges as a splinter of KDU and forms an electoral coalition with ODS	29 73	Splits and merges with ODS and KDU-ČSL	-
ČSSD - Czech Social Democratic Party	4 11	Unsuccessful in 1990 under the name Social Democracy-coalition of three Czech and Slovak social democratic parties-renames itself and contests elections as Czechoslovak Social Democratic Party	6 53	Changes name to Czech Social Democratic Party	26 44
KSČ - Communist Party of Czechoslovakia	13 24	Splits into SDL in Slovakia and LB in the Czech Republic	-	-	-
LB - Left Block	-	Emerges as a splinter and successor of KSČ in the Cz Rep . in an alliance with small left-wing groups	14 05	Splits into SLB (Party Left Block) and KSČM	-
KSČM - Communist Party of Bohemia and Moravia	-	-	-	Emerges from the LB	10 33
SPR-RSČ - Association for Republic-the Republican Party of Czechoslovakia	1	Changes name from the All People's Democratic Party and SPR-RSČ to simple SPR-RSČ	5 98	No major developments	8 01
HSD-SMS	10 03	Splits, but reemerges again as one party	5 87	Splits and merges into other small parties	-
LSU - Liberal Social Union	-	Emerges as a coalition of the Cz Socialist Party (ČSS), the Greens and the Agrarians	6 52	Splits and merges into a number of small parties	-

Table 3.8: Main Slovak parties between 1990 and 1994 (results of elections to the Slovak National Council/National Council of the Slovak Republic)

Name of the party	Period / Election June 1990	Between elections	June 1992	Between elections	September 1994
VPN - Public Against Violence	29 34	Splits into a number of parties	-	-	-
HZDS - Movement for a Democratic Slovakia	-	Emerges as a split from VPN	37 26	Splinter group forms DÚ. HZDS forms electoral coalition with the Agrarians	34 96
DÚ - Democratic Union	-	-	-	Splinter group from HZDS, also incorporates NDS-NA - a splinter group from SNS	8 57
SNS - Slovak National Party	13 94	No major developments	7 93	Splinter group forms NDS-NA, which merges with DÚ	5 4
KDH - Christian Democratic Movement	19 2	Splinter group forms Slovak Christian Democratic Movement	8 89	No major developments	10 08
KSČ - Communist Party of Czechoslovakia KSS - Communist Party of Slovakia SDL - Party of Democratic Left	13 34	KSČ splits and becomes, in Slovakia. KSS Reform continues and KSS becomes SDL	14 7	SDL forms electoral coalition Common Choice (SV) - with the Greens and Slovak Social Democrats, a splinter forms ZRS	10 41
ZRS - Association of Workers of Slovakia	-	-	-	Splinter group from SDL	7 37
ESWMK - Egyutteles and Hungarian Christian Democratic Movement	8 66	No major developments	7 42	Joins other Hungarian parties to form MK	-
MK - Hungarian Coalition	-	-	-	Emerges as an electoral coalition of ESWMK and Hungarian Civic Party	10 18

The second aspect relates to the role of the post-communist state in party development. In Western Europe, in various aspects, the relevance of the state in the dynamics of parties and party systems is generally recognized and emphasized in the literature (see Müller, 1993a; Mair, 1994), as it is in the development of parties in Eastern Europe (see Malová, 1994b; Lewis and Gortat, 1995). Especially relevant with regard to the party grass-roots is state financial support for political parties, which allows parties to insulate themselves from their membership base, at least with respect to financial concerns. As has been argued in another study, except in highly programmatic parties, state subsidies lead to a decline of activities at the grassroot level (Mendillow, 1992). Eastern European experiences show that the causality can also work in the other direction: state subsidies are partly introduced as a form of compensation for the low activity of parties on the ground, an act which merely preserves the existing situation, especially in the newly created parties. In other words, a decline in, or absence of, parties' activities on the ground can lead to an increase in state subsidies.

In both the Czech and Slovak Republics, parties showed a remarkable consensus on the desirability of state subsidies. In our survey, only 24 percent of the Czech MPs, and 33 percent of the Slovak MPs agreed with the statement "parties should do their own fund raising and not rely on the state for financial assistance". Also in both countries, the state has provided subsidies to the parties in proportion to their electoral results (reimbursement of electoral campaign) and, in the Czech Republic, the number of seats they hold in parliament. Besides that, Czech and Slovak parties represented in parliament receive extra funds allocated for the activities of their parliamentary parties.[22] Indeed, the increases in the sums per vote were the most important changes in electoral and party laws in both countries. For the 1992 elections, parties were entitled to 15 crowns for every vote for the Czech and Slovak National Councils, and the Chamber of Peoples and the Chamber of Nations of the Federal Assembly. Assuming that most of the voters gave a party vote for each of the three separate lists, the total sum per vote was thus 45 crowns (about $1.50) per vote. After the split of Czechoslovakia, the new Czech and Slovak states have assumed the responsibility of reimbursing their own parties with exactly the same sum of money. Parties thus also received money for votes to the Federal Assembly which no longer exists. Only parties that did not poll at least two percent of votes in one of the two republics were not entitled to a state subsidy.

The total sum of money parties received after the 1992 elections is presented in Table 3.9. Most of the Czech and Slovak parties claimed that

Table 3.9: State premiums for Czech and Slovak political parties according to electoral results and number of seats (in $)[1]

Czech parties	1992 elections	1996 elections
ODS/KDS	3,146,920	10,583,333
KDU- ČSL	594,379	3,334,000
ČSSD	680,785	9,473,333
LB (KSČM)	1,387,457	4,010,000
ODA	485,844	2,690,000
SPR-RS Č	610,666	3,320,000

Slovak parties	1992 elections	1994 elections
HZDS	1,425,211	1,777,439
SDL	588,169	-
Hungarian coalition	302,218	516,946
KDH	363,135	511,742
DÚ	-	434,901
ZRS	-	372,919
SNS	363,370	274,162

Sources: own calculations; for 1994 elections in Slovakia *Sme*, October 4, 1994; for 1996 elections in the Czech Republic, *MF Dnes*, June 11, 1996. Figures represent amounts of money for the whole electoral period (4 years).
Note[1]: all exchange rates applied in this chapter are as of August 1998: 1$ = 30Czk = 34Sk.

their campaign costs exceeded the state subsidy and, therefore, that they were heavily in debt. Neither private sponsors nor individual members could compensate for the financial costs of running a party. Therefore in both countries the state premium per vote has been increased, and the necessary amount of votes to be entitled to a state subsidy was raised. In Slovakia, parties polling at least three percent of votes countrywide receive 60Sk (about $1.70) per vote, payable shortly after the elections as a reimbursement of campaign expenses. Thanks to the early elections in 1994, the Slovak parties had to run on this smaller state subsidy for only two years, which improved their economic situation vis-à-vis their Czech counterparts, who had to wait for the 1996 elections to obtain new major resources. In Slovakia, the effect of increased subsidy can best be demonstrated by situation of HZDS and KDH. As can be seen from Table 3.9, in 1992 the HZDS received 1.4 million dollars for 57 federal MPs and 74 Slovak National Council MPs. In 1994, it was almost 1.8 million dollars for only 61 MPs in the Slovak parliament. The

KDH received $363,135 in 1992 for 14 federal MPs and 18 Slovak National Council MPs; in 1994 it was almost $512,000 for 17 MPs in the Slovak parliament.

However, even these figures pale compared to the sums cashed by the Czech parties after the 1996 elections. The new regulations, which partly took effect in 1995 to provide parties with extra money before the 1996 electoral contest, granted state subsidies in several forms: firstly, each party polling at least three percent of the votes nationwide receives 90CK (about $3) per vote as a reimbursement towards the electoral campaign costs. Secondly, each party polling at least three percent nationwide receives an annual state subvention of three million CK (about $100,000), plus an extra 100,000CK ($3,333) for each one-tenth of their vote above three percent, allocated up to five percent of the votes (the maximum per year for is thus five million CK, that is about $166,666). This is a subsidy for the functioning of the party. Finally, each party having a seat in the parliament receives annual subsidy of 500,000CK (about $16,666) per seat, also as a form of subsidy for the functioning of the party. The effect on the overall income of parties is apparent in Table 3.9. Despite a marginal change in the number of obtained votes and seats between 1992 and 1996 elections, ODS more than tripled its four-year income from the state. The new regulations responsible for such huge increases in state subsidies were agreed upon with a remarkable consensus on the political scene, where the only contested issue was the level of the vote threshold for receiving reimbursement of electoral campaign expenses.[23]

The third aspect, closely linked to the two previous considerations, concerns internal party politics, and in particular the way membership is likely to be evaluated by parties themselves. Most of the Czech and Slovak parties are top-down parties, which originated within the parliament or at the elite level, and thus the establishment of a strong organizational network on the ground involves a significant organizational endeavor for them. Given that post-communist parties operate in an era of mass communication, whereby party leaders can appeal to voters directly through television and modern campaign technologies, the need to mobilize new members, who would perform all traditional functions like canvassing and organizing public meetings is apparently much smaller than the effort it would involve. Furthermore, it may be unappealing for the leaders of the party, who in most cases are also the founders of the party, to strive for a large membership, and thereby create a potential powerful source of conflict inside the party. If militancy is likely to be a by-product of mass involvement in the party

(Bartolini, 1983), the actual costs of a large rank and file might be viewed negatively by the party organizers, particularly in the absence of any significant financial and political rewards.

On the whole, therefore, there are good reasons to expect the presence of the parties on the ground to be relatively marginal. Not only are the conditions in which contemporary parties operate unfavorable to mass political mobilization, but the strategic necessity of doing so is also less compelling. This is not to say that the members are not and will not be of any value, even for the newly emerging parties in modern times (for relevant discussion see Katz, 1990; Scarrow, 1994). On the contrary, we might be able to expect some structures of the party on the ground to be organized so as to recruit candidates for office at national as well as local levels. The membership may also help to legitimize the new party as such but, as experience shows, the new parties in post-communist democracies tend to seek legitimization more through what they have done in reconstructing political and economic systems or their ability to maintain stable electoral popularity, rather than in terms of their ability to organize themselves on the ground and integrate citizens into their organizations.

The data in Table 3.10 show a rather large variation among the Czech and Slovak parties concerning the number of individual members (i.e. paid-up members). Compared with the rest, continuous parties (KDU-ČSL and KSČM in the Czech Republic and SDL in Slovakia) can be characterized as mass membership parties and therefore they clearly deviate from the picture above. Membership in the newly emerged SPR-RSČ and ZRS is actually very high too, but the caution as to the realistic value of this figure is warranted in this case. Assuming that members are also party voters, the figures on member/voter ratio show that every fifth voter of these mass-affiliation parties was a party member, which indicates that they rely on a relatively stable base of supporters. The explanation of these findings is undoubtedly at the heart of our classification: the organizational legacy. All three parties fall into the category of continuous parties: that is, parties with a long-term uninterrupted existence. All three parties have had an extensive country-wide structure, and are therefore well organized at the local level. The members of these parties are generally from an old guard with identity links going back well into the pre-war period.

However, as can also be seen from Table 3.10, while the continuous parties have a membership base higher than any of the newly emerged or revived parties, all of them seem to have suffered a decrease in membership.

Table 3.10: Party membership in the Czech and Slovak Republics

	Number of direct members (thousands)		Member/voter ratio (%)[1]
	1993/1994	1995/1996	1995/1996
Newly emerged and revived parties			
ODS	22.0	22.0	1.2
KDS	4.0	2.2	n.a.
ČSSD	13.0	13.2	0.8
ODA	n.k.	2.5	1.4
SPR-RSČ	60.0	55.0	11.3
HZDS	n.k.	34.0	3.4
KDH	25.0	27.0	9.3
SNS	7.0	8.0	5.1
DÚ	n.a.	1.7	0.7
ZRS	n.a.	20.0	9.46
MKDH	7.0	7.0	n.a.
Continous parties			
KSČM	35.0	200.0	31.9
KDU-ČSL	100.0	80.0	16.3
LSNS (formerly CSS)	17.0	7.0	n.a.
SDL	48.0	40.0	n.a.

Sources: Czech parties: my own interviews in party headquarters (1993 and 1995); *Lidové Noviny*, 16 April 1996; Slovak parties: my own interviews in party headquarters 1995 and 1996.

Notes:

[1]Using electoral results of the 1994 elections to the Slovak parliament and 1996 elections to the Czech parliament.

n.k. = not known; n.a. = not applicable, either due to the non-existence of the party, or because it was impossible to make measure when parties contested elections in large electoral

In the case of the former Czechoslovak Communist Party (now KSČM and SDL), the drop in membership is astronomical, from almost two million before 1989, to 242,000 currently for KSČM and SDL together. Also the LSNS (formerly ČSS) suffered a remarkable loss of members: more than ten thousand. The sharp decline in Communist party membership is best be explained by its status under the old regime. Many of its members only joined the party to further their personal careers under the communists. As this ceased to be necessary after the regime change, most people left the party immediately. Moreover, all of the continuous parties face the problem of adjusting their ideological profile to the new circumstances after years of functioning under the communist regime. Especially in the Communist Party and the Socialists, this led to factional conflicts and subsequent party splits. The members joined new parties or left active politics altogether. Those that remained are the true loyal supporters, but their number is much lower than at the beginning of democratization. According to personal interviews with party organizers in both countries, the decline in membership in the continuous parties is likely to be progressive, since most of the party members are older, and the resulting natural decline has not been compensated for by the recruitment of new members.

The organizational legacy of the continuous parties also explains the relatively high level of organizational density in the contemporary Czech and Slovak Republics. If we take the available data on party membership of all Czech and Slovak parties, not just these listed in Table 3.10, the total membership in the Czech parties represents just over 6 percent of the electorate, and just over 5 percent in Slovakia. Perhaps surprisingly for a new democracy, the figures are close to the average for 11 Western European democracies at the end of the 1980s (see Table 3.11), and are substantially higher than levels of party membership in Hungary, Ukraine and Russia (all about 2 percent of the electorate, see Wyman et.al, 1995), or in Poland (1.5 percent of the electorate, see Mair, 1997).[24] However, it is precisely KSČM

Table 3.11: Party membership (% of electorate)

Country	Membership	Country	Membership
Netherlands	2.9	Belgium	9.2
United Kingdom	3.3	Italy	9.7
Germany	4.2	Finland	12.9
Ireland	5.3	Norway	13.5
Slovakia	5.5	Sweden	21.2
Czech Republic	6.2	Austria	21.8
Denmark	6.5		

Source: Except for Czech and Slovak figures, Mair (1994).

and KDU-ČSL that accounted for about 74 percent of party members in the whole country, yet they polled only some 20 percent of the votes in both the 1992 and 1996 elections. Likewise, the SDL in Slovakia accounts for 29 percent of all party members, yet the party polled 15 percent of votes in 1992 elections (to the Slovak National Council). Should the trend of declining membership continue, the current high level of organizational density in both countries would decrease as a result.

This is particularly plausible if we look at the membership figures for rest of the parties, that is, the newly emerged or revived parties. After an initial influx of new members, which many parties worked hard for in order to secure both the functioning of the organization and its basic legitimization, the membership seems to have become relatively stable. However, it is stabilized at a level far below any mass scale, as is underlined by the low scores on the member/voter ratio of parties involved, and there is no indication of further progress on recruiting new members. In fact, for some of the parties, like ODA in the Czech Republic and SNS in Slovakia, the minimal level of membership represents an obstacle for their active involvement in local politics. If we take into account the results of the municipal elections in both countries, the parties with at least 15,000 members were the most successful. And among these, of course, the most successful have been the continuous parties with an established local organization. The small parties were often unable to put up candidates outside the larger city areas, and local elections were characterized by a strong presence of independent candidates and personalities, running either on their own or on the lists of established parties.

It seems that the crucial explanatory variable for the low level of political involvement in new parties lies in the reluctance of the Czech and Slovak citizens to take political action through such conventional means as party membership, rather than in deterring actions of parties themselves. There are several elements involved. Wyman et.al. (1995) report that even though the citizens of the Czech and Slovak Republics are not particularly hostile to party competition, political parties as a whole were trusted less than other institutions. Party members who are male, over 30, and former members of the Communist party outnumber other members by 2:1 in each category. Given an established correlation between levels of party identification and party membership (see Katz, 1990), reported high levels of Czech and Slovak citizens with no attachment to a party (see Rose, 1995) adds to the mosaic of sociological factors underlying the low levels of party membership in both countries.

Indeed, if we reflect on the actions of party elites themselves, we find that, in general, the parties do not impose any significant barriers for new members. Although there were very few Czech and Slovak parties strategically committed to recruiting new individual members and building an extensive membership organization (ČSSD is an example), there is no evidence that parties deny party membership or are overly demanding of their members' time and energy. Members in all parties must be at least 18 years old (exception is the Coexistence in Slovakia - minimum age 16); they must be citizens of the country and their membership in one party precludes membership in others. The only usual obligation is to accept the program of the party and to obey the party rules as stated in the party statute. Moreover, most of the parties were, in one way or another, trying to expand links with various organizations and anchor their party structures within society. This is a strategy followed by almost all parties but, as the party organizers often admitted in personal interviews, nowhere has it led to results beyond the confines of a minimal level of membership, structured in a few professional clubs, youth and women's organizations.

With a few exceptions (KSČM, ODS), most of the Czech and Slovak parties also include provisions in their statute for the creation of ancillary organizations, that is, units that have direct organizational overlap with the party. Some parties (KDH, SDL, HZDS in Slovakia) give similar rights and status to professional clubs and organizations as they give to their district organizations, including the right to propose candidates for elections, to receive financial contributions from the party budget, and to participate in executive bodies of the party. ČSSD in the Czech Republic stands out in its efforts to organize ancillary organizations in this way. The party intends to develop itself as a party which is "open towards society and defines its terms of success in cooperation with as large a number of citizens as possible (including those who are not members of ČSSD). Therefore, it is possible to organize ancillary (and affiliated) organizations at all organizational levels" (Party statute, 1991, p.7). A special provision also exists in the party statute for an internal movement of Social Democratic Women and a club of Young Social Democrats. According to the party, it has succeeded in organizing about 80 clubs, constituting about 1,200 members. Since the party remains programmatically and ideologically committed to the mass organizational style of its pre-war predecessor, the attempts at organizational expansion have been typical of its post-communist existence. But again, as the officials stated in a personal interview, in Czech conditions this is very unlikely to be realized extensively as "the era of successful mass politics has passed".

Furthermore, membership fees are so low that it is difficult to imagine how potential members could be deterred by them. With the exception of KSČM (0.5 percent of annual income), the membership fees in the Czech and Slovak parties range from $3 to $18 yearly.[25] In order to keep the members in, LSNS even lowered dues from 4 percent of monthly income to $18 maximum per year. Some parties do not require membership fees at all. The insignificant revenues from membership fees obviously underscore the importance of state subsidies for political parties. For example, according to public information on parties' finances, the ODA in the Czech Republic received about $5,886 from membership fees in 1994, while the state subsidy for polled votes in 1992 was $485,844 and the costs of the electoral campaign in 1992 alone were about $1.5 million. In the Czech Republic, similar imbalances between marginal economic benefits from membership and the high costs of electoral campaigns were typical for all newly emerged or revived parties. This said, for the continuous parties, the membership fees may still represent a significant source of finances. KDU-ČSL, for example, received about $249,998 from its members in 1994, while the state subsidy for gained votes in 1992 elections was $594,379 and the costs of the 1992 electoral campaign were $566,667. Most important, however, is that continuous parties with a large membership tended to conduct the least expensive electoral campaign. Thus, for the continuous parties, members were not only rewarding financially in direct terms (large revenues from membership fees), but, given their size, also provided the party with a stable electoral base, which did not have to be mobilized through an expensive electoral campaign.

The actual difference between relatively low revenues from membership fees and state contributions on one hand, and parties' expenses on the other, explains the demands for an increase in state contributions. It proves that the Czech and Slovak parties are exceptionally dependent on external sources of finance. It also shows that despite successful attempts to procure more and more money from the state, parties have to seek additional financial contributions. In Western Europe, parties on the left have traditionally relied on the financial and human resources of the trade unions, parties on the right on the resources of business associations. Especially for the left-wing parties, this sometimes led to *en block* incorporation of outside organizations into the party structure, as in the case of the British Labour Party. Some parties thus became representatives of a particular interest in society, with individual membership enlarged by a collective membership of an ideologically friendly affiliated organization.

The Czech and Slovak parties, however, display no signs of such an organic link between interest associations and their party organization. KDU-ČSL has very loose contacts with Christian trade unions and a few entrepreneurial circles. Also, SPR-RSČ and KSČM are known for their close contact with friendly trade union organizations, but these are so marginal in terms of membership and influence that it is hard to talk about mass organizational encapsulation. A possible exception to this pattern are the Hungarian minority parties in Slovakia. They maintain very close contacts with Csemadok, the cultural union of ethnic Hungarians living in Slovakia. This organization already existed during the communist regime in Czechoslovakia, with the aim of promoting Hungarian cultural identity. Since 1989, the union's membership has been around 80,000 people. It has been deeply rooted in the social and political life of the Hungarian minority, providing for its preservation, development, and representation (Malová, 1995b). Although it does not support a specific party, Csemadok has been in close contact with all Hungarian parties, basically backing them collectively before the elections. The union also sponsored a petition urging the Hungarian parties to form an electoral coalition before the 1994 early elections in Slovakia.

The exception of the Hungarian parties stems from the segmentation of the Hungarian ethnic minority in Slovakia and its specific problems. As a clearly defined segment of Slovak post-communist society, the Hungarians provide a pervasive, though limited, basis of electoral support on which parties can build. Although the three Hungarian parties differ in their ideological orientation (MKDH is a Christian conservative party; MOS is a liberally oriented party; and Coexistence is predominantly nationalistic), the common denominator for their actions is the representation of ethnic Hungarians in Slovakia. This is also evident from parties' conception of membership. Despite the fact that the Hungarian parties do have (a few) direct registered members, they explicitly consider all supporters to be the party members. In line with this conception, Coexistence does not even register individual members.

The Czech parties and the rest of the parties in Slovakia can hardly rely on such homogeneous subculture and the development of their links with interest associations is strongly influenced by two factors. The first factor relates to the apolitical character of interest associations in both countries. In the Czech and Slovak Republics, there appears to be a strong belief that interests should be represented directly within the state hierarchy, without the mediation of parties. As such, it is a clear legacy of the past, in which the organic links between the trade unions and the Communist party (there were no business associations under the communist regime) were seen as an instrument of the latter in retaining a monopoly on power. The post-communist trade union leaders have been very conscious to distance their organization from the Communist party, resulting in a situation in which they cannot afford to link it to any other party, even if they would find it desirable. Wracked by a loss of credibility and cohesion, the Czech and Slovak trade unions are composed of members whose bitter memories of the politics on the shop-floor as well as a general distrust of other social organizations make them exceptionally reluctant to be associated with any one party. This legacy has been exhibited most clearly in the fate of the Social Democratic parties' attempts to forge links with the (re-structured) trade union organizations. ČSSD in the Czech Republic, owing to its attempted organizational style, has repeatedly expressed sympathy towards the labor organizations and offered various forms of cooperation. However, the largest Czech labor organization - the Czech and Moravian Council of Trade Unions, has continuously stated that (they) "will try to keep good contacts with all political parties, including those who do not like unions that much...(we) unconditionally agree that our position must be above any political party".[26] SDL's similar attempts in Slovakia ended on very much the same note.

The reluctance of interests groups to affiliate with a party has been reinforced by the second factor: the effect of tripartite, or what we could call corporatist, arrangements. Such mechanisms of mediation between the state and interest associations were introduced to the political process in the very early stages of democratization - by October 1990 in federal Czechoslovakia - and have continued to function in the Czech and Slovak Republics since the split (see Mansfeldová, 1996). It did not arise from a conflict between the state, employers and employees, but was simply introduced top down, out of the elite concept of social partnership which was deemed necessary for a peaceful economic transformation. Most importantly, however, the establishment of tripartite mechanisms preceded or coincided with the development of political parties. In functional terms, therefore, the existing and emerging interest groups could directly channel their demands to the state and other bargaining partners, without seeking help from a friendly party organization. Paradoxical for these early stages of democratization in the former Czechoslovakia was that many interest associations registered and behaved like political parties, while remaining reluctant to connect with any party. In order to secure their interests, they presented candidates in the national elections.[27] The distinction between interest groups and parties became blurred, and the political scene became exceptionally undifferentiated and unclear.

As the web of interest associations crystallized and became somewhat more organized, and as the party systems started to settle down too, these excesses receded into the remote past. Nevertheless, the combination of historical legacies with the simultaneous emergence of party systems and corporatist mechanisms have so far produced a large organizational and ideological split between parties and interest groups. Groups with certain claims tend to approach government or central bureaucracy directly. They bypass parties completely, create their own parties, or approach office holders who have something immediate to offer. In combination with parties' compelling need to secure finances from sources other than the state or membership, it appears to have unfortunate consequences for the growth of party and government patronage and the occurrence of various cases of corruption. Pragmatically oriented pressure groups do not necessarily support ideologically friendly party organizations, but rather those who are momentarily in the position to redistribute benefits. In the Czech Republic, the only parties which admitted at least minimal signs of contacts with organized interests have primarily been the parties in the government (Kopecký, 1995a). The same parties have also been involved in financial scandals between 1992 and 1996. And all of these scandals were, one way or the other, connected with fundraising and financial debts with influential business organizations: ODS failed to identify its largest sponsors, who gave gifts of 3.75 million crowns. When the press searched for declared donors, both from abroad, one was found to have died several years ago, the other distanced himself from the financial support. ODA declared a sponsorship gift of 3.3 million CK from Liechtenstein, only to see the press report later that the gift came from the Virgin Islands. The chairman of ODA's central office was also investigated in the matter concerning the payment of a 52 million CK loan from a certain Czech bank.[28]

In Slovakia, open financial scandals have been avoided, not least because the post-1994 Mečiar government turned out internally cohesive and, via the complete party control of the majority of state control organs (see next chapter), able to prevent public investigations. However, the Spring 1996 almost saw a break up of the coalition of SNS/HZDS/ZRS, when SNS vehemently protested the methods of privatizing the biggest Slovak insurance company. Reportedly, the SNS leadership had close interests in the matters of a company closely linked to the party. In a similar way, the ruling HZDS signed an agreement on political cooperation with the Party of Businessman and Entrepreneurs in October 1996. It came as a surprise to many observers, since HZDS declares itself to be a left-of-center party, and the businessmen had run in the last Slovak elections in a coalition with the liberal opposition Democratic Party. However, when this particular electoral coalition failed to make it into parliament, pragmatically oriented leaders of the businessmen party undoubtedly sought a more appropriate ally and hence chose the leading government party. The evidence from Slovakia is more incomplete and fragmented, but it does not mean that the situation is less explosive. Prior to the 1998 elections, the opposition declared that, if in power, it intends to re-open all cases of direct sales privatization conducted under Mečiar's government - a declaration which only further increased the sharp elite polarization that has characterized Slovak politics since 1992.

Whether such financial scandals are in any way going to deter citizens from closer identification with, and an active involvement in, the parties remains to be seen. But our evidence in this section points to the generally underdeveloped character of parties on the ground in the Czech and Slovak parties. The recorded levels of membership are relatively low, even though there is a difference between the continuous and newly emerged parties, with the former having at least for the middle term a comfortable mass basis, while the latter for various reasons have not succeeded in recruiting new members. With the exception of the Hungarian minority representation, the parties are by and large also lack a complex web of ancillary and affiliated organizations.

The implication is that the capacity of parties, which are seen at least by elites as the main representative bodies mediating between the state and citizen, to penetrate grass roots of Czech and Slovak societies have so far been very limited. Parties have been able to monopolize the sphere of representation as well as decision-making processes, while they remain weak as membership organizations. This obviously does not mean that parties do not represent citizens. But it appears that acts of representation are primarily confined to pre-election mobilization of voters, conducted with the help of modern and expensive electoral campaigns, with little additional activity shown in this sphere by parties and citizens alike in the period between successive elections. Moreover, the occasionally hypothesized possibility that party-geared forms of representation would be complemented by active involvement of citizens in other intermediary organizations (see Kopecký, 1995a), such as interest associations or various social movements and pressure groups, proved in reality optimistic. The lack of robust and active civil society is perceived as one of the major shortcomings of the new Czech and Slovak political systems (see Green and Skalnik-Leff, 1997; Malová, 1997; Kopecký and Barnfield, 1999).

Conclusions

The empirical material presented in this chapter points to the fact that political parties, rather than individual MPs or other organizations of civil society, are destined to be the crucial agents in linking the state with citizens in the Czech and Slovak Republics. This is our first important finding on the direction of parliamentary institutonalization. The electoral systems, which are very similar in both countries, provide an important institutional context favouring the dominance of political parties in the process of representation. It is the parties who compete for votes, in a relatively large electoral districts, and it is only registered parties who are allowed to contest national elections. The elements of personalized voting, embedded in both electoral systems in the form of preferential voting, make little difference to the general tendency for candidates in both countries to become elected based on how they appear on the lists determined by political parties themselves. This, in combination with growing numerical and organizational strength of parties, makes recruitment to both parliaments heavily party-contingent, at least in comparison with 1989-1992, where recruitment structures were relatively open due to a lack of both professional party cadres and candidates willing to stand for elections.

In addition, the 1989-1992 period was also characterized by a considerable confusion, both legal and normative, as to deputies' representative roles. As our examination of MPs' own views on representation showed, the party largely filled the gap in the periods which were to come. Owing parties their political career, and working in a system where party strength plays a crucial role, the MPs' roles in representing both local constituencies and various professional and social interests have largely been subordinated to the tasks associated with their work in parliament, such as legislating in certain policy areas, or simply living up to the party mandate. Although elements of the former representative models can be detected and may even further develop in both countries, the prevailing conception is that a deputy wins election on a specific program of a specific party and has therefore a right and duty to carry it out.

Our evidence from analyzing parties as membership organizations suggests that their capacity to become strong representative agencies is quite limited, however. The parties' linkage function, in the sense of being a vent for civic activity and a channel of communication, founders on the low level of citizens' direct involvement in political parties, if not on the parties' indifference to forging solid links with their constituencies. This is an important finding since, as we shall see in our following analysis of both the executive-legislative relationships and relationships inside the parliaments, the parties' ability to penetrate and organize state institutions appears significantly greater than their ability to penetrate society at its grass-roots level. Given the strong predisposition of both political systems to rely on intermediary forms of representation, and given that civil society organizations other than parties appear to be weak, this raises some concerns. The delegative principle inevitably involved in intermediary representation is echoed in a gap between party elites and their members and supporters, which reduces the whole process of (intermediary) representation to the single electoral act conducted at four-year intervals.

Notes

1. This is not say that a single-member constituency electoral system would necessarily produce the opposite. On the contrary, the study edited by Bogdanor (1985) concludes that a dominance of "partisan representation" is marked in plurality and majority systems as it is in proportional systems, depending on the strength of political parties in the given political system.

2. Andeweg (1997) argues that this institutional context provides essential limits to an analysis of role models developed in the American literature.

3. Note that the first elections to the Senate - the upper chamber of the Czech Parliament were conducted in November 1996, under an entirely different electoral system than those analyzed here for the four parliamentary elections before July 1996. After lengthy discussions, which delayed the establishment of the Senate for 3 years, Czech parties reached a compromise in 1995. The electoral law provides for the two-round formula similar to that used in France for the election to the National Assembly. Accordingly, a candidate is elected in a single-member constituency (each representing about 100,000 inhabitants) if he or she receives more than 50 percent of votes. If no one in a given constituency receives over 50 percent in the first round, the second round is to be held a week later, consisting of run-offs with the two most successful candidates.

4. Alex Pravda classifies elections in communist Czechoslovakia as "plebiscitary elections" (as opposed to "limited-chance elections"), that is elections with one candidate per seat, with high pressures for unanimity, and with selection of candidates usually determined by executive decision, except occasionally at the lowest local levels.

5. The partial exception to this pattern of elections were shot-lived electoral reforms in 1967.

6. In principle, the Droop quota (Votes/Seats+1) helps to achieve more complete distribution on the district level than the Hare quota (Votes/Seats), since it creates fewer remaining votes (see Krejčí, 1994:144-145; Lijphart, 1994:23).

7. The legal threshold, that is the explicit minimum level of support which a party needs in order to gain representation, should be distinguished from the effective threshold, which is determined by district magnitude and, to some extent, electoral formula and the number of competing parties. For discussion and different measures see Taagepera and Shugart (1989) and Lijphart (1994).

8. Note that a similar debate occurred before the 1996 elections. The Electoral Commission, consisting of the representatives of all participating parties in equal proportion, had to rule on the status of the coalition between the Free Democrats - Liberal National Social Party (SD-LSNS) and the Party of Entrepreneurs, Tradesman and Farmers, both of which merged shortly before elections. While initially agreeing to consider the coalition as one party, the Commission later decided that it should contest elections as a coalition of two parties. The SD-LSNS tabled a complaint with the Constitutional Court which, after a public debate and protests from party leaders and President Havel, overruled the Electoral Commission's decision. The last word, nevertheless, rested with voters, who did not give the party sufficient support to pass even the 5 percent threshold.

9. Nevertheless, this did not result in party fragmentation on the scale of the previous parliaments (see chapter 6). Only the coalition of Hungarian parties formed two parliamentary parties in the immediate aftermath of the elections, as they had done in the previous parliament as well. In fact, it was often argued in the run-up to the 1994 elections that the 5 percent threshold led to the unification of the Hungarian minority parties into a (safely electable) block. As this was seen as undesirable, some experts then argued for exempting the Hungarian parties from threshold requirements, or lowering it in general for all individual parties.

10. However, it is interesting to see that, in the Czech Republic at least, preferential votes are used as a test of personal prestige for the various leading politicians. Thus, while not necessarily owing their election to the personalized system of voting, some politicians used obtained preferential votes to enhance their bargaining position in the post-election selection of ministerial and top parliamentary posts.

11. Vladimír Mečiar noted: "The electoral system we have now is copied from the Italians, but unfortunately they have abandoned it. We are searching for a more stable system that would reflect the political will of the population and stabilize the work of parliament and the executive. We do not have a democratic structure like true democracies" (quoted in *Financial Times*, October 23, 1996)

12. Note that after the 1996 elections, the previous ruling coalition of ODS, KDU-ČSL and ODA formed a cabinet again, but initially two seats short of a parliament majority. A somewhat similar situation occurred after the 1998 early elections, but this time it was ČSSD who formed a minority cabinet with the support of ODS.

13. On the original formulation of the concept of focus of MPs' representation see Eulau and Wahlke (1959). The second important dimension which the authors introduce relates to the style of representation: a question whether an MP should be delegate, bound by mandates and instructions; or a trustee, freely making up his mind on the issues. Due to the lack of data, this second analytical dimension will not be considered here.

14. The Slovak constitution (Art. 72) states that "the deputies are representatives of the citizens"; in the Czech constitution, the oath of a deputy (Art. 23) states ".....to exercise my mandate in the interest of the people...".

15. It is interesting to note here that the lowest scoring category in both countries was 'specific social or professional groups'. Taking into account that cross-tabulation did not reveal significant differences among parties in this category, this implies that strong class or sectoral interests, as opposed to simply (undifferentiated) party voters, are barely considered to be a focus of MPs' representation.

16. The question was: "Could you tell me something about the way you specifically became a candidate for parliament during the elections in 1992? Which of the ways to be nominated applies to you?". The MPs could choose between the following categories: I put myself forward; I was active in my party and was subsequently nominated; I was not active in a party but was approached by a party; I was asked by a particular social and professional group; other.

17. Note that in the run-up to the 1990 elections, which were dominated by broadly based movements and freshly established parties, recruitment structures were rather open, with parties supplementing their lists with well known intellectuals and personalities, and even with a number of candidates simply putting themselves forward.

18. The disastrous floods in summer 1996 affected mainly the territory of South Moravia - a strong constituency of KDU-ČSL. It was interesting to see that the party MPs were remarkably and unusually active in questioning the government - of which they were part - about the solutions and steps taken to revitalize the area.

19. Moreover, in general, those MPs with other occupations spent very little time on them, with most of their working time being taken up by their jobs as MPs.

20. Our classification is similar to that of Waller (1996) who distinguishes between four categories: the communist parties, the 'block parties', the revivals, and the parties of the transition and the liberation myth. Although the author uses a broader criterion - that of the sources of party identity (organization, ideology, international links) - he arrives at basically identical categories, except that the communist parties will be grouped together with the 'block parties', since they all share uninterrupted organizational continuity. For other classifications of parties in post-communist Europe, organized around more conventional party families see Olson 1993b; Dellenbrandt 1993; Mudde 2000.

21. Moreover, (some of) the revived parties took material advantage of the existing party structures in exile and, while rebuilding their party organization, they could also rely on pre-war members either living in the locality or recently returned from exile. On Czech Social Democrats see the studies of Vermeersch (1994a,b).

22. Note that deputies' salaries are not included here as a source of state funding for political parties. This may distort the picture somewhat, for some deputies in both countries do pass part of their salary and/or constituency allowance to the central party office or, as we have seen in the previous section, use it to finance the local party (the KSČM is known to be particularly insistent in this practice).

23. Note that according to the opinion polls, only 23 percent of the Czech population favours state financing of political parties. It is absolutely unacceptable for 67 percent of the population, with the majority of 93 percent thinking parties should be financed from membership fees. See *Lidové Noviny*, 15 July, 1996. According to the source, the views of the Czech population on this issue have been very stable over time.

24. Note that figures on Eastern Europe from Wyman et. al (1995) are survey figures, whereas figures in Table 3.10 are figures reported by the parties themselves. We can nevertheless assume comparability, since the survey figures on the Czech and Slovak Republics correspond very closely to the parties' figures.

25. For an overview of the membership fees in the Czech parties see *Lidové Noviny*, November 30, 1995.

26. Interview with the chairman of the Czech and Moravian Council of Trade Unions in the daily *Rudé Právo*, May 5, 1994.

27. There were registered parties like the Beer Lovers Party, the Independent Erotic Initiative, the Movement of Pensioners for Social Security, the Political Party of Women and Mothers in Czecho-Slovakia, the Party of Handicapped People etc.

28. Note that further financial scandals involving ODS also led to the fall of a minority government and the split of the party at the end of 1997. This opened a chain of public and police investigations. Virtually none of the major Czech parties (including ČSSD and SPR-RSČ) avoided their own finance related problems. ODA paid perhaps the highest political price, spectacularly demising political scene after the severe press investigations proved party's links with the industry during the process of privatization.

4 Executive-Legislative Relations: Parliaments and Governments

Introduction

In chapter 2, we analyzed the choices made with regard to the constitutional position of the Czech and Slovak parliaments within the new institutional order. The previous chapter explored institutionalization of the relationships of two parliaments with one of the critical actors in their environment - the electorate. The concern of this chapter is the institutionalization of the relationships between the parliaments and another critical actor in their environment - the executive power. Having considered the causes of institutional design in 1992, we now need to know the consequences of these decisions. We need to know how basic constitutional choices, as well as other institutional and political factors, shaped institutionalization and political activity in the sphere of executive-legislative relations. What is the role of parties in structuring the relationships between parliament and government? To what extent do individual MPs and parliamentary committees enjoy policy-making autonomy? To what extent do Czech and Slovak parliaments act as cohesive institutions against the government? How do MPs see their role vis-à-vis the government? How do parliamentary and governmental majorities treat the opposition?

These are some of the most important questions we shall explore in the following analysis, using (a modified version of) King's typology of different modes of executive-legislative relations. King (1976) distinguished five modes of interactions between governments and parliaments: the non-party, intraparty, interparty, opposition, and cross-party modes. His analytical framework conceptualizes the influence of political parties on the relationships between government and parliament and, most importantly, shows that:

> "in fact it is usually highly misleading to speak of 'executive-legislative' *tout court* and that, if we wish to understand the phenomena subsumed under this

general heading, we need to identify and consider separately a number of distinct political relationships. We need, to put it another way, to 'think behind' Montesquieu formula" (King, 1976:11).

This disaggregate approach to the complexity of interactions betwen ministers and MPs, or parliaments and governments, is exactly what made King's framework attractive for country-specific application (see Saalfeld, 1990; Andeweg, 1992; Müller, 1993b), as well as for cross-national analysis of parliamentary structures in Western Europe (Andeweg and Nijzink, 1995). Particularly in Andeweg and Nijzink's comparative study, King's original typology was critically evaluated and modified into a typology with three modes of interaction between ministers and MPs.[1] The same redefined typology will be used in the remainder of this chapter to gain insights into the institutionalization of parliament-government relations in the Czech Republic and Slovakia. The typology consists of three modes:

1. an inter-party mode in which ministers and MPs from one party interact with ministers and MPs (or, if it is an opposition party, only MPs) from another party. Within this mode, two submodes can be distinguished: an intra-coalition mode in which ministers and MPs of one governing party interact with ministers and MPs of another governing party; and an opposition mode in which ministers and MPs belonging to the governing majority interact with opposition MPs. In the inter-party mode, parliament is not regarded so much as an institution but as an *arena* for party political struggles.

2. a cross-party mode in which cross-party coalitions of ministers and MPs interact with each other. These interactions are based on social interests, which not only cut across institutional boundaries, as in the inter-party mode, but also ignore party boundaries. In this mode parliament can best be regarded as a *marketplace* for the competitive trading of social interests.

3. a non-party mode in which ministers and parliamentarians interact with each other as members of two different *institutions*. This type of interaction is associated with the lack of political parties in the parliament, or with parties being nothing more than very loosely organized groups of MPs. It also most clearly conforms to Montesquieu's two body image, criticized by King as an inadequate description of the complexity of executive-legislative relations.

Each of these modes implies a different form of institutionalization of the links between parliaments and governments (and we shall devote one section to each in this chapter). It implies a different set of behavioral models (i.e. the cultural aspect of institutionalization), as well as different set of institutional preconditions (i.e. the structural aspect of institutionalization). For example, cross-party and non-party modes of interactions were typical of the parliament-government relations in the former Czechoslovak Federal Assembly (1989-1992), largely because of the organizational weakness of political parties and an individualistic style of politics among many then- new MPs. As Olson argued, the Assembly had "more in common with the American Congress than with any European parliament" (Olson, 1994b:45). The situation has changed since, however, and we may now expect the inter-party mode to become more important, if not dominant, in the interactions between Czech and Slovak ministers and MPs. If parties have become more organized and dominant in both countries - something which we implied in the previous two chapters - we should find empirical evidence for the situation in which "MPs and ministers see themselves as partisans, loyal to their party and its program, engaged in a democratic competition with ministers and MPs from other parties, and accountable to those party bodies that hold the power over their renomination" (Andeweg, 1992:163).

Parliaments as Arena for Party Political Struggles

The first way of checking our expectations and identifying the prevailing type of interactions between ministers and MPs in practice is to analyze attitudinal data of MPs. In both the Czech and the Slovak Republics incumbent MPs were asked to identify the mode that best describes the relationship between parliament and government.[2] The answers in Table 4.1 give an indication of the existence of the modes in both countries. We find that a large majority of 79 percent of the Czech and 73 percent of the Slovak MPs chose the inter-party mode as the best description of the interaction between parliament and government. Furthermore, both the Czech and Slovak MPs regard the non-party mode and the cross-party mode as virtually non-existent. The dominance of the inter-party mode is only slightly tempered by the answers of 16 percent and 20 percent of the MPs respectively, who were not able to identify a discernible pattern in the relations between parliamentarians and ministers. The data indeed indicate that the most salient line of interactions in the Czech and Slovak parliaments runs between parties which, in turn, points to a high degree of party unanimity in policy-making, and in voting in the parliament. Therefore, in the perceptions of MPs, our expectations about a shift from the non-party and cross-party modes seems to be authorized.

Table 4.1: Perceptions of relations between ministers and MPs

	Best description of relationship between government and parliament			
	Czech Republic		Slovakia	
	#	%	#	%
Non-party Mode	4	2.4	6	6.2
Inter-party Mode	132	78.6	71	73.2
Cross-party Mode	3	1.8	–	–
No discernible pattern	27	16.1	19	19.6
DK/No answer	2	1.2	1	1.0

However, this very high percentage of supporters of the inter-party mode certainly contains an element of normative bias, at least for two reasons. Firstly, in both countries, MPs who belong to opposition parties are particularly likely to emphasize their position as a powerless opposition, victimized by an unbreakable coalition machinery. The cross-tabulation, controlling for answers of opposition MPs in both countries, confirms the point, if only partly. Out of 84 interviewed Czech opposition MPs, 74 chose inter-party mode, whereas out of 82 interviewed coalition MPs, 58 did the same. The distribution amongst the Slovak coalition and opposition MPs was virtually the same. Secondly, regardless of the coalition/opposition division, the MPs are more likely to point to the inter-party mode, since it invariably fares well with a picture of stability and predictability in a functioning parliamentary system. To be loyal to their party and coalition, or to oppose the coalition, is a role the MPs voted for when choosing a parliamentary system of government. Would not they adhere to it at least verbally, even when reality is perhaps more complex?

The answer is probably yes, but the following evidence may help to clarify matters. Figures 2 and 3, based on the roll-calls from the Czech parliament, demonstrate the strength of the inter-party mode in voting behavior of the (main) parliamentary parties.[3] On the one hand, we can see that the coalition parliamentary parties, ODS, KDU-ČSL, ODA, displayed a

Figure 2: Voting Distances between Individual Parties I

Figure 3: Voting Distances between Individual Parties II

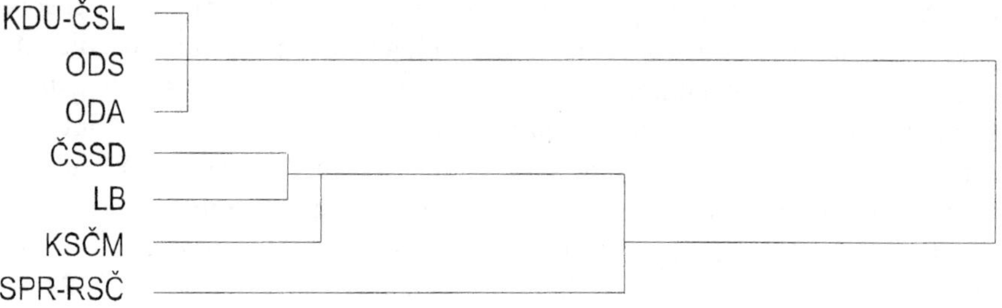

very high similarity in voting behavior in that they are clustered close to each other in the upper part of both figures. Within them as a group, the differences were virtually non-existent. On the other hand, the opposition parties, LB, KSČM, ČSSD, and the SPR-RSČ did have more in common with each other than with any other coalition party. They are clustered in the lower part of the figure. However, there were more apparent dissimilarities between them as an opposition block than within the coalition block of parties. We can see that ČSSD and LB displayed highest similarity within the opposition block (though not as strong as in the case of coalition parties), followed at a distance by KSČM (more dissimilar), and then by SPR-RSČ (even more dissimilar). In an aggregate form then, these data exemplify three prominent characteristics of the parliament-government relations in the Czech Republic between 1992 and 1996: an overall congruity of the coalition parliamentary parties which fostered governmental stability; a strong division between the coalition and opposition parliamentary parties; and divisions amongst opposition parties themselves.

This said, we have to take note of two problems which the aggregate evidence poses. In the first place, it tends to hide the presence of both inter-party submodes in parliamentary practice: intra-coalition (interactions between ministers and MPs within the coalition block of parties) and opposition modes (interactions between coalition ministers and MPs and the opposition MPs). The fact is that in most votes, the MPs and ministers belonging to coalition parties engaged *en block* in a struggle against the opposition parties. These opposition parties, as can be seen from Figures 2 and 3, were often divided among themselves. Some opposition parliamentary parties even came to vote fairly regularly with the coalition, thus increasing its legislative majority in the parliament. Nevertheless, there were cases when opposition parties succeeded in driving a wedge into the coalition, or, more often, when the coalition itself was divided, and a part of the coalition sought support of some opposition parties against a similar group of the remaining parties. Such was, for example, the case in the vote on a fundamental social reform in July 1995, when the missing votes of the governmental KDU-ČSL, which disagreed with raising the retirement age, were replaced by those of the opposition ČMUS. Another case was the vote on the restitution of the Jewish property in February 1994, when three coalition parties stood up against the ODS, which was supported by some opposition parliamentary parties, and even obstructed the vote by leaving the floor of the parliament. Similar events, though infrequent, always generated debates about the stability of the governing coalition and its political future, and showed that though largely cohesive, coalition MPs and ministers also clashed with each other.

In the second place, the aggregate evidence does not account for dissent within individual parties. The figure assumes that the 'party view' is that view supported by at least 50 percent of MPs within the parliamentary party. Obviously then, the aggregate evidence can distort reality, since internal parliamentary party cohesion can be relatively low (around 50 percent), and yet the figure treats it as one cohesive party. We shall deal with the cohesion of individual parliamentary parties in chapter 6. For now suffice to note that the Czech coalition parties were, in general, much more cohesive than their opposition counterparts, though, as was proven in a preliminary test, it was not particularly common to find roll-calls when the coalition parliamentary parties were not only united among themselves, but also highly cohesive (more than 90 percent) within themselves (see Plecitý, 1995). In other words, even if coalition parliamentary parties voted together, there were always some dissidents within their ranks who could endanger the governmental majority. In political terms, however, this did not cause the Czech government any serious troubles between 1992 and 1996, as the opposition was usually too fragmented to exploit conflicts inside the coalition.

The situation in Slovakia was initially somewhat different. Although roll-calls for 1992-1994 parliament were scarce, and therefore it is impossible to present here evidence comparable with the Czech parliament, two observations should complement the data from Table 4.1. Similar to the Czech situation, signs of a strong party mode of operation in the relations between parliament and government in Slovakia have been present. The parties nominated cabinet ministers, the MPs voted by and large along party lines and were also involved in the formulation of government policies, and the characteristic lines of conflict ran between ministers and MPs from the governing parties and the opposition. However, parliament-government relations during the 1992-1994 legislative term went through three distinct phases, very dissimilar to the Czech situation. In the first phase, from the elections in 1992 till April 1993, the country was basically governed by the HZDS executive (hereafter Mečiar I), with tacit parliamentary support from the SNS and (initially) SDL. There was neither a formal coalition agreement between the two parties nor, strictly speaking, any sharing of ministerial posts. In fact, the coalition-like appearance of the government was based merely on the participation of one SNS member, Ludovít Černák, as the Minister for Economy. In the summer of 1992 he was appointed as 'a non-political specialist' to the Mečiar I government, but later became the chairmen of the SNS, thus giving Mečiar's cabinet a sort of coalition form.

After the purges and resignations of ministers in March 1993 and the subsequent split of the HZDS parliamentary party, the second phase of the Mečiar I cabinet started, lasting till March 1994. Particularly important in this respect were the dismissal of the Minister of Foreign Affairs Milan Kňažko, on the Prime Minister's request, and the resignation of Minister for Economy Černák. Kňažko's dismissal caused a split in HZDS's parliamentary party (8 MPs left). At Černák's resignation, the SNS ended its support for the government and began its own internal disintegration. Afterward, the country was governed by a minority HZDS government, which attempted to bring SNS back on board. It was not until November 1993 that a proper coalition agreement between the two parties was reached and a revamped government, based on the sharing of ministerial posts and a tiny legislative majority in the parliament, was formed. Yet a month later, during the debates on the budget in December 1993, the SNS parliamentary party split, and a new minority government, this time composed of HZDS and SNS, remained in office until March 1994.

The third phase, from March 1994 till the early general elections in September 1994, was marked by a complete change of government. Although the HZDS/SNS minority government could initially rely on the selective support of the opposition SDL, or on frequent disunity of the opposition itself, it soon became clear that early elections would be called to solve the political crisis in the country. In due course, the HZDS parliamentary party lost another 10 MPs and two ministers, who were unwilling or unable to co-operate with Mečiar. Moreover, cabinet proposals were often defeated in parliament, which induced total executive immobility. After Mečiar rejected an offer to form a coalition with SDL, based on the condition that he would not personally take part in it, parliament cast a vote of no-confidence in the government. On March 11, 1994, the parliament finally voted the oft-reshuffled and reconstructed Mečiar I government down by a majority of 78 votes, with the deputies of HZDS and SNS ostensibly boycotting the plenary session. Less than a week later, on March 16, the new government was appointed. With the silent support of the Hungarian parties, the coalition of SDL, KDH, and DU, under the leadership of Josef Moravčík, held office until the new post-September election government (hereafter Mečiar II) was formed in December 1994, which held office until the 1998 elections.

This brief overview indicates that parliament-government relations in Slovakia were more turbulent than in the Czech Republic. This was so particularly because of the unstable nature of the legislative majority in Slovakia. Although the Slovak MPs and ministers, similarly to their Czech colleagues, interacted with each other predominantly in the inter-party mode during all three phases of political development, this was more apparent during Moravčík's broad coalition government, and most certainly under Mečiar II government, than during the period of Mečiar I government. Under Mečiar's premiership, the inter-party battles were complemented by conflicts between ministers and MPs from the same party, which set off the gradual disintegration of HZDS and a subsequent governmental crisis. As a result, the dependence of the Mečiar I government on ad-hoc majorities moved the parliament-government relations, at least initially, from the inter-party mode somewhat closer to the non-party or cross-party modes.

Therefore, the attitudinal data and an analysis of behavior in this section suggest a strong inter-party mode in the interactions between the Czech ministers and MPs and a somewhat chaotic appearance of this mode in Slovakia, at least between 1992 and March 1994. In order to advance our evidence, and strengthen it for the Slovak case in particular, we shall now turn to a number of institutional and political characteristics, which are presumed to bolster the inter-party mode by tightening links between ministers and their party colleagues in the parliament. Drawing largely on the empirical indicators used by Andeweg (1992) and Andeweg and Nijzink (1995), we shall specifically look at: the fusion between ministerial and parliamentary office and the subsequent recruitment of ministers; the process of government formation; and the institutional expression of consultations between party's ministers and MPs.

Ministerial recruitment

The Czech constitution does not prevent a politician from being a member of parliament and of the government at the same time. The combination of two offices was also allowed in the Czechoslovak Federal parliament. Despite a proposal (in 1990) to separate the functions of minister and MP, the fusion of the two offices continued in practice until the end of the Czechoslovak federation in 1992, and was inherited by the new Czech constitution. In itself, the provision provides a very important institutional precondition for strengthening the inter-party mode of interactions between executive and legislative branches, because government and parliament can effectively fuse together into one institution, as for example in the U.K. The only limit to a full fusion in the Czech case is that, according to the constitution, a deputy or a senator who is a member of the Government may not be the Chairman or Vice-Chairman of the Chamber of Deputies or the Senate, or a member of parliamentary committees, investigatory commission or commissions.

In practice, not all Czech cabinet ministers between 1992 and 1996 were MPs. Out of 19 cabinet ministers, only around half were parliamentarians. However, this stemmed from the nomination of candidates prior to the 1992 elections. The political heavyweights of the Czech parties, normally prospective ministers, were on the party lists to the former Federal Assembly, rather than on the lists for the then only 'second-rate' National Council (see also chapter 6). As a result, they did not hold a seat in what was in January 1993 to become the parliament of the Czech Republic, though a number of them, in the course of negotiations with the Slovak side, gradually assumed a position in the Czech government. This was possible given the old rule which did not preclude a mandate of the Federal MP with a position either in the Federal or one of the two republic's governments. The optimism of the Czech politicians with regard to the future of the common state with the Slovaks thus explains the relative infrequence of the combination of the two offices in the 1992-1996 Czech parliament. In the 1996 elections, the prominent party members were placed top on the lists again, and the government which was formed in the aftermath of this electoral contest made the fusion of offices more or less perfect.[4] All ministers were chosen from within the MPs' ranks.

Interestingly, the Czech MPs were considerably split in their normative views on the combination of offices. Around half of the interviewed MPs agreed with the statement: "MPs who are appointed as ministers should give up their parliamentary seats", while the other half disagreed or were not sure. With the exception of the Left Block (LB), in which the majority of MPs were against the fusion of offices, the split did not run between the parties, but rather through each individual party. This lack of consensus has been reflected in the many discussions on prohibition of the combination of two offices ever since 1992, though the reasons were not necessarily purely a matter of normative principles. A strong concern of many coalition politicians was that too many MPs in governmental positions posed problems for the management of parliamentary parties; it became difficult to maintain majorities in parliamentary committees, and ministers were frequently absent from the floor sessions of parliament. The relatively small number of ministers combining both mandates between 1992 and 1996 probably best explains why the opinion did not sweep in favour of the constitutional separation of mandates. However, the experience also shows that the fusion was very beneficial for government, in that when the ministers combined both functions, the executive had tighter control over what was happening inside their respective parliamentary parties. This control was almost total in the post-1996 Klaus government. And government parties were not eager to abandon such advantage, even though it meant a rather demanding coordination within their ranks, and higher work loads for ministers.[5] The situation in Slovakia closely corresponds to that in the Czech Republic. The majority of all new ministers in the post-1994 elections (Mečiar II) coalition government belonged, albeit very briefly, to the parliamentary party until they were appointed to a government position. This is to say that they first became MPs and as a result of coalition negotiations, were nominated to the cabinet.

Most importantly, the vast majority of the ministers in the Mečiar II cabinet also had parliamentary experience from the previous legislative periods, whether in the Slovak parliament or in the defunct Federal parliament. From the institutional point of view, however, the situation in Slovakia has considerably differed from that of their western neighbor. Article 77 of the Slovak Constitution states that "whenever a deputy becomes a member of the Government of the Slovak Republic, his parliamentary mandate does not become extinct; it is, however, not exercised during his tenure in governmental office". The designers of the Slovak Constitution probably looked at the recent parliamentary history of the common Czechoslovak state, as this is exactly the rule which a group of MPs (primarily from the Slovak movement VPN) unsuccessfully proposed in 1990 on the floor of the Federal parliament.

As the result of this new rule, the Slovak MPs who became ministers (5 ministerial appointments in the Mečiar I government) were replaced in the parliament by a person from a reserve list which, until 1994, was the person standing next on the electoral list in the preceding elections. When such a minister was dismissed from the government, he returned to the parliament and his replacement again lost the mandate. This principle of separation of power was also supported by a large majority of Slovak MPs, of which 74 percent agreed that ministers should give up their seat when becoming ministers. However, in one of the attempts to strengthen party grip on MPs and ministers, this provision was significantly modified by Mečiar's coalition in 1995: according to a new amendment, a vacant seat must be filled by a candidate from the same party and electoral district as the previous office holder. Crucially, it is no longer the order of candidates on the electoral list, but the party that determines replacement for a promoted MP, except in cases where any of the eligible candidates received preferential votes totalling at least 10 percent of the total votes cast for the party in that region.[6] Therefore, regardless of the question who choses a new MP (something Mečiar and his allies had particularly in mind to control when changing the law), this modification also became an in-built stabilizing factor for government: it is more difficult for a newcomer to vote against the minister (or government), since it could cost him his seat in parliament.

Overall, considering the two countries' constitutional prescription for the fusion of ministerial and parliamentary offices, there is a weaker precondition for the occurrence of inter-party mode in Slovakia. Yet, because there has been a common trend towards recruiting ministers primarily from the parliamentary benches, this important institutional difference between Czech and Slovak political systems has meant little in practice. Moreover, the strength of the inter-party mode has also been evident in another aspect of ministerial recruitment - its partisan footing. Even when the ministers were recruited from outside of parliament, they were usually members of the party which nominated them, had very close contacts with this party, or joined the party after ministerial recruitment. In other words, the appearance of non-partisan ministers in both countries was exceptional, though initially slightly more frequent in Slovakia than in the Czech Republic.[7]

Noteworthy is the fact that such political trends appeared in a situation where, in normative terms, MPs in both countries showed little sympathy for the British or Irish system of exclusive recruitment of ministers from parliament and, moreover, were considerably divided on the question of partisan ministers. Only six Czech and five Slovak parliamentarians agreed with the statement "Ministers should be recruited exclusively from parliament". About 57 percent of Czech and 42 percent of Slovak deputies agreed with the statement "Ministers should be members of a political party", whereas 20 percent and 29 disagreed. Probably the most plausible explanation is that, regardless of political practice, many Czech and Slovak MPs answered under a strong normative commitment to ministers as 'specialists', rather than as 'professional political appointees' at the mercy of their parties. This issue had a heavy bearing in many debates in the dissident circles, within the conception of anti-political politics, as well as being part of the criticisms of the overpoliticized and party-dominated democratic system of the First Republic. Post-communist elites always stressed publicly that appointments are based on specialist knowledge, rather than political experience or party affiliation. However, this normative conception or rhetoric has not translated into political practice, and we can thus conclude that our evidence of ministerial recruitment strongly supports a picture of the dominance of the inter-party mode of interactions between parliaments and governments in both countries.

Government formation

The potential strength of the interactions between ministers and MPs based on the inter-party mode is also clearly exhibited in government formation in both political systems. Article 68 of the Czech Constitution states that "the Government shall appear before the Chamber of Deputies within thirty days of its appointment and request a vote of confidence". Similarly, the Slovak Constitution states in Article 113 that "the Government is obliged to appear before the National Council of the Slovak Republic within thirty days from the date it has been appointed in order to submit its Programme and ask the National Council for a vote of confidence". From one point of view, the investiture vote could be interpreted as a sign for the non-party mode, since the act of voting pitches parliament against the government. However, we can argue with more plausibility that precisely because there is a mandatory vote of confidence, the establishment of a necessary parliamentary majority will require close consultations between both parliamentary parties and prospective ministers and between parliamentary parties themselves which, in turn, will strengthen the inter-party mode.

In reality, the extent of parliamentary party involvement in the negotiations on the formation of first governments in both countries is rather difficult to assess. First, there is not much information on the matter, because media coverage in the 1992 post-election situation focused predominantly on events related to the fate of the Federation. Moreover, the negotiations on the future of the Czechoslovak common state, and in particular the tense climate surrounding these events (see chapter 2), distracted the activities of political elites from questions of government formation to such an extent that once the prospective coalition partners agreed to work together, the leadership of the involved parties were given a free hand in the appointment of ministers. Parliamentary parties played only a passive role. This was particularly apparent in the case of Czech and Slovak governments formed below federal level; that is, those two national governments which were soon to become governments in two countries emerging from the split of the Federation. The secondary role of parliamentary parties also stemmed from an important provision in the federal constitution, which granted the Presidium of the Czech and Slovak National Councils the power to appoint the republics' governments. Only after 1993, in connection with the reconstruction of governments in Slovakia and changes on ministerial posts in the Czech Republic, were there clear signs of a more active parliamentary party involvement in government formation.

It must be noted, however, that in the Czech Republic the government parties signed the coalition agreement, defining the terms of cooperation of the prospective government parties for the whole legislative term. It is not a legally sanctioned rule, but parties involved in Klaus' first cabinet signed such a document in July 1992 after a month of negotiations, ostensibly in order to promote the stability of the emerging government. Besides a sketch of the governmental programme in various policy areas, the document mostly dealt with a distribution of government posts and basic rules of communication between the coalition partners. The experience showed that, though often disputed, violated, and even reformulated, the agreement became an important point of reference in all coalition negotiations. It set the basic rules for, and provided a battle ground in, a number of conflict situations that arose.[8] The inter-party mode acquired another institutional expression. Regular meetings between the chairmen of the coalition parties were established, and it was agreed that coalition MPs would not question ministers on the floor of parliament. Even proposed changes in the structure of ministries, something the Czech government championed in order to proceed with budgetary cuts, were skilfully avoided because, as the Prime Minister pointed out, "it is clear that a fragile balance of coalition forces does not allow the removal of a single minister, even if his entire department would be abolished".[9]

In Slovakia, the choice of ministers for the Mečiar I government was initially a matter of HZDS internal politics, since the cabinet (with one exception) was formed by its members or candidates. Therefore, no coalition agreement was needed, although on an informal basis certain political steps - such as division of committee and parliamentary chairs (see below) - were taken by HZDS and SNS in order to secure the tacit support of the latter party for the government. After further negotiations with SNS in November 1993, a new coalition agreement was reached but, unlike in the Czech Republic, it did not take the form of an elaborate written document. Although SNS had insisted on a written agreement with the HZDS, which would include precise rules of the game, the coalition partners were constantly coming up with new demands and there was never enough time and political will to agree on a final version (only a short preliminary version was signed). As a result, coalition business in Mečiar I government was dealt with on an ad-hoc, informal basis. Moravčík's provisional coalition cabinet, appointed in March 1994, also relied on an informal agreement, though there was a short signed document which established the so-called 'Coalition Council' (see below). The lack of time, rather than the lack of political will, explains the situation. Given that the government was formed within five days from the vote of no-confidence against the Mečiar I administration, it was already an achievement in itself to settle on the distribution of ministerial chairs and on governmental program. This means that, in comparison with the Czech Republic, the inter-party mode took a somewhat less institutionalized form between 1992 and 1994. However, having learned their lesson from previous years, the parties involved in forming the Mečiar II government signed a detailed coalition agreement in early 1995, thus making the situation similar to the Czech Republic.

Contacts between ministers and MPs

Even if parliamentary party involvement in government formation is marginal, and even if formal coalition agreements are not signed, the inter-party mode can obtain an institutional expression in the form of consultations between ministers and MPs. These can take the form of both parliamentary party meetings of the whole government majority to co-ordinate its activities vis-a-vis the opposition, as well as meetings between MPs and ministers from the same party. Indeed, while the coordination of the government majority in the Mečiar I cabinet focused primarily on consultations with party colleagues (see also below), during the term of Moravčík's cabinet a new institution - the Coalition Council - was established. The Council, comprised of the ministers and parliamentary party leaders, was set up to mediate the differing opinions of coalition parties on legislative proposals, and to facilitate support for governmental proposals in parliament. Without a written coalition agreement therefore, the inter-party mode was de facto instituted in the political process since, as Malová and Siváková (1996) point out, the Council considerably limited the powers of the parliament by making the legislative process heavily dependent on the bargaining of political parties outside the parliament.

The Czech Republic did not differ in this respect. In addition to the rules from the coalition agreement, the government parties established the so-called Coalition Thirteen. Similarly to the Coalition Council in Slovakia, the body comprised leaders of the coalition parties, the chairman and vice-chairman of the parliament (both representatives of the coalition), and the leaders of the coalition parliamentary parties. The aim of this unofficial body was to discuss legislative proposals before the floor meeting of the parliament, simply to find out whether there was enough support for a common course of action or, eventually, to reconcile existing disagreements. Additional devices established involved the so-called 'Parliamentary Nine'; that is, the Coalition Thirteen without the chairmen of the parties, which usually met twice a week, and the so called 'Four'; that is, the party leaders. If there was a disagreement between the parties in one of these consultative bodies, and if the conflicting proposal still found its way to the parliament, the existing divisions were usually reflected on the floor. In this way, the decisions reached or not reached in these institutions were important determinants of parliamentary politics.

Moreover, in both countries there were other information channels to make sure that the MPs would be in harmony with the decisions of government ministers. Our survey data indicated that the ministers and MPs were in close contact to coordinate party strategies, although the extent of institutionalization and intensity of contacts differed between the two countries as well as from party to party. On the whole, 93 percent of the Czech coalition MPs stated that they talked at least once a week to a minister from their own party. The frequency of talks with the ministers from other parties was lower: 37 percent of the MPs had such talks at least once a week, but a plurality of 41 percent had them only "a few times a year". Obviously it is difficult to determine the nature of such talks as in the Czech parliament it can include very popular and informal background corridor or smoking room talks, committee hearings, as well as the parliamentary party meetings. The party and government strategy must, however, be known to all involved, and hence our battery of questions on the frequency of the meetings of ministers and the parliamentary party should be a better empirical guide to the reality of consultations between ministers and MPs.

A large majority - 85 percent of the Czech coalition MPs - stated that their parliamentary party meets at least once a week with ministers from their own party. The breakdown of answers by party, summarized in Table 4.2, suggests that these meetings took place on a regular basis, at least once a week, in the three coalition parties. Additional interviews with parliamentary party leaders indicated that these meetings were not strictly regular, e.g. in an institutionalized form, but that the ministers were invited to parliamentary party meetings to present the government's point of view. For example, the statute of the ODS parliamentary party provides for ministers to participate at parliamentary party meetings whenever they think it necessary or when they are invited by the chairman. Technical parts of proposals or initiatives of individual MPs are usually discussed on these occasions. On more general policy matters, coordination between MPs and ministers is achieved in the

Table 4.2: Frequency of meetings between ministers and parliamentary parties: Czech coalition parties (%)

	ODS	KDS	ODA	KDU- ČSL
More than once a week	11.8	–	18.2	16.7
Once a week	80.4	28.6	72.7	75.0
Once a month	7.8	57.1	9.1	8.3
Few times a year	–	14.3	–	–
Hardly ever / never	–	–	–	–
(N)	(51)	(7)	(11)	(12)

meetings of party executives, where MPs regularly delegate their representatives, or at least (ex officio) the parliamentary party chairman (see chapter 6). As one MP remarked in a personal interview, "although there is a certain flexibility, the resolutions of the Executive Council should basically be binding for all of us." These guidelines for parliamentary parties are understood by the leaders of parliamentary parties, and the MPs themselves indicated this fact. The majority of the MPs in all coalition parties stated that the parliamentary party leader gives regular accounts of the meetings with the ministers. We could add that these meetings usually took place during either the sessions of party executives or in the abovementioned institutions like the Coalition Thirteen. Conversely, with the exception of KDS (see below), most MPs said that the parliamentary party leaders were regularly instructed on the stance to adopt in such meetings.

To what extent the parliamentary parties actually influence their ministers is of course open to question. But it is clear and documented in real cases that government proposals were drafted with the participation of coalition parliamentary parties or were in later stages, significantly changed after meetings with the parliamentary party. The MPs themselves said that their parliamentary parties have a rather high level of influence over ministers from their own party. On a scale from 1 (no influence) to 7 (a lot of influence), the mean value of influence for all coalition MPs was 4.88, with a standard deviation of 1.1. Table 4.3 summarizes the findings by party, indicating that the KDS parliamentary party had a lower influence over its (two) ministers than the other coalition parliamentary parties. The feeling that there should be more influence, however, was common to all coalition parties,

Table 4.3: Actual and desired influence of parliamentary party over 'own' ministers: Czech coalition parties (mean scores and standard deviation)

	All coalition parties		ODS		KDS		ODA		KDU- ČSL	
	Score	S	Score	S	Score	S	Score	S	Score	S
Actual influence	4.88	1.10	5.10	1.02	3.71	0.76	4.45	1.13	5.00	1.13
Desired influence	5.78	0.91	5.86	0.80	6.00	0.58	5.09	1.30	5.92	0.90
Difference between actual and desired influence	0.90	1.03	0.76	0.91	2.29	0.76	0.64	0.81	0.92	1.31
(N)	(81)		(51)		(7)		(11)		(12)	

although the actual difference between empirical and normative statement was, except for KDS, not very big. Perhaps this small gap between reality and ideal could help us to interpret the fact that in ODS, KDU-ČSL, and ODA there were only a few MPs dissatisfied with the communication between the parliamentary party and the party's ministers, whereas more than half of KDS MPs were dissatisfied.[10]

The data for the meetings of the parliamentary parties with ministers from other parties suggest a lower frequency of contacts, but nevertheless confirm that such meetings take place. Except for the KDS, the majorities of MPs in all remaining coalition parliamentary parties stated that their parties meet with ministers from other parties a few times a year. Most of the disagreements between coalition parties seemed to have been aired in Coalition Thirteen, and the solutions were then conveyed to parliamentary parties by the ministers or parliamentary party leaders from the same party. Only on few occasions did ministers attend hearings for other parliamentary parties, usually when they have been criticized persistently in a parliamentary committee or in the government.

If we move to the Czech opposition parties, meetings with ministers display an even lower frequency. This adds to the picture of divisions between coalition and opposition parties (i.e. a manifestation of a strong opposition submode in inter-party struggles) in the Czech parliament. Although a large majority - 73 percent of the opposition MPs - claimed to talk individually with ministers at least once a month, meetings of ministers with opposition parliamentary parties were scarce. The data in Table 4.4 show that with most opposition parliamentary parties the meetings took place only a few times a year - in the words of one MP only when "the ministers want to hammer out

Table 4.4: Frequency of meetings between ministers and parliamentary parties: Czech opposition parties (%)

	ČSSD	LSU	LB	HSD-SMS	HSDMS	SPR-RSČ
More than once a week	–	11.1	–	–	–	–
Once a week	–	–	–	–	–	–
Once a month	7.1	–	20.6	–	14.3	12.5
Few times a year	50.0	55.6	79.4	–	85.7	–
Hardly ever / never	42.9	33.3	–	100.0	–	87.5
(N)	(14)	(9)	(34)	(7)	(7)	(8)

something important"- and there were never meetings with the far right SPR-RSČ or HSD-SMS. More contacts were probably maintained through the meetings of ministers with the leaders of opposition parliamentary parties. This was confirmed by majorities of all opposition MPs, with the exception of the SPR-RSČ. The MPs also indicated that the parliamentary party leaders gave them regular accounts of such meetings, although the leaders were apparently not always instructed by the parliamentary party meeting on which stance to adopt in meetings with ministers.

Turning to Slovakia, one finds a somewhat different picture, at least with regard to the period of the Mečiar I government.[11] A large majority (76 percent) of their MPs stated that they talk individually with their own ministers at least once a week. However, here the similarity with the Czech colleagues in coalition parties ends. While 15 MPs stated that ministers meet with the parliamentary party at least once a week, 18 said once a month, and three a few times a year. The explanation rests in the nature of the HZDS party executive, which was, perhaps more than in the case of the Czech governmental parties, used as a means of communication between ministers and MPs, and as a tool to enforce the party line. This explanation can be supported by the views of HZDS MPs themselves, who stated they were given regular accounts of the meetings of their parliamentary party leader (an ex officio member of the party executive) with the ministers, and that the leader was, more regularly than incidentally, instructed on the stances to adopt in such meetings.[12]

It is also tempting to suggest from comparison with the Czech coalition parties that less intense contacts between the HZDS ministers and MPs may lie behind much of the troubles of the Mečiar I government. The mean value for the deputies' influence over ministers from own party, as stated by HZDS MPs, was 4.67 with 1.19 standard deviation. The stated mean value for the influence deputies should have over their own ministers was 5.81, with 1.17 standard deviation. Thus the gap between actual and desired influence was higher for the HZDS MPs than for the Czech coalition MPs. What partly militates against this explanation is that, similarly to most of the Czech parties, there was only a small number - 4 out of 36, of MPs who were dissatisfied with the communication between the parliamentary party and the own ministers. If, however, we pursue this topic further, looking at data on consultations between ministers and opposition parliamentary parties, we can uncover more of the background. Except for SDL, the majority of all opposition MPs, stated that ministers never meet with their parliamentary party, although a majority in each case confirmed regular meetings between their parliamentary party leaders and ministers. The exception of SDL is understandable, since this party often provided selective support for the Mečiar I government, hence the existence of consultations. Yet relying on one party alone, and keeping the others in strict opposition when the government's own majority was shaky provides us with a good background evidence for the turbulent nature of parliament-government relations during the June 1992 - March 1994 period. As after the 1994 elections, the Mečiar I cabinet tried to act as it had a strong majority, but unlike in that later period, the balance of parliamentary forces hardly allowed them to do so.

Under Moravčík's coalition government, consultations between ministers and MPs assumed a different character, pointing to the appearance of a strong inter-party mode. In KDH, for example, the party's ministers met with the parliamentary party whenever the government proposed a bill, and the KDH MPs, if they initiated their own policy or bill, consulted the government in advance.[13] Policy proposals of ministers from other coalition parties were usually presented to the parliamentary party by its own ministers. Also, as we indicated above, the Coalition Council mediated between coalition partners on the level of top party representatives. Moreover, a strong division between opposition and coalition parties was present (opposition submode), because HZDS and SNS were in practice unwilling to support any of the governmental proposals, often boycotting parliamentary sessions, blaming coalition parties for enacting a state coup, and declaring the government illegitimate. Needless to stay, the same sort of government-opposition polarization, if not a worse one, occurred during the Mečiar II government, but this time it was the parties from the former Moravčík government which stood in sharp opposition to virtually all proposals originating from the coalition.

All in all, there are grounds to suggest that the inter-party mode of interaction between MPs and ministers has been well promoted and has found a stronger institutional underpinning in the Czech Republic than in Slovakia. In the former, combining of ministerial and parliamentary offices is allowed; there is a tendency to recruit ministers from the parliament who are also representatives of political parties; a mandatory investiture vote exists; coalition parties sign coalition agreements and establish important institutional devices to mediate between each other; ministers and MPs are engaged in close consultations with each other. In Slovakia, though the mandatory investiture vote exists, the formal institutional preconditions for the occurrence of inter-party mode are slightly less favorable, since MPs have to give up their seats once they become ministers. However, it is important to note that the appearance of the inter-party mode in Slovakia differed from government to government. In other words, the character of parliament-government relations changed over time. From July 1992 to March 1994, under the Mečiar I administration, the inter-party mode was the least expressed mode of interaction between MPs and the ministers: government parties were fragmenting; MPs were in less intensive consultations with the ministers; coalition agreements with SNS were largely informal. From March 1994 to September 1994, under Moravčík's premiership, the situation migrated into a more pronounced inter-party mode, particularly in that the government enjoyed a relatively stable majority, nurtured by close consultations between ministers and MPs, as well as by inter-coalition mediating institutions (the Coalition Council).

Clearly, Slovakia's admittedly more polarized, and initially also more fragmented, political scene has gradually produced a shift towards the inter-party mode of interactions between ministers and MPs, and in particular towards its strong opposition sub-mode. The HZDS adversarial style of politics resulted not only in an inability to maintain its political partners in the first government, but also speeded up the process of crystallization and internal consolidation of other parties. The omnipresent attempts by Mečiar to make inroads into the leadership of opposition political parties fabricated an undesired side-effect - a propensity for higher internal cohesion among opposition parties and, gradually, a willingness to cooperate with each other.[14] The political situation after the September 1994 elections is telling in this respect. HZDS turned out its second successive victory in the general elections. Although they failed to gain an absolute majority that would have let them form a one-party government, they still won enough seats in the parliament that realistically no coalition with a parliamentary majority could be formed without HZDS participation. The government took almost three months to form and the result was coalition of HZDS, SNS, and the Association of Workers in Slovakia (ZRS), controlling 83 seats out of 150.

A move of ministers and MPs into the inter-party mode of operation was apparent from the very first meeting of the new parliament in November 1994. In a famous night-long session, HZDS, SNS, and ZRS (at that time not even yet established as a formal government coalition), replaced virtually all personnel in key parliament-appointed oversight bodies and state media with their own candidates.[15] Having done so, the government formation in Slovakia was predetermined. The other parties, namely SDL and KDH, walked out of negotiations, claiming that the political style of the election winner precludes any stable coalition government with their participation.[16] The same parliamentary majority also determined the composition of the parliamentary committees to its advantage. The original proposals of the opposition parliamentary parties were changed on the floor of the parliament, so as to give the coalition a majority on all committees except the less important Committee for Environment.[17] The opposition deputies were shifted into this committee against their will and without their consent. The strong division between the coalition and the opposition parties was completed, with the opposition excluded from virtually all oversight or investigatory committees and commissions.

Moreover, after the government was officially formed in January 1995, similar changes in favour of coalition parties began to take place on the level of ministries and branches of state administration. The Mečiar II government could rely on a firm and cohesive majority and, until June 1996, when the coalition itself was divided over the issue of bank privatization, no government bill was defeated in the parliament. In a press release, the opposition DU criticized the work of the Slovak parliament as a "tyranny of the majority",[18] while the Prime Minister criticized opposition parties for not co-operating with the government, saying that only his coalition partners were willing to work together.[19] As a result of this hostility and infighting, what was initially a polarization between various individual parties rapidly became a sharp polarization between two mutually hostile and increasingly cohesive blocks of parties. KDH and DU formed the so-called Blue Coalition in the summer 1997, agreeing to co-ordinate their oppositional and electoral strategies and, three months later, included the other three smaller parties in the agreement under the umbrella organization called the Slovak Democratic Coalition. It is also telling that a similar agreement was also signed with the Hungarian minority parties (which themselves formed a coalition), although the Hungarians had hitherto been treated by *all* Slovak parties with a suspicion and kept at a distance.

It is very tempting to conclude after all this that the Czech and Slovak parliaments were transformed primarily into arenas for party political struggles. However, the word "primarily" is crucial here. As indicated above, the translation of institutional arrangements into political reality was not always without problems. In at least three important areas - the restitution of church property, the establishment of the Senate, and the administrative division of the country, the Czech coalition parties, and very often even MPs and ministers, could not find a common course between 1992 and 1996, regardless of the agreements, institutional preconditions, and objectives of the governmental programme. Autonomous decisions of individual MPs existed, and the activity of parliamentary committees constituted a challenge for government-sponsored bills. Two scholars concluded that:

> "their existence has proved that the Parliament still occupies a strong position within the political system and that it is able to extricate itself from the grip of the decision-making of the executive power and of political parties" (Reschová and Syllová, 1996:98).

In a similar vein, one observer of the Slovak political scene concluded in the light of the governmental crisis in 1994 that recent events in Slovakia show how a strong Parliament can complicate cabinet formation and undermine executive power, particularly when political parties are fragmented and undisciplined and the political elite is unsettled and adversarial (Malová, 1995a). This indicates that cross-party interests or individual MPs might not have lost their influence altogether and, in turn, leaves our analysis with an important question to answer: even if the inter-party mode is the dominant mode of interaction between Czech and Slovak ministers and MPs, are there any institutional arrangements and political conditions which can prompt the existence of cross-party and non-party modes?

Parliaments as Market Places for Trading of Social Interests

The system of parliamentary committees is undoubtedly the most important indicator of the existence of the cross-party mode. It has been argued that "[c]ommittees are critical to the deliberative powers of parliaments...[s]trong committees, it appears, are at least a necessary condition for effective parliamentary influence in the policy-making" (Mattson and Strøm, 1995:250). Committees enable deputies to develop specialization in specific policy areas and to acquire necessary information and are, therefore, not only an important indication, but also an important precondition for the existence of the cross-party mode (Andeweg and Nijzink, 1995). The Czech and Slovak parliaments have at their disposal just such a system of permanent parliamentary committees. A snapshot picture in Table 4.5 shows that in 1994, structural differences between the two parliaments were negligible, both in the number of committees and in their membership. The committees are specialized and subject-based, though they do not strictly correspond to ministerial departments (see also Table 4.6 below). Some bills are referred simultaneously to two or more committees, which may meet together and present a common report. All bills without exception used to be referred to the

Table 4.5: Permanent Committees in Czech and Slovak parliaments, 1994

Czech Parliament		Slovak Parliament	
Committee	No of MPs	Committee	No of MPs
Mandate and Immunity	14	Mandate and Immunity	15
Constitututional and Legal Committee	20	Constitututional Committee	20
Economy	21	Economy and Budget	20
Budget	18	–	–
Agriculture	18	Agriculture, Forest and Water Economy	10
Public Administration, Regional Development and Environment	23	Civil Service, Regional Management and Nationalities	15
–	–	Environment and Protection of Nature	9
Social Policy and Health	22	Health and Social Affairs	16
Legal Protection and Security	18	Petitions, Law, Protection and Security	15
Petition, Human Rights and Nationalities	13	–	–
Foreign Affairs	15	Foreign Affairs	12
Science, Education, Culture, Youth and Physical Training	19	Education, Science and Culture	17
–	–	Privatization	12

Source: Malová and Siváková (1996) for the Slovak parliament; *Parlamentní Zpravodaj*, 1(2), 1995 for the Czech parliament.

Constitutional committees to check their compatibility with the constitution.

According to the Czech constitution, the committees have to be constituted at the beginning of every legislative term, though it is not specified exactly in what numbers and structure. These, together with the committees' procedures and powers, are specified in parliamentary standing orders. The Slovak constitution does not say much about parliamentary committees, and their structure, procedures and powers are primarily regulated by the standing orders. Until recently, in both countries, the only mandatory committee to be established was Mandate and Immunity. The new standing orders of the Czech parliament, passed in April 1995, provide also for the mandatory establishment of the Budget and Petition committees. The new standing orders of the Slovak parliament, passed in October 1996, also establish a mandatory Constitutional Committee, and the Committee for Incompatibility of Mandates.[20] The chairmen of both parliaments are not allowed to be committee members: neither are (in the Czech Republic) MPs

Table 4.6: Committee Structures, Powers and Procedures

	Czech Republic	Slovakia
correspondence with ministerial departments	subject-based, approximate correspondence between most committees and ministerial departments	subject-based, approximate correspondence between most committees and ministerial departments
mutlitple membership	double membership allowed	neither mandated nor prohibited
sub-committees	allowed	no
chairs selection	by committees, but must be approved by majority voting on the floor	by parliamentary parties, must be approved by majority voting on the floor
member selection	by parliamentary parties according to PR principle	by parliamentary parties, must be approved by majority vote on the floor
committee meetings	public, unless decided by committee otherwise	public, unless decided by committee otherwise
commitee stage of deliberation process	after plenary stage	after plenary stage
minority reports	possible, if requested by at least one fifth of committee members	possible, if requested by at least one third of committee members
legislative initiative	no	yes
authority to rewrite bills	no, commitees only present amendments	no, commitees only present amendments
timetable	minimum 60 days for a bill, can be extended by another 20 days if agreed by bill initator	minimum 30 days for a bill, can be extended by majority vote on the floor
hearings	ministers and civil servants obliged to participate if asked by	ministers and civil servants obliged to participate if asked

who simultaneously serve in the cabinet.

As the above citations indicate, the activity of parliamentary committees presumably exerted a significant influence on the legislative process in both countries and, at first sight at least, there is some evidence to support such views. To take a broad view of both parliaments, the existence of parliamentary committees clearly fostered both the cross-party agreements and conflicts between individual MPs and their parliamentary parties. Consequently, governmental bills were modified and successfully amended in the committee stage of the legislative process: the estimates talk about 20 percent of changes to each passed bill in the Czech Republic, the changes being recommended in the often large committee reports presented on the floor of parliament.[21] MPs regularly exercised their right to request ministers' personal attendance, inviting them for informational hearings about the situation in their policy area. The work of MPs in committees is now monitored by the office of the chairman of parliaments - an indication that absenteeism in committees became unacceptable from the view point of the full exercise of MPs' mandate. Moreover, in the Slovak parliament, the committees used their constitutional right of legislative initiative to successfully propose bills. Out of a total of 232 passed bills in the 1992-1994 legislative period, two such committee-sponsored bills were passed by the parliament.

The Czech and Slovak MPs themselves were keen on emphasizing committee activity in the area of legislative deliberation. In response to the question "Which, in your experience, is the single most important function the permanent parliamentary committees perform at this moment", large and equal majorities of 76 percent of MPs in both countries answered "to prepare legislation for plenary debates". Answers in the category "check on government" and "channel demands of social and professional groups" scored distinctly less: 12 percent and 4 percent respectively in the Czech Republic, and 9 percent and 10 percent respectively in Slovakia.[22] In normative terms (which function *should be* performed), the percentages went up for the category "check on government" - 32 percent of Czech and 27 percent of Slovak MPs - largely at the expense of the category "prepare legislation for plenary sessions". Not surprisingly, the cross-tabulation by party showed that it was by and large opposition MPs who accounted for the slight shift of answers in normative compared to empirical terms.

However, preparing legislation for plenary session is, in fact, a sign of the relatively weak position of committees in both parliaments, rather than, as the picture above might suggest, of their strength. There are a number of institutional and political factors in play here, which supports this contention.

The first obstacle to developing strong committees, and hence a strong cross-party mode of interaction between ministers and MPs, can be detected in the institutional arrangements themselves. Although the standing committees in both parliaments enjoy the right to invite ministers, experts and civil servants for hearings, the professional support granted to them has been quite weak. Apart from a secretary and one administrative employee, the standing committees did not have permanent professional background facilities at their disposal. In practice, it increased both the importance of party facilities and resources (see chapter 6) and the dependence of legislation on governmental drafts, which were much better prepared than comparable private member or committee proposals. Interestingly, the MPs themselves did not feel that increasing resources for parliamentary committees was a priority: in a response to the question "If there are resources for administrative backup for parliament, where should the money primarily go?", only 11 percent of Czech and 20 percent of Slovak MPs said it should go to the committees. A plurality of Czech MPs (44 percent) preferred money to be spent on personal staff for MPs (19 percent of MPs in Slovakia) and a plurality of Slovak MPs (35 percent) would have preferred money to go for parliamentary parties (20 percent of MPs in the Czech Republic).[23] Indeed, it is worth pointing out that the largest increases of financial resources granted to parliaments in subsequent years were distributed exactly according to the preferences of the corresponding pluralities in both countries, even though also the less preferred committees slightly benefited from extra financial backup.

Furthermore, the institutional character of committees was the subject of numerous debates, especially as the MPs in both parliaments started work on new parliamentary standing orders. And the changes made in both countries do not lend much support to the idea of strong parliamentary committees. The legislative process in both parliaments was significantly changed by the introduction of the so-called 'principle of three readings'. From the committee viewpoint, the most important consequence is that the bill is assigned to a committee only after it has been debated on the floor. If the majority on the floor agrees with the general principles of the bill, then the Organizational Committee or the Chairman of the Parliament in the Czech Republic, or the Chairman of the Parliament in Slovakia, can recommend it be passed on to one or more committees. Compared to the previous legislative procedure in both countries, whereby the bill was first referred to the committee(s), the committees have lost complete discretion over the proposed bill, since the prior agreement on the floor limits their competences to details and specifics (though it is still possible for committees to recommend rejection of the bill during the second reading).

Moreover, in the Czech Republic, the new standing orders allow an MP to acquire membership in two committees. The introduction of double membership was a result of the difficulties the coalition experienced between 1992 and 1996 with maintaining majorities in all committees. Holding governmental posts or positions in the leadership of the parliament, precluded membership in the committees. This could also explain why the Slovak elite, undoubtedly keen on a strong majority rule, did not introduce double membership (though standing orders also do not strictly forbid it): as we have seen above, Slovak MPs do give up their seat if they become ministers. This puts significantly less stress on the availability of personnel for parliamentary committees. Given their small size, parties in the 1992-1996 Czech government, such as ODA and KDS, were not able to cover all existing committees with at least one MP from their ranks and a simple change of rule was seen as possible remedy to this situation. From the committee view point, however, a possible consequence of double membership (essentially a result of the promotion of a majority rule) is that it waters down the effect of specialization and, therefore, impedes the prospect for the emergence of the cross-party mode.[24]

Needless to say, the changes mentioned above did not come out of the blue. On the contrary, they are very good reflections of political elites' conceptions of the role different parliamentary institutions should perform. In a sense, the changes in the structure of parliamentary committees should supplement our evidence on the dominance of the inter-party mode in the parliamentary practice in both countries, and in particular on a strong tendency to institutionalize majority rule. To be sure, a skilful use of the prerogatives in the old standing orders had the same effect. For example, in 1994 the Slovak coalition government shifted opposition MPs from one committee to another (see above), simply using the rule that "committee membership is decided by the majority vote on the floor". In a similar vein, the Czech parliament did not introduce any substantial changes to the standing orders for a long time, because parties, and particularly coalition parties, were happy with the status quo. However, the enthusiasm of many MPs, who saw the need to modernize the old and discredited standing orders was simply used by ruling majorities to (try to) institutionalize their dominant position. Although committees retained many prerogatives (see Table 4.6) to foster a climate of cross-party cooperation and specialization, and even gained in some respects (e.g. minority reports), it is clear that their weakening was as important as the alleged modernization the changes were supposed to achieve.

The institutional rules were engineered in a specific political context of Czech and Slovak executive-legislative relations, and this context proved a further major hindrance to the strength of committees in both parliaments. In any parliament, the committees may fall victim to a number of outside pressures, limiting their impact on the legislative process and, thereby decreasing their potential for fostering the cross-party mode of relations between MPs and ministers. A seminal study on parliamentary committees has argued that the single most important factor in this respect is the (parliamentary) party (Shaw, 1979). Even in a legislature traditionally associated with very strong committees, such as the US Congress, they may be seen as merely the instruments of a majority party and its leaders (Cox and McCubbins, 1993). However, although party affiliation is probably the single most important factor, and is certainly vital for us to consider here (i.e. the interplay of inter-party and cross-party modes), it is not the only limiting factor. The work of procedurally very strong committees in the Japanese parliament, for example, suffered from a lack of interest and independent initiative on the part of its members (Baerwald, 1979).

The lack of interest does not seem to be the Achilles heel of Czech and Slovak parliamentarians, even though it was not unusual in the first years to see committee meetings cancelled because of poor attendance (i.e. lack of quorum). In itself, the problem was rooted in the chaotic organization of the legislative process, in particular the many overlapping agendas with which MPs had to cope, rather than in unjustified absenteeism. The introduction of new standing orders in both countries could, in this respect, potentially help a good deal. Committee sessions, plenary sessions, international journeys, and surgery weeks are now organized into more neatly separated blocks and the MPs are under obligation to notify committee chairs in written if they will be absent from its sessions. However, while procedural clarity may be an important element in eventually strengthening the position of committees, the streamlining or, as Illonszki (1996) calls it in her survey of Eastern European parliaments, "rationalization", should not be viewed in isolation from the interests of (governing) political parties.

In any case, the work of parliamentary committees was influenced less by attendance than by the dominant position of governments and the marginal input of extra-parliamentary actors in the legislative process. The dominance of governments could be explained by disproportionate advantages in administrative backup available to the ministerial departments, as opposed to those of the committees, or individual MPs. When asked whether they agreed or disagreed with the following statement: "committees are under pressure to give most attention to government bills", the answers of our respondents were nevertheless fairly divided. Fifty percent of Czech and 44 percent of Slovak MPs agreed or agreed completely with the statement, while 25 percent and 33 percent either disagreed or disagreed completely; 21 percent of Czech and 23 percent of Slovak MPs were of neutral opinion (neither agree nor disagree). Cross-tabulation by coalition/opposition showed that opposition MPs in both countries, and particularly in the Czech Republic, were more likely to agree with the statement, while coalition MPs were in the opposing camp. This is hardly surprising given that the opposition MPs were rarely involved in preparing coalition legislation and, as we shall also see later, their way of influencing legislation by presenting private member bills achieved only marginal success. Government bills, drafted with more developed legal services, fared better than often poorly developed bills from committees or individual MPs, even those prepared by coalition MPs themselves.

Committees in both countries also suffered from the sheer volume of legislation they had to process within a relatively short period of time, which had the obvious effect of limiting their chance to make substantial changes to the proposed drafts. Although a fast-track legislative procedure had been possible in exceptional cases in both countries since the introduction of new standing orders, it was not used very often. However, committees were flooded with mostly government sponsored legislative proposals and were requested to deal with them as quickly as possible. In the Czech parliament, a large majority of 84 percent of MPs either agreed or agreed completely with the statement "the government too often exerts pressure on committees to discuss bills quickly," and the division between coalition and opposition MPs was marginal. In Slovakia, a majority 60 percent of MPs agreed or agreed completely, but unlike in the Czech Republic, responses were divided between coalition (more likely to disagree) and opposition (more likely to agree). In technical terms, the limitation of committees' time to consider a bill was the result of a tight legislative program, agreed at the beginning of each year between government and parliament, to which committees had to conform. If a bill was to be discussed in a plenary session, the committees were under informal obligation to report the bill, even if they had less time to devote to it than was desired. Committees had to function almost like law processing factories, because governments were pushing to pass as much legislation as possible in a short time, driven by the rapid pace of social, political and economic reforms for which they were held responsible.

In light of the above, the lack of consultations between committees and organized groups, and between committees and various non-governmental organizations, was at least partly a blessing. Legal chaos could well have ensued if committee work was slowed down even further as a result of lengthy bargaining with outside parliamentary organizations. However, the exclusion of external actors from the legislative process also meant that committees deprived themselves of vital sources of information and expertise with which to challenge their respective governments, and the legislative process in both countries provided only a limited support for external actors seeking to influence the state. In consequence, this exclusion undermined, and continues to undermine, a cross-party mode of operation between the parliaments and governments. Analyzing this problem from the view point of weak elite-mass linkages in the Czech Republic, Green and Skalnik Leff (1997:77) write:

> "The legislative process itself offers little additional access to the policy process. The opportunity for external input, which could occur only at the committee level, is itself uninstitutionalized: involvement by outsiders occurs only by invitation of the committee majority, and is often limited to being present; only rarely does an outside actor have the opportunity to answer questions or provide information of any kind".

The answers of Czech MPs tend to confirm the situation described by Green and Skalnik-Leff: 57 percent of respondents answered 'low' or 'very low' to the statement "How do you rate the chances of social and professional groups of influencing the decisions in your committee", while 34 percent said 'high', and only 4 percent answered 'very high'. There were differences between individual committees, though, in that, for example, Constitutional and Foreign Affairs committees scored very low on outside influences, while the Agriculture committee, often lobbied by one of the better organized interest groups, scored higher. Even in the cases of arguably more exposed committees, however, answers of MPs were split, and significant numbers of deputies said that the influence of social and professional groups was low or very low. Interestingly, very similar (actually almost the same) results yielded answers to the statement "How do you estimate the chances of civil servants to influence the decisions in your committee": 57 percent of respondents answered 'low' or 'very low', whereas 38 percent said either 'high' or 'very high'. This is a paradoxical result, because close observation of committee work would surely reveal that civil servants were, via their more or less regular hearings and by defenses of governmental bills on behalf of ministers, more likely to influence the work of committees than were social and professional groups. In all likelihood, our respondents provided socially desirable answers to one or both questions, since they did not want to be viewed as either dependent on civil servants, sometimes associated with the old 'nomenklatura', or as representatives of particular interests and lobby groups.

In Slovakia, the answers of MPs to the above statements were even more puzzling. The respondents were more equally divided in terms of the influence of both professional and social groups, as well as civil servants: 45 percent said chances of social and professional groups to influence the work in their committee was high or very high (47 percent low or very low); 49 percent said chances of civil servants were high or very high (42 percent low or very low). The cross-tabulation by committee was truly puzzling, since, for example, the influence of professional and social groups was seen high or very high in Constitutional and Foreign Affairs committees which, similarly to the Czech parliament, were both the exclusive domain of MPs and minsters, with traditionally little outside influences. At the same time, a majority of respondents gave low or very low scores to the Budget committee, which was more likely to be influenced by economic interest groups or, for that matter, also by civil servants. It is difficult to find any explanation other than that our question was misconceived, or answered at least partially in a socially desirable way. The reality was, nevertheless, strikingly similar in both countries, and the lack of influence, if not deliberate exclusion, of social and professional groups from committees was even higher in Slovakia (except for those groups sanctioned, supported and financially dependent on the government) than in the Czech Republic, especially under the Mečiar II government.

The lack of interest groups participation in committee work (and in the political process in general) in the Czech and Slovak Republics is usually associated with groups' weak basis in society, poor organization, and a lack of elaborated strategies of action. But this has also been reinforced, in both countries, by the technocratic approaches of governments, political parties and their MPs, who were unwilling to open the policy-making process to outside groups, and to face challenges from experts not immediately accountable to party machines, or holding opposing views to that of government majorities. This exclusion was obviously possible only because committees could hardly renounce their (party) political character, and the committee assignment procedure is the first indicator in this respect. For while the formal designation of committee members is made by voting on the floor, the real decisions are made within the parliamentary parties. In our survey, 57 percent of the Czech MPs said that the meeting of the parliamentary party decides on the membership in the committees.[25] Only 18 percent of them stated it is the MP's own decision, while another 18 percent answered "somebody else decides", pointing (in open-ended answers) to a combination of an MP's own wish, ability, professional experience and party interest. Beside that, and as indicated above, composition of committees in the (1992-1996) Czech parliament was preceded by the parties' attempt to provide both a majority of government deputies in all committees and, at the same time, to maintain obligatory proportional representation. The abovementioned question yielded very similar percentages for the Slovak MPs: 54 percent for the parliamentary party meeting, 19 percent for the MP himself, and 15 percent for a combination of party interest and professional expertise.

The distribution of the committee chairs also reflects party line divisions. None of the committee chairmen in the 1992-1996 Czech parliament came from the opposition parties. The new standing orders from 1995 even make this the rule, in that the principle of proportional representation must be applied in the designation of MPs to the committees, yet all chairmanship positions in the parliament, including those in the committees, are decided by the committee and the parliamentary majority.[26] In Slovakia, the gap in formal rules has been filled by political decisions and, in the parliament elected in September 1994, none of the opposition deputies chaired a committee. As shown above, the coalition even went so far as to substantially violate a hitherto observed informal rule of PR representation of individual MPs on committees and, by voting on the floor, changed original opposition parties' proposals as it felt appropriate. However, during the 1992-1994 parliament, opposition parties (except of Hungarian parties) were given at least one committee chairmanship in the immediate aftermath of the 1992 elections. This was part of a broader package of concessions made by the leadership of HZDS in order to the secure support of the opposition for the new Slovak constitution, and also in the investiture vote. The political impact of this decision was felt during the Mečiar I government, as some committees assumed an important role in challenging the government and, in fact, became one of the principal means of influence the opposition parties could bring to bear on the administration. It is therefore not all too surprising that the first thing the Meciar II government did after its 1994 victory was to secure a clear majority in all parliamentary positions, including parliamentary committees. These changes were not only a matter of political revenge, but also a conscious attempt to exercise safe coalition control in all positions were it mattered.

The lack of relevant data is a major obstacle in the study of actual behavior of MPs at the committee stage. To what extent do MPs feel free from the party line at the committee stage? And, conversely, to what extent does the specialization in the committees enhance individual MP's chances of determining the party line in the parliamentary party meeting? On the one hand, a significant indication in the direction of specialization is provided by the designation of re-elected MPs. Reschová and Syllová (1996) report that from 60 re-elected deputies in the Czech parliament, 41 were elected to the same committee and some of them even became chairman of that committee. On the other hand, it cannot be easily judged whether the MPs became primarily the representatives of that committee, or whether, with the centralization of party management, they became merely representatives, supporters, and advocates of party policy. The survey does not help much in this respect: 39 percent of the Czech and 51 percent of the Slovak MPs stated that the parliamentary party meeting is a crucial determinant of their position in the committee stage of the legislative process. Nonetheless, 39 percent of the Czech deputies, and 27 percent of the Slovak ones, said that this depends on their own decision; 19 percent and 17 percent respectively, stated that "somebody else decides", usually pointing to an interplay of factors like the issue on agenda, or a particular party interest. Neither in the Czech parliament, nor in the Slovak, did the cross- tabulation reveal substantial differences between the parties.

One plausible hypothesis involves differences between individual MPs. Andeweg and Nijzink (1995) argue that ministers and MPs may specialize in one mode or another, which can explain the coexistence of modes. In our case, some of the MPs - those deputies taking the party position at the committee stage - would be party representatives, the others would perhaps be representatives of special social, professional and regional interests, or just true parliamentarians, who believe checking on the government to be the main role of the committees. The data from a preliminary test, however, do not support this hypothesis. We divided the MPs who answered the question "What do you consider to be the most important tasks you have to fulfill as an MP" into two groups: those saying that the most important task is to fulfill the party program (presumably party representatives), and those saying, in some form, that the most important task is to represent a certain region or to be involved in a particular policy area (presumably specialists).[27] We then cross-checked them with their answers as to who determines the position they take on the legislation in parliamentary committees. We might have expected 'party representatives' to say that it is the parliamentary party, whereas we would expect 'specialists' to say that it is their own view. Although the Czech 'party representatives' had a tendency to say their view was determined by the parliamentary party, 'specialists' were equally divided between 'party view' and 'own view'. The Slovak 'party representatives' were equally divided between 'party view' and 'own view', 'specialists' even had a tendency to say their view was determined by the parliamentary party.

Thus, we are still left with a hypothesis which is thrown into doubt by yet another important aspect of Czech and Slovak parliamentary reality - the relatively small size of both the parliament and parliamentary parties. In combination, these can obstruct the specialization of MPs, since in reality there is not much of a difference between a specialist in a certain policy area and the party representative. Indeed, the author's own interviews with the members of smaller parliamentary parties in Slovakia (KDH and the Hungarian parties) indicated that the view of the party is usually the view of the specialist, who is the party spokesman on the issue as well as a member of the relevant parliamentary committee. On the other hand, the bigger parliamentary parties, like ODS in the Czech Republic, established a system of intra-party committees, or ad-hoc groups of specialists, which worked out the standpoint of the party before and during the committee stage of the legislative process. In both cases, and in both parliaments, this again indicates that the development of the cross-party mode was obstructed by the strength of the inter-party mode, either due to the small size of some parties, or due to the growing *intra-party* specialization. Calda and Gillis (1995) report, for the Czech parliament, that although committee members may propose amendments, only one-sixth of all proposed amendments have been accepted and passed into law.

What could not be done on the level of officially instituted parliamentary committees was at least partly provided by informal networks of individual MPs. The existence of such networks or groups in both parliaments was confirmed by our respondents. Ninety percent of the Czech MPs said that there are informal groups of deputies from different parties who have a common interest in some problem or issue. Sixty percent of the MPs indicated that they participate in one or more of these groups. Apart from groups interested in a particular policy area, groups of MPs representing a certain region were also frequently mentioned in the answers to a question that was aimed at identifying these groups. There were also visible examples of ad hoc groups of MPs, created to discuss and even prepare legislation concerning, for example, the regulating of prostitution; there was also a group of women representatives. In the Slovak parliament, the percentage of MPs stating that there were informal groups was lower (67 percent), and so was the number of participating MPs. As in the Czech parliament, regional groups as well as policy area groups were frequently mentioned in open-ended answers to this question.

However, in the words of Czech and Slovak MPs themselves, it was equally apparent that the role of all these informal groups was relatively marginal in the legislative process. Informal networks nurtured the sense of cooperation and collegiality between deputies from different parties which, in the post-1994 Slovak parliament, was surely an achievement in itself, given the hostility between opposing blocks of parties. Nevertheless, there were few structural preconditions for cross-party groups to proliferate. In neither of the two parliaments have they been officially recognized in either the constitution or parliamentary standing orders. Moreover, their possible influence was negatively retarded by the way electoral laws and the nomination procedure of candidates for the parliament worked in practice. As we saw in the previous chapter, in both countries the MPs are elected by a system of proportional representation, based on large electoral districts. The constituency is usually represented by more than 20 MPs from different parties which, together with other factors, has so far tended to minimalize direct links between MPs and their constituencies. The link is provided by the party, which nominates an MP to parliament. Therefore, the prospect for cross-party groups are more dependent on the extent to which the nomination procedure within the parties is decentralized, and any links the local party makes between a particular regional issue and the renomination of an MP.

From the perspective of the parliaments elected in 1992, both countries had a centralized nomination of candidates. This was not necessarily connected to oligarchical tendencies within parties, but more to the fact that parties were still building local organizations and their choice of candidates was severely limited. That said, it turned out to matter that the Slovak parties before the split of Czechoslovakia in 1992 nominated their top candidates to the Slovak National Council parliament, whereas the Czech parties nominated theirs to the Federal Assembly (see also chapter 6). As a result, the Czech MPs nominated to the Czech National Council were, by and large, selected from the growing local party organizations in the regions. This may have fostered their propensity, compared with the Slovak MPs, to advocate issues connected to various cross-party interests, and perhaps explains the somewhat higher response of the Czech MPs on the existence of informal groups. It may shed light as well on a spectacular cross-party division on the floor in April 1995, when a proposal from a group of MPs on the establishment of administrative units in the country was discussed. Regardless of party affiliation, a number of the Czech MPs formed groups behind a proposal or amendment, which would split the country into such units that would grant their home cities the status of regional administrative capitals. The proposal was defeated, primarily because parties mustered enough obedient members to avoid potential embarrassment to the official government line, but it showed that at least some forms of cross party cooperation were possible.

In sum, the relatively marginal importance of informal groups of MPs is symptomatic of the whole issue of cross-party cooperation in the Czech and Slovak parliaments. Our evidence suggests that the cross-party mode of relations between MPs and ministers is, in institutional as well as political terms, largely overshadowed by the dominance of inter-party interactions, and there is very little to suggest that this might change dramatically in the near future. Whether the non-party mode of interactions displays similar characteristics to cross-party interactions is subject of the following and last section of this chapter.

Parliaments and Governments as Two Separate Institutions

The Czech and Slovak parliaments provided clear examples of parliamentary meetings in which ministers and MPs interacted according to the non-party mode; that is, situations in which parliament acted as an institution against the government. The Czech parliament, for example, almost unanimously rejected a governmental proposal for the privatization of the parliamentary buildings. The government's intention was to move the Czech parliament into the building of the former Federal Assembly, which had been empty since the split of the Czechoslovak Federation in January 1993. The government planned to offer the potentially lucrative historical buildings of the National Council in the center of Prague to foreign investors. This proposal met with fierce resistance from Czech parliamentarians, who were reluctant to move to the place where their rivals used to sit, and was voted down. Another example of the non-party mode appeared during the debates on the new Parliamentary Standing Orders. Although opposition MPs frequently accused coalition MPs of devising the document in accordance with their own needs, all MPs seemed to be united in that they regarded the whole debate as a parliamentary matter, in which the government should have no say. The government's interventions were seen as undesirable by all parliamentarians. Similarly, Slovak MPs surprised the government when they decided to increase their wages and other parliamentary subsidies in 1992, which Mečiar and his cabinet colleagues vehemently opposed. Such debates, which pitched the MPs against ministers, occurred also in the Czech Republic whenever salary questions were dealt with on the floor of the parliament.

The legislative activity of individual MPs, or group of MPs, is another reason to believe that the non-party mode of interaction between MPs and ministers found some expression in the Czech and Slovak parliamentary practice. In just one year, 1993, the Czech parliament passed 79 bills in total, of which 16 were private member bills (Reschová and Syllová, 1996). The Slovak parliament, from August 1992 to August 1994, passed 227 bills in total, out of which 55 were private member bills.[28] Although not all of these bills concerned very important matters, the activity of an individual MP in seeking support for his/her bill at least put the issues on the political agenda. Interestingly, the individual MPs' initiatives in both parliaments shared certain policy attributes. For while economic issues were predominantly covered by the government, on issues related to reform of the state administration or constitutional matters (electoral law, law on political parties) we witnessed greater activity from individual MPs. This is understandable, since more lawyers than economists tended to sit in the parliament and, as mentioned above, parliaments had less administrative resources to make qualified decisions in the economic sphere. Equally, it is arguable that MPs had a better chance of attracting public attention in frequently televized parliamentary sessions, by advocating more general issues rather than technical economic proposals.

It is crucial to note, however, that the vast majority of private member bills were, in fact, bills proposed by parliamentary parties. This points back to the dominance of inter-party rather than non-party mode of relations between MPs and ministers. Since most private member bills were opposition bills, and since parliamentary parties in both countries are not granted the right of legislative initiative, they had to assign an individual MP if they wanted to put a proposal on the legislative agenda. Parties usually did not object to designated and respected specialists if they came up with their own legislative initiatives, but it was equally rare for an MP to pursue an initiative against the will of his own party. In this respect, life was even more difficult for coalition MPs, who understandably had to consult the government in advance. Using the right to comment on all draft laws, the Czech and Slovak governments provided their opinions on private member bills, which regularly resulted in the bills' defeat on the floor. As a result, the proportion of private member to governmental bills has been decreasing: Malová (1998) reports a decrease from 30 percent in 1990, to 25 percent during the 1992-1994 legislative period, to a further 18 percent after the 1994 election in Slovakia. In particular bills of opposition MPs did not stand much chance of getting through once the government expressed its negative opinion. Private member bills were often prepared together with a relevant ministry and, as seemed to be the case of the bill on the illegality of the communist regime in the Czech Republic, the government was quite happy to shift the responsibility for a controversial proposal onto the parliament. In addition, the Slovak government also used the right to request the president to return a law to the parliament for re-consideration (Article 87 of the Slovak Constitution), if the bill slipped through the parliament against its will.

The use of the right to question government ministers is another indicator of the activity of individual MPs. Again, however, this right was used predominantly in the inter-party mode. One of the articles of the coalition agreements in the 1992-1996 Czech parliament was that the MPs belonging to the governmental majority would not question ministers on the floor. In consequence, and to much criticism from the opposition and the media, the questions of coalition MPs were shifted to the closed sphere of parliamentary party meetings, while question time on the floor was dominated by inquiries from opposition MPs. Moreover, only in exceptional cases was minister's answer to a written question not approved by the majority on the floor. This practice, pointing to the inter-party mode, largely overshadowed the influence of individual MPs in their function of overseers, though a large majority of the Czech MPs (82 percent) stated that they would not ask prior approval (of the parliamentary party meeting or the parliamentary party leader) before asking a written question. A similar large majority of 81 percent of the Slovak MPs stated the same and, it must be noted, the MPs under the Mečiar I and Moravčík governments did question ministers on the floor regardless of their status as governmental or opposition MPs. However, and very predictably, this situation changed after 1994 elections: although government MPs continued to question ministers, this was done with the clear intention of overwhelming questions from the opposition with far more comfortable and answerable questions from within the coalition parliamentary parties.

The right to form an ad hoc investigative commission to carry out parliamentary inquiries, another weaponry of individual MPs to oversee the administration, is also provided for by the parliamentary standing orders of both parliaments. In both cases, a majority in parliament is needed to form such a commission. According to the new standing orders of the Czech parliament, the support of a minimum of one-fifth of the MPs is required to even propose its installment. Therefore, the influence of this power of administrative oversight depends on the will and cohesion of the governmental majority. In practice, this proved fatal for the attempts of the Czech opposition to establish the few investigatory commissions it proposed, since the governing majority turned all of them down. Only one commission was formed between 1992 and 1996, on a multi-party basis, investigating the involvement of the former state security police in anti-regime demonstrations in 1989. In Slovakia, two such commissions were formed between 1992-1994, also on a multi-party basis. One commission investigated violation of foreign trade, and one was concerned with privatization. Nevertheless, Malová (1998) notes that neither commissions' reports brought any conclusive results, except that one commission decided to refer matters to the government. In neither country did parliamentary inquiry caused the resignation of a minister, partly because of the influence of political parties on their representatives in the commission, and partly because the subject of inquiries was not necessarily connected to the competencies of a particular cabinet member.

This said, the Slovak parliament elected in September 1994 established three investigatory commissions which were, in their own way, of utmost importance. Two investigatory commissions were established in the November 1994 overnight session of parliament. One was charged with examining the alleged constitutional crisis in March 1994; that is, the vote of no-confidence in the Mečiar I government and its replacement by the Moravčík government. The other one, formed under the auspices of the Mandate and Immunity Committee, was supposed to investigate allegations of fraud in collecting the 10,000 signatures necessary for the opposition Democratic Union (DU) to register for the 1994 elections. Neither of these commissions included representatives of opposition parties, however. Both commissions were a tool of the governing majority to enhance its rule and undermine the legitimacy of the opposition. Similarly, the commission formed in September 1995 to investigate the tragic death of Alexander Dubček (the former dissident and Chairman of the Federal Assembly) was installed on the proposal of an opposition MP, who nevertheless failed to be elected to it.

In other words, the investigatory commissions formed in Slovakia were not only an expression of an inter-party mode, but they were also clear examples of an unprecendented rule of majority exercised by the Mečiar II government. The commission investigating alleged frauds of signatures concluded that DU assembled only 8,219 signatures, but its findings were ridiculed by the parallel police report, which concluded that only about 2,500 signatures were invalid from the total of more than 14,000! Moreover, the opposition petitioned Constitutional Court, arguing that investigatory commissions gradually assumed executive powers. The Court ruled in favour of the opposition, but its ruling was initially ignored by the coalition representatives.[29] The activities of both commissions were eventually suspended, regardless of the fact that the second commission concluded that the events in March 1994 resulted from a conspiracy. They obviously served the purpose of the ruling elite in that they produced at least important political-symbolic outcomes. However, somewhere down the line, the institution of the investigatory commission completely lost its original purpose: to be a body investigating matters of public concern on a multi-party basis.

The political (rather than constitutional) elimination of investigatory commissions was as successful as the political elimination of another constitutional power held by the Slovak MPs scrutinizing the activity of a minister: the right to request a vote of no confidence in an individual minister.[30] This prerogative is based on two articles of the Slovak Constitution. According to Article 88, "the National Council of the Slovak Republic must discuss a proposal to put the confidence in the Government whenever such a proposal is supported by at least one-fifth of all deputies."; and, according to Article 116, "members of the Government are individually responsible for the execution of their duties to the National Council of the Slovak Republic". This means that Slovak MPs can dismiss individual ministers, or prohibit the Prime Minister from recalling them. Depending on how the Slovak constitution is interpreted (see next chapter), the President may also refuse to approve candidates for ministerial posts. This is unthinkable in the Czech Republic. There the government can be collectively voted down by the parliament, but the fate of individual ministers is solely in the hands of the Prime Minister (and politically in the hands of intra- and inter-party negotiations).[31] In Slovakia, the result of these provisions and of a weak governmental majority was the resignation of two ministers from the June 1992-March 1994 Mečiar government. Votes of no confidence, or attempts to incite them, became a frequently practiced method of opposition and, as Malová (1998) reports, in one case 16 ministerial posts were subjected to votes of noconfidence, including the positions of premier and his deputy. Due to the high cohesion of the governmental majority after 1994, however, this tactic ceased to pay dividends. The three opposition attempts to vote down a minister failed, and even though three ministers were replaced in the

Mečiar II government, these were internal matters of HZDS and interventions of the Prime Minister, rather than the work of parliamentary opposition.

In light of the above, it is not surprising that the most important indication of the institutional expression of the non-party mode - control of parliamentary agenda - also gives us a pessimistic picture of the position of parliament vis-a-vis the government (or governmental majority). Although in procedural terms the control of the parliamentary agenda differed significantly between the two parliaments, in both cases it fell victim to the influence of the government and political parties. In both parliaments the legislative agenda for each parliamentary year must be prepared on the basis of government agenda, which immediately creates a certain dependence of the parliament on the government, hence the weakness of the non-party mode. The final decision of the Slovak parliament on the legislative agenda, as well as on the programme for each session, was taken by the Presidium of the National Council. The Presidium consisted of the chairman and vice-chairmen of the parliament and the chairmen of the parliamentary committees. However, the so-called Political Gremium, consisting of the parliamentary party leaders, had a crucial influence on the Presidium. Despite the fact that the resolutions of the Political Gremium were merely recommendations, the Presidium did not in practice proceed against the Gremium's will.

As could be expected, the functioning of the Presidium, and its relation with the Political Gremium, depended to a large extent on its political composition. During the 1992-1994 parliament, the opposition was allocated one parliamentary vice-chairmanship and a few committee chairmanships (see above), which weakened the government somewhat, and at least partly increased opposition political influence on the formation of parliament's agenda. In the parliament elected in September 1994 this did not apply anymore, as all chairs were given to the governing coalition, very much in line with the overall (inter-party) character which the parliament-government relations took on. Moreover, the coalition abolished the old Presidium, and replaced it with a four-member chairmanship of the parliament, with all seats occupied by HZDS and its coalition partners. In the same vein, the new standing orders give powers to the chairman of the parliament to set the parliamentary agenda for each parliamentary session, which is difficult to change unless a majority votes otherwise. And since the chairman of the parliament has been one of the key party-political figures, rather than a neutral representative of parliament, this leaves little room for non-party mode of interactions between parliament and government to occur.

The Czech parliament did not differ too much in this respect, except that decisions concerning the agenda for each session have been made in the Organizational (or Steering) Committee since 1992, when the old Presidium was abolished. This body consists of the chairman and vice-chairmen of the parliament, and the representatives of the parliamentary parties designated on the basis of proportional representation. According to the old standing orders, valid until September 1995, the parliamentary parties could nominate one representative for every 10 MPs affiliated to the party. The new standing orders do not specify this number, but clearly state that parliamentary parties nominate their representatives in the same way to every specialized parliamentary committee; that is, according to the principal of proportional representation. Consequently, the inter-party mode is directly built into the agenda-setting procedure of the Czech parliament, though it is also obvious that, in comparison to post-1994 Slovak parliament, the opposition's representation on these high decision-making bodies is secured by law. However, as in the Slovak parliament, the chairman of the Czech parliament between 1992 and 1996 was a representative of the biggest government party, and although he acted in a much more subtle and non-confrontational way than his Slovak counterpart, his behavior could hardly counteract party-political character.

Conclusions

What can the evidence presented in this chapter tell us about the institutionalization of parliament-government relations in the Czech and Slovak Republics? The first important general point concerns the link between party developments and the overall structure of parliament-government relations. The empirical evidence presented strongly suggests that the inter-party mode and its opposition sub-mode are predominant. This means that parliament-government relations in both countries are clearly driven by political parties and, within this structured system of interactions, they show signs of elite inclinations towards a culture of strong majority rule. This does not leave cross-party interests, individual MPs, or parliament as a whole completely impotent, but makes them arguably far more contingent on party politics than was the case in the first parliaments elected after 1989 under the common Czechoslovak state. Particularly with regard to the internal consolidation of political parties, and their ability to strengthen their grip on the parliament, the government and individual MPs, we can conclude that their positions have become stronger in both countries. Chapter 6, which analyzes internal functioning of parliamentary parties, will return to these issues in more detail.

This said, we also have to point to the differences between the Czech and Slovak Republics, and this brings us to the second important point. Regardless of the current strength of party domination in parliament-government relations (in both countries), or a relative richness of formal institutional devices to foster it (in the Czech Republic), there has been a tendency in both countries to engineer institutions in such a way as to make institutional preconditions for the inter-party mode (and its opposition sub-mode) even more favorable. The Czech political elite were successful in changing the parliamentary standing orders, impeding the power of parliamentary committees and institutionalizing the dominance of the current parliamentary majority. In Slovakia, the HZDS elite, dissatisfied with the minority status of their own government between 1992 and 1994, went so far as to start advocating an entire change of the institutional system (i.e. from parliamentary to presidential), with a clear goal of providing for a stronger rule by majority. This difference between the two countries is very important. While the institutional changes in the Czech Republic basically conform to the logic of the system within which they were implemented, (some of) the changes advocated in Slovakia would turn the system upside down. Thus, in the Czech Republic, we witness a piecemeal institutional development and readjustment, whereby the existing rules are adapted to the exigencies of the moment, either via a partial reformulation of formal rules, or by their extension using set of complementary informal rules. To be sure, the adaptation of rules to the exigencies of the moment holds also for Slovakia, but the changes already proposed there are indicative of the existence of a clear expectation in a part of the elite that institutional arrangements should produce majorities, and if this cannot be achieved, it is better to change the whole system rather than to focus on legislative bargaining for a coalition.

The short period of the Moravčík government proves that paraconstitutional devices, like the Coalition Council, may effectively help to maintain a legislative majority without any major institutional changes. In fact, one could argue that evidence from the Czech Republic also makes this case. For although the formal institutional rules may appear more favorable to the party and executive dominance than in Slovakia, it is definitely the paraconstitutional devices for mediation between coalition ministers and MPs and their parties (and the willingness of elites to negotiate them) that underlined much of the stability of the 1992-1996 Czech government.[32] Later on, these informal rules also enabled parties and parliaments to adapt to significant environmental changes, like minority governments after the 1996 and 1998 elections, without major institutional turnarounds. In contrast, the Slovak situation shows that dominance of parties in relations between parliaments and governments, arguably fully achieved during the Mečiar II government, does not necessarily guarantee a stable parliamentary government (see Andeweg, 1992). And this is the final observation we wish to emphasize. The majority-rule culture gained such a divisive momentum in Slovakia under the Mečiar II government that both cooperation between political parties and the whole institutional framework gradually became endangered by the severity of the underlying political conflict. Thus, despite the fact that the direction of institutionalization of Czech and Slovak parliament-government relations appear more similar than dissimilar, it is the substantive issues, or the degree of institutonalization, which makes the Slovak situation arguably more tense and turbulent. It is in the following chapter, where we turn to explore the role of presidents in executive-legislative relations, that these differences will become even more apparent.

Notes

1. The term 'interactions' captures all types of relations: co-operative on one side, and conflictual on the other side.

2. The question was as following: "How would you describe cabinet-parliament relations in general"? The choice of answers was as following: "parliament as a whole opposes the cabinet" (non-party mode); "the cabinet and parliamentary parties in the coalition oppose the opposition" (inter-party mode); "professional ministers and parliamentary specialists in a particular area of policy oppose their colleagues in other areas", "professional ministers and parliamentary specialists in a particular area of policy oppose generalists like the prime minister, minister of finance, and parliamentary party leaders" (both cross-party mode); "no discernable pattern."

3. The figures are dendograms, demonstrating average linkage (voting correlations) between parties, calculated by the squared Euclidean measure method. Figure 2 is based on 4197 roll-calls recorded between the 16th and 43rd session of the Czech parliament (February 1993 - April 1995). Figure 3 draws on data from the same sessions and includes the Republicans as an important opposition party. However, as a result, the number of roll-calls on which the figure is based had to be reduced to 2999, because the Republicans did not participate on many votes taken on the floor of the parliament (for additional reference see Table 6.4. in chapter 6). In addition, since parties like HSD-SMS, ČMUS, and LSNS were frequently spliting during the parliamentary term, they could not be included to these figures (for additional reference see Table 6.1. in chapter 6). The same is true at KDS,

which merged with ODS before the June 1996 elections. However, one of the reasons for both parties to merge was precisely their similarity and, therefore, the inclusion of KDS into these figures would not make any difference to the overall picture. For confirming these trends, the reader should consult all numbers of *Parlamentní Zpravodaj,* which provide analysis of the distances between parties for each individual parliamentary session.

4. Note, however, that this government, led again by Klaus, resigned in December 1997 and was replaced by a temporary caretaker government, in which the recruitment from outside of the parliament (and outside of the parties) was given a high political priority.

5. Some ministers felt the high workload of two offices was too much to bear. The ODS-nominated ministers of Finance and Foreign Affairs in the post-1996 government, for example, voluntarily gave up their parliamentary seats.

6. The application of this rule sparked a huge controversy in 1997, in the so-called Hruška affair, when SNS announced the name of the candidate from the reserve list to fill a seat vacated by the death of one of its deputies. SNS decided, against the law, to fill the seat with a candidate in good standing within the party, despite the fact that there was an another candidate from the reserve list who obtained more preferential votes, but after the elections distanced himself from SNS. To be sure, *both* prospective candidates exceeded the total of 10 percent of preferential votes, but in such cases, the law declares that the vacant seat is to be filled by the eligible candidate receiving the greatest number of preferential votes. The SNS violated this principle. A year later, the Constitutional Court ruled that parliament had violated the constitution and electoral law and asked for a redress of the situation. However, as with the case of HZDS deputy stripped of his mandate (see chapter 6), the governing majority ignored the ruling, arguing that the Court cannot dictate to the highest authority in the state.

7. The Mečiar I cabinet had altogether four non-partisan ministers. Two (Defense and Interior) were nominated by HZDS (and joined the party in 1994, after the government was voted down). The third (Minister of Economy) was appointed as a "non-political" specialist, but was a member of SNS, which supported the government, and later even became party chairman (see above). The fourth one (again Minister of Economy), was appointed after the reshuffles in the Mečiar I government in November 1993. In the caretaker government formed in March 1994, none of the appointed ministers was non-partisan. The same applies to Mečiar II coalition government formed in winter 1994. The Czech Republic witnessed only two non-partisan ministers between 1992 and 1996 (Minister of Education, Youth and Sports and Minister of Culture). However, as mentioned earlier, the temporary caretaker government formed in January 1998 contained more non-partisan appointees.

8. Note that a similar agreement was signed between the same coalition partners after the 1996 elections. It was an even more detailed document, and particularly the junior coalition partners (ODA and KDU-ČSL) insisted on listing all possible details in order to offset the strength of ODS, which had been seen as too dominant in previous years.

9. Interview with Václav Klaus in *Lidové Noviny*, September 8, 1995.

10. This deviation of the KDS from other parties might be explained by the existence of two parliamentary party factions, one of which was strongly associated with two ministers (see Kopecký, 1995b). Therefore, the part of the parliamentary party in opposition to this faction probably felt that their influence over own ministers was marginal.

11. Note that consultations between ministers and MPs from governmental parties will be considered for HZDS alone. This means that the cabinet will be considered as a one-party government which, as we saw above, was not completely true. Unfortunately, the answers of SNS deputies, who formed a proper coalition with HZDS only in November 1993, are very difficult to interpret. By the time the MPs were interviewed, their experience with the coalition government was limited to one month and, moreover, the (parliamentary) party itself was in the process of disintegration. Data for most of these questions therefore provide ambiguous evidence. Even data for HZDS are not without problems, at least with regard to interpretation. The parliamentarians were uncooperative and requests for additional open-ended interviews with parliamentary party leaders were refused.

12. The prohibition for functioning as both deputy and minister in Slovakia played an important role in this respect. If ministers cannot be parliamentarians, and hence cannot naturally belong to this institution, this may be the cause for parties to find a functional equivalent for communication outside the parliament. This has opened the way to more complicated and antagonistic communication between ministers and parliamentary party than would be the case if direct participation of ministers at parliamentary party meetings were permitted.

13. Information from author's personal interviews in party headquarters conducted in Bratislava in October 1994.

14. It could be argued that a dominant style of Czech coalition government between 1992 and 1996 had a similar effect on the opposition parties. They had option no other than to unite internally in order to mount a challenge to the coalition parties. However, in comparison to Slovakia, Czech opposition parties never joined into a stable and cooperative block pitted against the governing coalition.

15. Particularly important changes in this respect were the reconstitution of the Special Supervisory Board - an institution charged with supervision of the Slovak Intelligence Services, and of the Presidium of the Fund of National Property - a body overseeing activities of the institution dealing with privatization of state assets. In the case of both institutions, their composition changed so as to exclude all previous opposition deputy members, who were replaced by members of HZDS, SNS and ZRS. In the same vein, the newly appointed Councils for the Slovak Radio and for the Slovak Television completely excluded voices hostile to the coalition, the chairman of the Slovak radio was replaced by a HZDS deputy and, somewhat later, the parliament appointed a new chairman of the Slovak Television with strong links with HZDS. It is important to note in this respect that all these bodies included at least some opposition representatives during Moravčík's government, and that similar bodies in the Czech Republic have done the same.

16. The Hungarian parties were not considered as the prospective coalition partners at all. The DU was absolutely unacceptable for both HZDS and SNS, because it was formed by the former members of antecedent parliamentary parties.

17. This was possible in procedural terms, since the nominations to parliamentary committees must be approved by the majority on the floor. For more details see following section in this chapter.

18. Reported in *Sme*, July 18, 1995.

19. From Prime Minister Meciar's evaluation of the cabinet's first 100 days, reported by *OMRI Daily Digest*, March 30, 1995.

20. This committee primarily investigates whether MPs do not exercise functions incompatible with their mandate, or whether civil servants comply with the civil service code of conduct. The committee was established by HZDS, basically as an extra weapon to control behavior of MPs and civil servants.

21. My own interviews with Czech MPs and with the editors of *Parlamentní zpravodaj* - the magazine devoted to the analysis of the Czech parliament.

22. 7 percent of Czech, and 3 percent of Slovak respondents said "others".

23. The remaining 17 percent of Czech and 18 percent of Slovak MPs said it should go to staff for parliament as a whole, while seven percent of Czech and six percent of Slovak MPs said "somewhere else".

24. However, it is interesting to note that the rule on double membership does not necessarily have to help the majority - which is exactly the reason why it was introduced in the Czech Republic. As Italian experiences showed, MPs with double assignments may be put under high pressure as the different committees meet at the same time. In consequence, the unwillingness of one MP to attend committee meetings or the impossibility of doing so may, to the embarrassment of the government, alter the actual ratio between government and opposition MPs (see D'Onofrio, 1979).

25. The question was: As far as your parliamentary party is concerned, who decides which MP will be member of which committee? Is it parliamentary party meeting, the parliamentary party leadership, the party's national executive, the MP himself or somebody else?

26. However, after the 1996 elections and the formation of minority government, the hitherto ruling coalition had to swallow a bitter pill and share the committee chairmanships with the Social Democrats, who made their support for minority government conditional on the chairmanship of the parliament and few key committees. This was a typical minority government situation, but it was interesting to see that while the Social Democrats argued before the 1996 elections for a strict application of the PR principle in distribution of committee chairs, they were happy to scrap it once they faced the prospect of offering chairs to the Republicans and Communists as well.

27. The remaining MPs (63 out of 167 of the Czechs and 46 out of 95 of the Slovaks), who gave answers such as to "represent democracy", or "to be a safety valve against the return of totalitarianism", or "to represent the interests of the electorate in general", were not included to the test because of the difficulty in assigning them a specific role.

28. Information from the Department of Information and Analysis of the Slovak National Council.

29. It is interesting to note, however, that the new standing orders, passed by the Slovak parliament in 1996 and largely the work of Mečiar's coalition, mentions commissions only in a vague form. There are no rules as to how such commissions should be established, and it is noted that commissions can investigate only in matters concerning parliament's jurisdiction.

30. A vote of no confidence in the Prime Minister is equal to a vote of no confidence in the whole government. If successful, the entire government resigns with the Prime Minister.

31. In procedural terms, the ministers are appointed and dismissed by the President on the Prime Minister's suggestion (see next chapter).

32. It is worth quoting the words of the Vice-Chairman of the 1992-1996 parliament, who assessed the cooperation between government parties (ODS, KDU-ČSL, ODA and KDH) in the following way: "That the coalition was able to cooperate for four years derives, among other things, from the system of regular meetings, preparations for plenary sessions, and the sessions of the Steering Committee. We informed each other about sensitive issues. We met together in about 200 coalition negotiations...Bilateral negotiations between only two partners, behind the back of the third party, were the exception, not the rule". See *Lidové Noviny*, May 15, 1996.

5 Executive-Legislative Relations: Presidents

Introduction

This chapter continues our exploration of parliamentary institutionalization by focusing on the position and role of presidents in executive-legislative relations. As we saw previously (chapter 2), the governments are constitutionally declared supreme bodies of the executive power in both countries. The presidents are elected by parliament and are, *de jure*, supposed to perform largely ceremonial functions.[1] Nevertheless, it is clear that in any political context both the overall role played by the president, as well as the form of institutionalization of his relationship with the government and parliament, may differ substantially from what is actually written in the constitution. In post-communist circumstances, there are three elements of particular importance.

Firstly, the newness of institutional structures means that the roles of the two executives are as yet undefined in political practice. The formal institutional framework is thus likely to become a battlefield on which presidents and governments will struggle to define their influence and position. Secondly, presidents in the new democracies in East Central Europe are or were persons who played an important role in the opposition against the old regime and in the dramatic period of transition to democracy. This gives them an additional source of legitimacy and can prove a political asset in shaping their institution, which may extend well beyond the confines of formal rules (Holmes, 1993/1994; Baylis, 1996). Thirdly, if other institutions are infirm and fragmented, even a constitutionally weak president may wield a decisive influence on the political process. Even parliamentary systems, like the Czech and Slovak Republics, provide for the relative security of presidents once in office. This factor may provide presidents with considerable influence in the context of fractious parties and unstable governmental majorities.

The following analysis is divided into two sections. The first section provides evidence on the presidents' relations with their respective governments. The second section deals with relations between the presidents and their respective parliaments. This distinction is of course largely artificial, because presidential powers towards parliament and government are, particularly in parliamentary systems, often fused together under the banner of the president's relationships with parliamentary and governmental majorities. But it will enable us to show how the contrasting experiences with presidencies in the two countries run through the entire system of executive-legislative relations. Knowing the initial ideas of different parties on the shape of presidency (chapter 2), we will also be able to examine empirically any changes in these conceptions, and the influence president's activities may have had on elite views of the current shape of the presidency.

Presidents and Governments

The Czech president's relations with governments can overall be said to be based on relatively well developed and accepted informal norms and behaviors which complement the formal constitutional rules. At the start of Havel's term in 1993, there were substantial tensions between the two institutions, as both were translating their formal competencies into practice. This had smoothed out during the 1992-1996 term, to the extent that Havel's influence in day-to-day governmental processes was practically marginal. After the formation of a minority government in 1996, the president became again more active and, at the end of 1997, was heavily involved in the fall of Klaus' minority coalition and the subsequent formation of a caretaker government led by the non-partisan Tošovský. Formally speaking, the Czech president appoints the Prime Minister and, on his suggestion, appoints other members of the government and entrusts them with managing the ministries. The president dismisses members of the government if this is proposed by the Prime Minister. Finally, the president dismisses a government which does not offer its resignation when it is obliged to do so (after a vote of no confidence). Although these formal powers could give the president an important role to play, particularly during the formation of the new government, established practice shows that is the parties, their leaders, and the prime minister who hold the trump cards.

The appointment of the Czech prime minister after the 1992 elections was made before the president was elected. More specifically, the Czech government was appointed by the Presidium of the then Czech National Council - a procedure which was embedded in the federal constitution. Havel certainly had a lot of experience with forming or reforming governments during his tenure as federal president. Yet, at that time, government formation was not only based on the results of the elections, but also constrained by the need to balance appointments between candidates of Czech and Slovak nationality (see chapter 2). This was the principle which stood above, or was at least as important as, the electoral positions of different parties. Nothing of that informal legacy was obviously carried over into the Czech Republic. Instead, the common understanding among the Czech elite is that the candidate for the post of prime minister is the chairman of the party which wins the election - that is the party which receives most votes. He or she is supposed to be entrusted with the formation of a government. This informal rule is well apparent in the country's political discourse, in that it is normal to talk about the leader of a particular party as the prospective prime minister. The president is thus constrained by this basic guideline for his activity in government formation, whether to his liking or not.[2] Moreover, even if the president objected to the leader of the winning party, his room for manoeuvring is limited, because the power to nominate the prime minister falls to the chairman of the parliament (Chamber of Deputies), if the parliament votes in two successive investiture votes against the governments proposed by the president.

With regard to the choice of individual ministers, the constitution stipulates that the president recalls the cabinet member who is proposed for dismissal by the Prime Minister. The power to appoint a new minister also follows initiatives by the Prime Minister. Indeed, Havel has rarely tried to assume these prerogatives of the government's chairman. All dismissals of ministers from the 1992-1996 Klaus government were approved by the president without any objections. The same holds for the appointment of the new ministers proposed by Klaus in that period, though Havel occasionally invited a newcomer for an informal talk in his office. This was, for example, the case with the appointment of the new Minister of Defense in September 1994, or appointments of the Minister(s) Of Foreign Affairs. Since Havel as the president is the commander-in-chief of the armed forces, and since he also represents the country internationally, he was understandably more active in personnel changes in the administrative departments close to his constitutional prerogatives than was the case with changes in the ministries not falling directly under his jurisdiction.

In fact, the biggest tension between the government and the president occurred precisely in the sphere of foreign policy, particularly at the beginning of Havel's first term in 1993. According to the constitution, the president represents the state in external affairs and, in particular, negotiates and ratifies international treaties. Havel's dissatisfaction with the term 'Czech interests' in the official government formulation of foreign policy, his long-term open support of military intervention in Bosnia, his (initially) different views on Czech-German relations, and official audiences he gave to some world politicians and personalities[3] all provoked hostile reactions from the Klaus government and the Ministry of Foreign Affairs. The disputes centered around Havel's insistence on his constitutional right to be involved in (some of the) government's policies, or at least to express his views, and the countervailing attempts of government to relegate him to a purely ceremonial representative role. At stake was not just communication between two executive centers, or harmonization of official statements of presidential and governmental offices. On the contrary, what was at stake was the actual content of foreign policies and the locus of responsibility for their formulation. Although the Czech constitution clearly names presidential activities which require the counter-signature of the prime minister (or a minister accredited by him), the document remains open to interpretation with regard to the president's role in foreign affairs.

These tensions have been significantly eased by a semi-institutional compromise. The first attempt to solve the problems between ministers and the president came as early as February 1993. The president has the right to participate in cabinet meetings and also to demand reports from individual ministers. The constitution-makers thought that this would solve the problems of communication. However, because of the president's normally tight schedule, the presidential office proposed regularly sending a delegate or aide to the cabinet meetings. The proposed law on the Presidential Office, which would enable its head to perform this function was, nevertheless, refused by the government. Instead, the government came to an agreement that the prime minister would come every Wednesday (after the cabinet meeting) to the Prague Castle (the official residence of the president) to inform him about the government's activities. The idea came from Klaus who said that "[W]e (the government) took this decision which was inspired by my visit to Great Britain. I was sitting with John Major, who suddenly looked at his watch and said: I have to go to visit the Queen".[4] The political practice of informal meetings, which has developed since the establishment of this paraconstitutional device, has certainly enhanced the cooperation between the president and the government. Even though the meetings between the president and the prime minister have not been as regular as was envisaged at the beginning (or as is the case in Great Britain), the fact that they were put to work supplied the formal constitutional rules with an important informal device for enhancing mutual relationships between the two executive centers.

The cooperative or at least cordial nature of the relationship between the president and the government was further facilitated by Havel's active approach towards the Czech political scene. In addition to his meetings with the prime minister, the president initiated numerous rounds of talks with politicians from all sides of the political spectrum. These informal meetings were usually held on Friday and became one of the ways for Havel to be informed about the political atmosphere, as well as presenting an opportunity for the president to present his views on crucial issues on the political agenda. Thus, party leaders, trade-union leaders, delegations of parliamentary parties, individual ministers, and (less frequently) representatives of non-governmental organizations and media have all been regularly seen in the Castle exchanging views with the president. The far-right Republicans, whose invectives against Havel in the parliament during the televized presidential elections provoked one citizen to threaten the parliament with a bomb attack, and the Communists were virtually the only key political actors excluded from meetings with the president.

This political practice enabled Havel to maintain his influence on the political scene, and also prevented Havel's surprise moves which used to shock (party) elites and public alike in the past years. He himself wrote: "[the president] should operate as a background moderator of political negotiations, as an occasional seeker of consensus, as a concealed stimulator, as a framer of the space for mutual understanding, as something like a watch dog of political culture".[5] Our survey data captured the practical implication of Havel's desired role nicely, in that he was indeed perceived principally as a mediator breaking impasses (32 percent of respondents). Only 16 percent of MPs saw him as a statesman.[6] However, in the answers to the same question framed in normative terms, the MPs were fairly consistent in preferring a statesman and symbolic protector of the constitution above other categories (69 percent of the respondents). It simply indicates that in seeking a role for the Czech president, Havel retreated from a kind of solo game that his office played during the Federation to a more active backdoor negotiations and channels of influence during his tenure as the president of the Czech Republic. But the fact that the MPs would like to see the president more in the role of statesman, rather than mediator, also shows that the established political actors were more than keen to limit the effect of his personality.

The relations between the president and the government in Slovakia were problematic from the beginning of Kováč's tenure in office[7] and, unlike in the case of the Czech president, underwent a further dramatic deterioration. These relationships turned into struggles of a personal nature between Kováč and

Mečiar, as well as struggles over the shape of the presidency as such. They became the most visible embodiment of Slovakia's adversarial elite behavior and institutional conflict, and they also demonstrate the tendency of these conflicts to move towards the use of unconstitutional methods. The only period of a smooth relationship between the president and the government was during the short rule of Moravčík's broad coalition in 1994 - a cabinet which came into being with heavy presidential support (see below). After Mečiar returned to government in the winter of 1994, his new administration engaged in numerous attempts to dismiss the president from the office and, when this proved unviable, attempted to curb presidential powers under the current parliamentary system.

For example, in February 1995, and then again in 1996, the government slashed the budget of the president, to the extent that part of the presidential staffing had to be financed from private donations. In April 1995, a bill was reapproved by the parliament (after Kováč's veto), transferring the power to appoint and remove the director of the Slovak Intelligence Service from the president to the government. From 1995, the state television stations, which were controlled by Mečiar's government, refused to broadcast presidential speeches. Another political stalemate appeared on May 5, 1995, when the government's allegations against the president prompted a no-confidence vote against him in the parliament (see below). On September 19, 1995, the Slovak government again issued a statement calling for Kováč's resignation. The government argued that the president's rejection of an invitation to discuss with the government his remarks against the cabinet and the representatives of the coalition had damaged the prestige of the head of state as a symbol of Slovakia.

It would simply take too long to list all squabbles and exchanges between the Slovak government and the president between 1993 and March 1998 - the date Kováč officially ended his five-year tenure in office.[8] How have these conflicts evolved, and what are the conditions underlying it? Formally, the powers of the Slovak president vis-à-vis the government are quite similar to the Czech president. This means that the Slovak presidency was established and intended as an institution with relatively limited powers. According to the Slovak constitution, the president appoints and recalls the prime minister and other members of the government, and puts the ministers in charge of their departments. The president also appoints and removes the principal officers of national bodies and high officials as defined by law. The president recalls the government if it receives a vote of no confidence by the parliament. The same must be done in the case of individual ministers. The president has a right to attend the sessions of the government, to chair these sessions and to demand reports from the government and its members. With regard to policy formation, as with the Czech president, the Slovak president represents the country internationally, and negotiates and ratifies international treaties.

As with relations between the Czech president and government, the political problems in Slovakia initially arose from the differing views of the president and the Mečiar I government in the sphere of foreign policy (as early as in 1993). However, unlike in the case of the Czech presidency, this tension soon assumed the tenor of a sharp conflict about who is in charge of the personnel changes in government and Slovak embassies abroad. When, after several personal clashes within HZDS, prime minister Mečiar proposed the dismissal of the Foreign Minister Kňažko in March 1993, the president expressed satisfaction with that minister's performance. Although he later accepted Mečiar's proposal to recall Kňažko from his post (19 March 1993), this event opened a series of presidential involvements in the recalls and nominations of individual ministers - a situation largely unknown in the Czech Republic.

The role of the Constitutional Court was very important in this respect. Kováč asked the Court for a ruling on an unclear constitutional provision concerning the appointment and dismissal of individual ministers at the prime minister's request. According to the constitution, a proposal to recall a member of government may be submitted by the prime minister and on the advice of the prime minister, the president shall appoint and recall members of the government. The Court decided that the president was not obliged to follow the prime minister's requests and thus set the stage for the president to exercise his powers of appointment and recall of ministers independent of the government. In light of the growing antagonism between Mečiar and Kováč, which was very much underlined by the latter's distaste for the prime minister's confrontational style, and in light of the government's instability (see chapter 4), the president started to reject the prime minster's candidates for ministerial posts.

The first veto came on 5 November 1993. The HZDS and the SNS agreed to reshuffle the coalition government. Mečiar submitted to the president a list of new cabinet ministers, adding the condition that the president must not refuse to appoint any single person from that list. Instead, the president was given a choice of either rejecting or accepting the entire list.[9] Kováč declared this condition unconstitutional and refused the nomination of Ivan Lexa for the post of the Minister of Privatization. Mečiar withdrew the whole list and the next day submitted all the candidates again, except Lexa. The prime minister himself took on the role of managing the privatization ministry and the National Fund for Property on a temporary basis, until a new candidate could be appointed. The second rejection came in February 1993, shortly before Mečiar's government lost a vote of no confidence in the parliament. Kováč refused to appoint SNS member and then-Deputy Prime Minister Josef Prokeš as Minister of Foreign Affairs. Mečiar proposed him as a replacement for Josef Moravčík (the then member of HZDS), whose forced resignation was accepted by the president a few days before.

The ruling of the Constitutional Court also had an important impact on the president's power to appoint and remove principal officials of high state bodies. As mentioned above, in 1995 HZDS proposed an amendment which would transfer to the government the president's power to appoint the chairman of the Slovak Intelligence Service and the chief of the general staff of the army.[10] To a certain extent, the impetus behind this amendment was the Mečiar II government's continual campaign to eliminate the president from the political process. However, the amendment also reflected a more fundamental problem with the text of the constitution, which does not make clear which "central bodies and high state officials" fall under the president's jurisdiction, or who decides the scope of the president's power to appoint and remove. The verdict of the Constitutional Court was that the parliament itself can decree by a simple majority which government agencies are considered "central bodies", although the army's chief of the general staff remained (under the Court's ruling) under presidential jurisdiction. In turn, the parliament voted in favour of HZDS' 1995 amendment and the president lost the power to nominate the director of the Intelligence Service. Given this particular decision of the Court, the parliament, and the government majority, can now exercise practically unfettered control over most appointments in the state administration.

Kováč also proved remarkably active during the formation of new governments. In March 1994, after the vote of no confidence in the Mečiar I government, the president met with all opposition parties to discuss the formation of a new cabinet. After the negotiations, Kováč said that he accepted the proposed Moravčík cabinet as a whole, since all personnel questions were discussed with him and he met personally with most of the candidates for ministerial posts.[11] He faced a more difficult task after the September 1994 general elections. HZDS, the winner of the elections, had made clear already during the electoral campaign that they would initiate proceedings to dismiss the president from office. When the polling rooms closed and the electoral commission announced the results, Kováč first invited top representatives from all parties, without making clear whom he would name to lead the negotiations to form a new government. In doing so, he undermined an informal rule similar to those then guiding these processes in the Czech Republic - an informal rule which was very much perceived by HZDS and its allies as given, and which then became included in numerous HZDS's attempts to change the formal wording of the constitution so that leaders of winning parties would be automatically nominated by the president to form the coalition.[12]

In addition to the active role he took in government formation, Kováč showed willingness to play an important part in day-to-day politics, more independently of the government than was expected at the beginning of his term in office, or than has been the case of Havel in the Czech Republic. For example, he initiated round-table talks with the country's ethnic minorities. The first round of such negotiations, known under the name Round Table for National Minorities, occurred in 1993. In September 1995 the president also met with representatives of the Union of Romani Political Parties to discuss problems related to what is the biggest ethnic minority group in Slovakia. In particular the Romani representatives stressed that the president was the only constitutional representative to understand their problems and that the prime minister had not responded to four letters they had sent him in 1995.[13] Thus, while the leaders of the ethnic groups evaluated these negotiations positively, the government's reaction to them was rather hostile. Most importantly, the president started to mediate actively in the struggle of political parties. In his televized New Year address in 1994, he expressed the wish that a broad coalition of political parties be established to solve the political problems in Slovakia and tried to push this idea in political circles. In this way, Kováč began to undermine the fragile coalition of HZDS and SNS. The president's speech in the parliament in March 1994, in which he heavily criticized the Mečiar I government (and the prime minister personally), for their inability to administer the country, was the final impetus for the opposition to cast a vote of no confidence in the cabinet. Shortly before the September 1994 elections, Kováč mildly expressed his hope for a continuation of Moravčík's coalition in governmental office, saying: "I think that not only Slovakia, but also other post-communist countries need in this transformative period a coalition government...in other words, they need to involve all important political bodies in these historical changes".[14]

To be sure, Havel was as active in politics as Kováč and, particularly after the 1996 elections, his sharp criticisms of political parties, as well as his open statements on substantive policy issues, generated a great deal of tension between him and the government (and party leaders). However, Havel always tried to concentrate on addressing issues of a broad character and where this proved impossible, he consciously attempted to avoid overt involvement in the day-to-day squabbling of political parties by framing his speeches in a general way. In contrast, Kováč showed more willingness to air openly and directly his opinions about the government from the very beginning of his tenure. His petition of the constitutional court about the president's prerogatives to name the ministers is a good indication of this. In January 1994 Kováč also said that: "[I]n a democratic system, it is normal for there to be a coalition and an opposition. This does not mean that the opposition is inferior. And precisely in this area, the president can show that the political actors can be put together to find solutions for the problems... Clearing the existing political atmosphere is in the hands of politicians, deputies, ministers, and the president".[15] It is then no surprise that the principal role performed by the Slovak president, as perceived by the MPs, was that of a mediator (42 percent of the respondents), though 31 percent of MPs (more than in the case of Havel) saw him as a statesman representing the interests of the nation. Also not surprisingly, there was a fairly consistent support (68 percent of MPs) for the president's role as a statesman.

Paradoxically for the Slovak's president role in general, however, his activity in executive-legislative relations has directly undermined his possibilities for success as a mediator in breaking political impasses. Because of his involvement in the personnel changes in the Mečiar I government, and because of his sharp criticism of this same government, part of the political spectrum in Slovakia subsequently cut Kováč out of any further political negotiations. There is no doubt that the context of politics in both countries played a crucial role and we will return to these issues in the conclusion. Suffice it to say now that the relationship between the presidency and the government in Slovakia shows signs of instability, whereby the informal norms and customs, as well as the formal constitutional prerogatives continue to be subjected to sharp controversies. In contrast, the Czech constitution was supplemented with few informal rules and practices which seem to make relations between the two executives less controversial. Given that presidential powers vis-à-vis the government are inevitably mirrored in the president's relationships with parliament, the next section will add further evidence to this emerging portrait.

Presidents and Parliaments

What are the most important formal powers the Czech and Slovak presidents can exercise vis-à-vis their respective parliaments? First of all, both presidents can dissolve the parliament. The Czech president can dissolve the Chamber of Deputies (not the Senate) only if: a) the government's prime minister was appointed by the president on the suggestion of the chairman of the Chamber (the third round of appointment procedure) and the Chamber of Deputies passes a vote of no confidence in the newly appointed government; b) the Chamber of Deputies fails to decide within three months on a bill with which the government has linked to a vote of confidence; c) a session of the Chamber is adjourned for a longer period than admissible; d) the Chamber fails to reach a quorum for longer than three months, although the Chamber's session is not adjourned and it is repeatedly called to session. Similarly, the Slovak president can dissolve the parliament only when the programme of the government is rejected three times within six months of the elections, and after the president hears the opinion of the chairman of the parliament. Therefore, in both countries, the presidents can dissolve parliaments, but only in a few strictly defined circumstances. Their prerogatives are not a particularly powerful tool against the parliament, since neither president has the absolute authority to terminate the parliament. In other words, once a government in both the Czech and Slovak Republics is installed, the parliaments are practically undissolvable.

Second, perhaps a more powerful tool in the hands of presidents is the legislative veto. According to the Czech constitution, the president has the right to return adopted bills (except constitutional bills) within fifteen days of its advancement, if he gives an explanation for its return. However, the president cannot submit specific amendments, and if the parliament reapproves the returned bill with an absolute majority of all deputies, the bill becomes law. The Slovak president can return the bill to the parliament with comments. The president must do so within fifteen days of the bill's advancement and, unlike the Czech president, he can also return constitutional bills. The Slovak constitution then states that the parliament shall discuss the pertinent bill again and, if approved by a simple majority, such a bill shall be declared law. Therefore, in both cases the president has a suspensive veto rather than an absolute veto on legislation. The president's decision to return the bill can be overridden by the parliament.

Both presidents used their right of suspensive veto. Not surprisingly, Kováč used his right to veto legislation quite frequently, and more so after the

September 1994 elections than either during the June 1992-March 1994 period or the March 1994-September 1994 period. Before the Mečiar I government was ousted from office in March 1994, he vetoed 4 bills. However, these were returned to the parliament at the request of the government, which saw its own bills modified so drastically by a fluctuating parliamentary majority that it resorted to the last possible constitutional means to advance its own agenda.[16] The president did not veto any bill during the (short) rule of Moravčík's coalition government. However, once the war between the Mečiar II coalition government and the president broke out, the legislative veto became the order of the day. In 1995, for example, Kováč returned seven bills to the parliament (three in March, one in July, and three in September), all of which were reapproved by the coalition majority in the parliament.

In most instances, the presidential veto became effectively the veto of the opposition parties, which were normally unable to break the cohesive coalition block in the parliament. The two bills vetoed by Kováč in 1995 - one on investment funds, the other on the state control over strategic industries - were reapproved by the coalition majority, and the opposition parties decided to take them to the Constitutional Court. This happened already in October 1994, when the new coalition of HZDS, SNS, and ZRS cancelled several direct sale privatization projects approved by the previous Moravčík government. Kováč first returned the bill to the parliament, and after it was reapproved, the opposition advanced it to the Constitutional Court. In essence, this became normal legislative practice in Slovakia: governmental bill passed the parliament, it was vetoed by the president, reapproved by the parliamentary majority, and then advanced, either by the president or the opposition, to the Constitutional Court. The presidential veto thus became a veto of the opposition, on whose side Kováč firmly resided until the end of his tenure.

In the Czech Republic, Havel refused to sign seven bills between 1993 and 1996 (one bill in 1993; two in 1994, four in 1995; none in 1996) and returned them to the parliament. On one hand, one could say that the activity of Havel was the result of an incomplete institutional system in the country. Since the second chamber of the parliament was not elected until the end of 1992-1996 legislative period, the president supplied the function of a legislative corrective vis-a-vis the lower chamber, which would normally be performed by the Senate. On the other hand, at least four of the vetoed bills - on import and export duties (July 1993), on state levies (December 1994), on rewarding resistance fighters from World War II (May 1995), and on an extension of the so-called "screening law" (October 1995) - all contained provisions which clashed strongly with Havel's vision of politics and society. He would probably have vetoed them even if these bills had been approved by the Senate. Four of the presidential vetoes between 1993 and 1996 were overridden by parliamentary vote; three times parliament failed to reapprove returned bills. In one instance of a reapproved bill - an amendment to the law on the profession of architects - Havel used his right to ask the Constitutional Court's opinion.

However, compared to the Slovak president (particularly in the later period), Havel's use of the suspensive veto did not stir up much controversy on the political scene. After the president returned two bills to parliament in December 1994 (both reapproved), the vice-chairman of the parliament resolutely rejected hints at escalating tensions between parliament and president (though one coalition deputy remarked that the president should be more active earlier on during negotiations with the government, rather than relying on a legislative veto later).[17] Thanks to Havel's informal talks with the delegations of parliamentary parties and the government, it was usually clear in advance that he was going to veto a particular bill. Only when the majority in the parliament was determined to pass a bill, as was the case with the extension of the screening law in October 1995, even the anticipated veto did not force parliamentarians to consider the president's objections. Yet some of Havel's vetoes, and the reasons he gave for them, were taken on board by parliament in the form of new amendments in the subsequent reapproval vote. Perhaps most crucial for good relations between parliament and president was Havel's ability to avoid being seen as vetoing the bills at the behest of the opposition. He was actually petitioned a few times by some of the opposition parties to return a bill to parliament, but in none of these cases did he actually do. All the president's vetoes were perceived as his own vetoes and accepted as such by the parliament and ruling majority.

Havel's addresses to the parliament, the third important prerogative of president vis-a-vis the parliament, were more problematic. According to the constitution, the president has the right to take part in sessions of both chambers of parliament, their committees and commissions, and he must be given the floor any time he requests it. From January 1993 till October 1995, for example, Havel used his constitutional right three times, giving lengthy speeches to parliament. In particular his March 1995 speech, when the president (among other things) addressed the financing problems of political parties and proposed the institution of an ombudsman did not receive many warm comments from coalition politicians. Most importantly, however, Havel was caught in a quarrel with the government and some of the coalition MPs because of the intended conception of his speeches. In November 1994, in his regular Sunday radio address, he announced that he would like to launch a tradition of regular March speeches in the parliament, meant as a "State of the Republic" address. The then-prime minister Klaus rebuffed him saying that "such a tradition does not mesh with our constitutional system", and that such a report could only be composed by the government.[18] The president replied with a reference to his constitutional rights, but backed down by noting that his speech certainly cannot, and was not intended to question the accomplishments of the governmental's program.[19]

Kováč's formal position in this respect was similar to Havel's in the Czech Republic, with the exception that the Slovak president is actually expected by the constitution to deliver crucial speeches. According to the constitution, the president submits to parliament reports on the state of the Slovak Republic and on major political issues. The Slovak president indeed delivered two important addresses which, unlike Havel's earlier speeches, directly confronted the government. As was mentioned above, his speech in the parliament in March 1994 dealt a mortal blow to the Mečiar I coalition. After a series of criticisms of the government's performance and Mečiar's style of politics, parliament voted down the coalition of HZDS and SNS. The hesitant and divided opposition did not have much choice but to cast a vote of no confidence, since Kováč's account on the state of the country was devastating. In a second major speech, delivered in September 1995, the president again addressed the question of the functioning of government and parliament. While welcoming Mečiar's efforts to create a stable coalition government, he stressed that government's policy was not consensual. He referred to majority control over all important parliamentary posts, expressed fears for the right of the opposition to express its opinion in parliament, and condemned the ruling elite's tendency to question or disregard decisions of the Constitutional Court.[20] Neither the prime minister nor any government member was present for the address, and this was a normal pattern whenever the president addressed the parliament.

We also have to note that while presidents can exercise some powers over the parliament, parliaments can do the same over presidents. The position of the Czech president is safe since, once elected by the parliament, he is not accountable for the discharge of his office. The only way to remove the president from office is to charge him with high treason before the Constitutional Court on the basis of an indictment by the Senate. The Slovak president may also be prosecuted for treason before the Constitutional Court, if a suit is brought by the parliament. However, unlike in the Czech Republic, the Slovak president is actually responsible for the execution of his duties to the parliament. A very unusual and unclear constitutional provision follows, stipulating that parliament may recall the president from office if his actions threaten the sovereignty and territorial integrity of the Slovak Republic, or if his activities are aimed at removing the democratic order of the country. A proposal to recall the president can be submitted by a simple majority of all deputies and a three-fifths majority of all deputies is needed to remove the president.

Indeed, on 5 May 1995, pursuant to this article of the constitution, one coalition (SNS) deputy initiated a no-confidence motion against the president. The motion was based on the allegations that in 1994 the president employed the Slovak Intelligence Service to monitor activities of some HZDS members and the prime minister Mečiar.[21] Eighty coalition deputies voted to approve the motion, one HZDS deputy abstained, and 40 opposition deputies voted against. Therefore, the required 90 votes (a three-fifths majority) were not amassed and the president continued in office. As we saw, however, the unsuccessful vote of no confidence did not deter the governing majority from carrying on with its attempted impeachment of the president and further attempts to weaken the institutional set-up of the presidency. On October 5, 1995, the prime minister Mečiar said that the nicest way to remove the president would be to pass a law ending his office. But he also said that if this does not work, a referendum on public confidence in the president will be considered.[22]

Nevertheless, the referendum on removing the president was not carried out, not least because the government knew that Slovak citizens who supported Kováč slightly outnumbered those who preferred his removal from the office. Instead, the president and the parliamentary opposition took a concerted action at the end of 1996 to force a different referendum - on the direct election of the president. The opposition anticipated (correctly, as we know now) that, after the end of the five-year presidential term, the divided parliament would not be able to agree on a new candidate. Many of the presidential powers would thus automatically devolve to the prime minister and his government, further increasing their powers within the political system. The coalition was thus not exactly keen to change the method of electing the president and blocked the proposal for a referendum in the parliament (a simple majority was needed to call for it). However, the opposition succeeded in collecting the necessary 350,000 signatures - an alternative way to compel the president to call for a referendum. Meanwhile, after a simple majority vote in the parliament, the Mečiar II government agreed to conduct a referendum on the entry of Slovakia into NATO. Thus, in March 1997, the president faced the need to call for two referendums. He opted to combine the three questions of the NATO referendum with the question concerning direct election of the president into a single four-question referendum to be held at the end of May 1997.

The result was chaos. The coalition, determined to eliminate the fourth question, asked the Constitutional Court to rule on the legality of changing the constitution by referendum. The Court issued an unclear statement, saying the referendum could take place with all four questions, but that the parliament would be under no obligation to actually accept a draft law of the constitution which was attached to the fourth question.[23] On the basis of this ruling, both opposition and coalition offered different interpretations. The opposition insisted on carrying on with the referendum in the four-question form, the coalition demanded the reduction of the ballot to the three questions only. The Central Referendum Commission, a body formally responsible for conducting the referendum and consisting of one representative from each parliamentary party plus the Interior Minister, decided on the four-question ballot. However, the Interior Minister claimed that the commission was merely a supervisory body, and that the commission fell under the government's jurisdiction. As a consequence, and against the will of the commission, the ministry distributed to all polling stations ballots containing only the three questions on NATO. The opposition, as well as many local mayors, called on people to refuse the three-question ballot. As a result, fewer than 10 percent of eligible voters actually cast their votes, rendering the referendum invalid. The commission declared the referendum was marred, while the government said it was just invalid. The Interior Minister was subsequently charged with several criminal complaints and law-suits, but was relieved of these charges later that year.

The dispute between the coalition and the opposition on this particular referendum embodied several highly controversial points, making it difficult to provide a neutral evaluation. It appears at the very least that, by using the loopholes in law and interpretable statements of the Court, the ruling coalition once again attempted to severe the links of horizontal accountability between institutions to enhance its unrestricted majority rule. However, even more important, from the viewpoint of this study is that the conduct of this referendum showed the extent to which the formal institutional shape of presidency in Slovakia is in question. Although merely moving to the direct election of the president would not necessarily alter the overall parliamentary character of the Slovak system of government, it is a potentially important institutional change. The extra legitimacy directly elected presidents enjoy may fire their ambitions, and hence increase their influence. Popularly elected presidents are also less likely to be held hostage by political forces (parties), because these are not directly responsible for their election.

Indeed, the following data partly reflect the extent to which the initial consensus on presidential powers in both countries in 1992 (see chapter 2) has largely disappeared in Slovakia. In our survey we looked at the formal powers of the president under seven headings, which reflect the possible powers a president can have in relation to parliament and the government and then compare these to MPs' answers about the specific powers which the president should enjoy. The possible powers are the following: to rule by decree, to initiate legislation, to nominate the prime minister, to dissolve parliament, to suspend legislation, to veto legislation and to dismiss the government.[24] The actual powers of both Czech and Slovak presidents with respect to these seven headings are the same. The answers of MPs are summarized in Tables 5.1 and 5.2.

Table 5.1: Views of Czech MPs on presidential powers (% yes)

	ODS	KDS	ODA	KDU-ČSL	ČSSD	LSU	LB	LSNS	Others
Rule by decree	0.0	0.0	18.2	16.7	0.0	0.0	2.9	0.0	0.0
Initiate legislation	46.2	37.5	81.8	66.7	85.7	88.9	80.0	75.0	61.2
Nominate the prime minister	65.4	62.5	72.7	83.3	57.1	66.7	80.0	50.0	61.2
Dissolve parliament	76.9	87.5	100.0	91.7	92.9	66.7	37.1	25.0	50.0
Suspend legislation	94.2	62.5	100.0	83.3	78.6	77.8	62.9	75.0	61.2
Veto legislation	0.0	0.0	0.0	0.0	0.0	0.0	2.9	25.0	5.6
Dismiss the government	25.0	25.0	36.4	66.7	64.3	33.3	34.3	25.0	27.8
(N)	(-52)	(-8)	(-11)	(12)	(14)	(9)	(35)	(4)	(18)

Table 5.2: Views of Slovak MPs on presidential powers (% yes)

	HZDS	KDH	SDL	SNS	Hungar.	Others
Rule by decree	0.0	0.0	0.0	0.0	0.0	0.0
Initiate legislation	64.9	73.3	75.0	33.3	66.7	66.7
Nominate the prime minister	48.6	60.0	70.0	83.3	88.9	77.8
Dissolve parliament	27.0	73.3	60.0	50.0	55.5	66.7
Suspend legislation	45.9	66.7	85.0	66.7	44.4	55.6
Veto legislation	0.0	6.7	10.0	16.7	0.0	11.1
Dismiss the government	13.5	53.3	70.0	50.0	33.3	44.4
(N)	(37)	(15)	(20)	(6)	(9)	(9)

To rule by decree

As can be seen from the data, there was a widespread consensus that the president should not be able to rule by decree. In Slovakia, the consensus was absolute, in that none of the respondents indicated the willingness to grant such a power.

To initiate legislation

The Czech and Slovak presidents do not have the right of legislative initiative, yet almost 65 percent of respondents in the Czech Republic and 67 percent in Slovakia answered that they should have this power. This is the only example in our data where the MPs' answers indicated a willingness to increase the power of the president. In the Czech Republic, there was more approval on the part of respondents from the opposition parties, which were already in favour of this prerogative during the negotiations on the constitution. They may also have thought that this presidential prerogative would provide them with more leverage in getting their legislation on the political agenda, particularly during the strong majority rule of the Klaus government between 1992 and 1996. In Slovakia, the major parties were in favour of the president's right of legislative initiative. As in the Czech Republic, this prerogative was disputed during constitutional debates, and was even included in the final draft of the constitution.

To nominate the prime minister

As we saw, the president's power would be more realistically described as "appointing" the prime minister. In the Czech Republic a majority of respondents in all parties endorsed the right of the president to nominate the prime minister. The answers to this question in Slovakia are less clear. The general picture across the parties, with the exception of Mečiar's HZDS, was one of approval of the presidential right to nominate the prime minister. The split answers of Mečiar's party probably reflected the debate within the party itself on the place of the president in the institutional set-up because, in 1993, Mečiar several times expressed his wish to change Slovakia into a presidential system. He argued that this would provide much needed governmental stability. It was of course at that time that his own party and government were disintegrating and facing a hostile parliamentary majority in the parliament. It could also reflect the personal antagonism between Mečiar and Kováč, which was growing at the time the interviews were carried out.

To dissolve parliament

Here again the answers of respondents from HZDS provide an explanation for the comparatively low percentage of positive answers to this question in Slovakia. For the rest of the Slovak parties, as well as the majority of the Czech parties, the powers of the president to dissolve the parliament under the circumstances described in the respective constitutions seemed to be generally endorsed.

To suspend legislation and *To veto legislation*

Only a negligible number of MPs in the Czech and Slovak Republics indicated they would like the president to have the right of absolute veto on legislation. Again Mečiar's own party and also part of his coalition partner SNS accounted for the lower percentage in favour of suspensive legislative veto in the Slovak Republic.

To dismiss the government

This is the only answer which received similar, relatively low scores in both countries, with most parliamentarians opposing the idea of the president having the power to dismiss the government. However, in Slovakia, the two main opposition parties (SDL and KDH) were largely in favour of this right, as were the then-opposition Social Democrats in the Czech Republic. This, of course, is not consistent with answers these MPs gave on other aspects of presidential powers, because granting the presidents the power of dismissing the government would significantly enhance their position within the system, or even change the system as a whole. The opposition MPs' answers may have been contextually biased, in that the opposition parties would have welcomed the chance to bring down the government by any means.

This evidence can be summarized in the following observations: in general, the lowest scores for approval of presidential powers were for the three headings under which neither of the presidents has powers. Thus there was a general agreement that the presidents should not have more powers than they already have, although the picture is less clear with regard to "dismissal of government". As indicated above, a breakdown of the responses per party supports the impression that, in some cases, the answers were clearly influenced by the experiences of MPs in the institutional and political set-up. They were normative answers, but strongly influenced by recent contextual factors. The other exceptions were the Czech and Slovak respondents' endorsement of legislative initiative - a power the Czech or Slovak presidents do not have. We argued that one possible explanation is also contextual. But it also indicates that original disagreements which surfaced during the constitution-making processes were still reflected in MPs' views at the time we carried out our survey.

There was also a tendency among the respondents to endorse the powers presidents already have, with agreement usually scoring above 50 percent. Where scores hovered around 50 percent, approval is less clear cut. This indicates a lack of consensus within parties, and particularly within Mečiar's HZDS, on nominating the prime minister and suspending legislation. It may have also reflected a lack of clarity as to the precise prerogatives of the president in a given area. However, it also indicates that elite views on presidential powers in Slovakia were controversial already at a time when the conflict between Mečiar and Kováč was relatively subdued. Given the later debates and, in particular, given that it was the opposition who in 1997 initiated the referendum on direct presidential elections (i.e. the same parties which seem to agree in our survey that the president should be indirectly elected), it indicates only that the views on the institutional framework are driven by momentary political conflict and actor's position. In other words, and as we have already seen with the electoral system (chapter 3), the attitudes of Slovak elites toward the country's fundamental institutions are flexible, rather than based on a firm normative commitment.

This stands in contrast with the Czech Republic, where contemporary political discourse on the presidency (and many other institutions too) does not appear to contradict a large normative consensus displayed by elites at the time of our survey. However, it should be noted that, after the 1998 elections, the Czech political elite made several constitutional proposals concerning the presidency. Although no concrete change was agreed at the time this study was finished, curbing of the right to nominate the prime minister was the major proposal regarding powers of the president. Similarly to Slovakia, (part of) the Czech political elites argued that the constituton should explicitly state that the president nominates the leader of the (electorally) largest party to form the government, rather than, as under the current constitution, leave it up to the president's judgment (or the hitherto respected informal rule). In itself, this is not a significant constitutional change - certainly not the same as those advocated (and partly implemented) in Slovakia. Yet, it shows that the Czech Republic is by no means immune to constitutional engineering, even if it the changes are only formalization of existing informal rules or their gradual improvment.

Conclusions

Shortly before the presidential elections in 1993, Havel wrote: "The Czech president will neither be a leader of the executive branch, nor a leader of the parliamentary majority, but only an indirectly elected constitutional subject with a very specific position and task".[25] Our evidence suggests that, in executive-legislative relations, he played precisely this limited role which was envisaged by, and embodied in, the constitution. The initial turbulent phase of transition where the head of state could perform an outstanding role was by and large over. The 1992-1996 Klaus government did not desire any presidential arbitration. After Havel was elected president of the Czech Republic, every step he made was closely monitored and commented upon by the political parties. In other words, the political structures in the country stabilized and this, together with limited constitutional powers, narrowed the margin in which the president could operate. Havel largely recognized this and did not intervene where it was no longer necessary. Moreover, and perhaps crucially, he did not have to face a fragmented legislature and unstable coalition government, which was precisely the situation faced by

Kováč in the 1992-1994 Slovak parliament. In Havel's political circumstances, the temptation to increase the powers of the president, or to play a more active role in the governance of the country, would have been difficult to justify. It was only after the 1996 (and 1998) elections, under conditions of increased governmental instability, that his involvement in executive-legislative relations again became more intensive (and controversial).

As for the question of institutionalization, it seems that the presidency was a chief beneficiary of Havel's reign. Our evidence suggest that the constitutional prerogatives of the president, as well as the basic understanding of the role president should play, find acceptance among politicians. The answers of MPs across all political parties were largely in favour of the existing powers. In addition, political debates in the country, as well as the activities of the president himself, do not indicate that the constitution will be dramatically revised. Although several constitutional changes concerning the presidency were proposed at the time this study was closing, they did not seem to contradict the existing institutional set-up. While politically motivated, these proposed changes appeared primarily to codify informal rules, such as those guiding the nomination of prime minister, which had developed as the complement to formal constitutional prerogatives.

Much of the evidence on the performance of the Slovak president is in contrast to that of Havel. In executive-legislative relations, Kováč played a much more active role. After the important ruling of the Constitutional Court, he became involved in personnel changes in the government, refusing to appoint candidates proposed by the prime minister. Neither did the formation of new governments occur without Kováč's intervention. While his involvement in the formation of the Moravčík cabinet was not problematic, his active approach to steering the formation of the government after the September 1994 elections damaged his relations with the Mečiar II government. As we saw, this episode gradually led to a bitter battle over presidential powers. Zifčák (1995) pointed out that the Slovak constitution itself set the preconditions for the Slovak political stalemate by not making clear which of the presidential powers should be exercised independently, and which only at the government's request. Indeed, these imprecisions in the constitution were an important precondition for the intensity of the conflict between the president and the government, since Kováč himself showed a remarkable willingness to expand the spheres of presidential influence. However, it would be wrong to attribute these attempts entirely to Kováč's personal ambitions. The president's activity had increased with the deepening of the governmental crisis at the end of 1993 and, therefore should be also seen as an attempt to counter political instability in the country. In the context of personal animosities between Kováč and Mečiar, and given the lack of established conventions regulating the relations between the institutions of the president and the prime minister, this vagueness caused an escalation of the conflict, which culminated in a meta-institutional clash over meaning of democracy and accountability.

Little good has come of this conflict between the president and government. Slovakia is searching for stability for the presidency which, perhaps more than any other institution, mirrors the struggles over democracy and the institutional framework. The implications of conflicts for the Slovak presidency are more far-reaching in formal institutional terms than are the implications of several comparable tensions which occurred in the Czech Republic. The largest Slovak political party (HZDS) at first advocated a presidential system, giving the institution of president extraordinary powers. When that proved impossible, the ruling elite briskly changed its strategy and started cutting presidential powers under the current parliamentary system, as well as blocking the elections of a new president after Kováč's term expired. To add to this malaise, the Slovak opposition which had been firmly behind the concept of a weak, indirectly elected president in the incipient period of Slovak democracy, launched a series of initiatives to introduce direct presidential elections (and succeeded in doing so after the 1998 elections). The institution of president has thus been under fire from all sides, and the common denominator behind these challenges is the attempt either to empower the momentary parliamentary majority (on the part of Mečiar's coalition), or to ensure at least some form of horizontal accountability between Slovak institutions (on the part of the opposition).

Notes

1. According to the Czech Constitution, a candidate is elected president if he/she receives an absolute majority of votes of all deputies and an absolute majority of all senators. If no candidate receives an absolute majority, a second round is held within fourteen days, in which the candidate(s) with the highest number of votes from the Chamber of Deputies and from the Senate must receive an absolute majority of all present deputies as well as all present senators to be elected. According to the Slovak Constitution, a candidate is elected president if he/she receives a three-fifths majority of all deputies' votes. Note, however, that, for the reasons we shall discuss below, the Slovak constitution was changed following the 1998 elections. The Slovak president is now directly elected.

2. Havel tried to question this rule before the 1998 early elections, when he remarked that he is under no constitutional obligation to nominate the leader of the (electorally) largest party to start coalition negotiations. Despite the fact that his remark was directed against the leader of the Social Democrats, and hence was of potential use to other parties in the electoral campaign, he was rebuffed unanimously by all parties. They insisted that the established informal rule be honoured and, in fact, Havel's influence in the subsequent coalition negotiations was marginal.

3. For example, Brokl and Mansfeldová (1994) refer to the visit of Salman Rushdie as one of the most strident squabbles between the president and the prime minister. Havel's invitation for Yasser Arafat to visit the Czech Republic, offered in October 1995, also met with sharp criticism from the premier and other politicians.

4. Reported in daily *Dnes*, February 27, 1993.

5. See Václav Havel, "Role českého presidenta", in daily *Dnes*, January 19, 1993

6. The question was "Could you tell me which of these statements, according to your own personal opinion, most closely resembles the role predominantly performed by the president?". Possible answers were "party representative"; "statesman; representing the interests of the nation"; "mediator"; "protector of the constitution"; "other".

7. Note that the election of Kováč was already a divisive issue in Slovakia. While Havel was supported by all major parties (the Republicans and the Communists excepted), most Slovak parties (HZDS, SNS, KDH, SDL) nominated their own candidate for the first round of the presidential elections in 1993. After an unsuccessful first round, in which parties voted for their own candidates and no candidate could thus master the necessary qualified majority, the negotiations between political parties started again. This is when the name of HZDS member and party co-founder Michal Kováč surfaced. His name did not appear among the first four candidates, because part of HZDS (including Mečiar) strongly opposed him and, for the first round, proposed a candidate with an identical surname - Roman Kováč. However, for the second round, the part of HZDS favorable to Michal Kováč prevailed, and, as he was acceptable also to a large part of the opposition, he was elected president for five years. He gave up his membership of HZDS (though this is not a constitutional obligation in either of the two republics).

8. It is worth pointing out that the peak of that crisis was reached in August 1995 when Kováč's son was kidnapped in Slovakia and left in his car outside of a police station in neighboring Austria (see Fischer, 1995). It was the peak of the crisis, because the kidnapping changed the terms of debate between the president and the government from legal constitutional squabbles into a series of illegal actions and wide-reaching criminal allegations. Kováč Jr. - a young Slovak businessman - was under prosecution in Germany, which demanded that he testify in a large fraud case involving the Slovak company Technopol. However, because the constitution guarantees that Slovak citizens cannot be deported to another country, he was awaiting further developments in the prosecution's case on home soil. After his sudden abduction and subsequent jailing in Austria (he returned to

Slovakia 6 months later), the Slovak Information Service came under immediate suspicion of being involved in the kidnapping. Although no clear-cut evidence exists to date, the kidnapping case has been widely interpreted as one of the most uncharitable weapons the Slovak government employed in the struggle with the president. The chain of events which followed the abduction included the removal of three investigators from the Bratislava police department, a car explosion and the death of a former policeman linked with the abduction, and ended with charges filed by the president against the prime minister for his media allegations that Kováč Sr. was also involved in the financial frauds within Technopol.

9. See *East European Constitutional Review*, Slovakia Update, 2/3 (3/1), 1993/1994.

10. See *East European Constitutional Review*, Slovakia Update, 4(3), 1995.

11. Interview with the Slovak president Michal Kováč in daily *Rudé Právo*, March 17, 1994.

12. Politically, the president's authority to exclude the HZDS from government proved too narrow anyway. Without Mečiar not participating in the talks, the HZDS walked out of the negotiations, claiming that the president should not have any say in the cabinet formation. Since none of the realistic coalition combinations made it possible to form a government without HZDS, Kováč could not but officially designate Mečiar to take the role of constructing the cabinet. Indeed, in December 1994, he endorsed the whole proposed list of cabinet ministers, and appointed a new coalition government of HZDS, SNS, and ZRS.

13. Information from *OMRI Daily Digest*, No. 187, Part 2, 26 September 1995.

14. Interview with the Slovak president in *Rudé Právo*, June 11, 1994. Citation is from an answer to the question "What chances do you give Moravčík's government of continuing in office after the elections?".

15. See "Bilancie a perspektívy", an interview with Michal Kováč in *Parlamentný Kuriér*, 2(1), 1994.

16. Note that according to the Slovak constitution, the president must return a bill to the parliament any time the government request him to do so. This rule was one of the means the Mečiar I government had at its disposal to express its opinion on the bills adopted by the parliament against the governmental will.

17. See *Rudé Právo*, December 28, 1994.

18. See daily *Rudé Právo*, November 15, 1994

19. It must be noted, however, that Havel's parliamentary address in 1997 could be interpreted as an evaluation of the governmental program. Though framed as usual in general terms, the speech was nevertheless a sharp criticism of Klaus' minority cabinet, and of ODS in particular, and contributed to the fall of the government. This event, along with Havel's involvement in the formation of Tošovský's caretaker cabinet (1997-1998), marked a

deterioration in the president's relationship with Klaus and ODS.

20. See *OMRI Daily Digest*, No. 174, Part 2, September 7, 1995.

21. Note that these allegations were made by the Special Control Agency, established as a special body of the Slovak parliament to monitor and check on governmental institutions. The agency was set up by a vote on the floor of the parliament and had five members - all belonging to parties in the Mečiar II government.

22. See *OMRI Daily Digest*, No. 195, Part 2, October 6, 1995.

23. The fourth question on the referendum ballot was: "Do you agree that the President of the Slovak Republic should be elected directly, according to the attached draft of a constitutional law?". The question included a supplement containing a draft law.

24. These are, of course, not exhaustive. Shugart and Carey (1992), for example, divide presidential powers between legislative (veto, partial veto, rule by decree, exclusive right to initiate certain proposals, budgetary initiative and power to propose referenda) and non-legislative powers (cabinet formation, cabinet dismissal, lack of assembly censure and dissolution of assembly). We have chosen those powers which we consider to be the most important in broadly defining a system as presidential or parliamentary.

25. See Václav Havel, "Role českého presidenta", in daily *Dnes*, January 19, 1993.

6 Inside the Parliaments: Parliamentary Parties

Introduction

This chapter will complete the empirical inquiry into the institutionalization of the Czech and Slovak parliaments by focusing on their internal functioning. It aims to substantiate the evidence presented in previous chapters by examining the organization and behavior of parliamentary parties[1] - arguably the single most important analytical unit in the internal functioning of Czech and Slovak parliaments. Chapter 4 showed that, within a relatively short period of time, the relations between parliament and government have become dominated by political parties in both countries. This was exhibited in a number of formal institutional features of their executive-legislative systems, but also in the actual interactions between ministers and MPs, which both, one way or the other, forcefully underpin the centrality of parties. Parliamentary parties in the two states have evidently matured into cohesive bodies, leaving cross-party interests, parliamentary committees, individual MPs, and parliamentary agendas contingent on party politics. How has this process occurred? Have the internal procedures of Czech and Slovak parliaments influenced parliamentary party cohesion? Has the parliamentary party leadership been able to sanction disobedience among their own MPs? To what extent is the cohesion of parliamentary parties influenced by their relationship with the external party organizations?

The chapter will address these questions by working with three key analytical terms: cohesion, discipline and fragmentation. Parliamentary party *cohesion* is defined as the extent to which, in a given situation, parliamentary party members can be observed to act together for party goals (Özbudun, 1970). It is distinguished from the term party *discipline*, which refers to a system of sanctions by which parliamentary party cohesion is attained or attempted. The distinction allows us to make clear that parliamentary party cohesion may well result from enforcement and punishment (disciplining measures), or may equally be spontaneous (voluntary behavior of parliamentary party members). However, our starting point is the analysis of parliamentary party *fragmentation,* that is the splits and mergers of individual parliamentary parties. As a persistent phenomenon in Eastern Europe, parliamentary party fragmentation represents an important dimension to the study of parliamentary institutionalization. In stable Western democracies the problem of party fragmentation can be easily glossed over, since the frequency of parliamentary party splits is relatively low and parliamentary parties can be expected to hold on to their original members (see Mair, 1990). As is apparent in many parts of this study, there would be little point to studying cohesion of Czech and Slovak parliamentary parties without first considering the changes of the 'units' themselves and the reasons for it.

Fragmentation of Parliamentary Parties

Table 6.1 shows that after the elections in June 1992 there were nine parliamentary parties in the Czech parliament. By March 1994, their number had gone up to twelve. By December 1995, the number of parliamentary parties had settled at ten and further decreased to nine prior to the 1996 elections. Apart from the merger of KDS with ODS, the coalition parliamentary parties remained largely unchanged, whereas opposition parliamentary parties underwent a process of restructuring. LSU and HSD-SMS disappeared altogether, and two new parliamentary parties were formed from them: the Czech-Moravian Union of the Center (ČMUS) and the Liberal Social National Party (LSNS). LB split into LB and KSČM. Furthermore, a few MPs became independent - without any formal parliamentary party affiliation; and some MPs engaged in 'fraction-hopping' or, as the Czechs call it, 'political tourism': moving from one parliamentary party to another.

The Slovak parliament started the legislative term in 1992 with six parliamentary parties. When the parliament was dissolved at the end of June 1994, eight parliamentary parties were in operation. The two new ones, the Democratic Union (DU) and the National Democratic Party-New Alternative (NDS-NA), were both splinters of the coalition parties. DU (initially named the Group of Independent MPs - KNP) consisted of MPs defecting from HZDS; NDS-NA was set up by a group of defecting SNS MPs. Both parliamentary parties merged before the September 1994 elections to form a new party named Democratic Union (DU). In addition, as in the Czech parliament, a few MPs remained without party affiliation, and some changed their affiliation in the course of the parliamentary term.

Table 6.1: Czech and Slovak parliamentary parties and number of seats (1992-1996)

	Czech Republic								Slovakia				
Party	June 1992 (elections)	Jan 1993	Jan 1994	Jan 1995	Jan 1996	May 1996	May 1996 (elections)	Party	June 1992 (elections)	Dec 1993	June 1994	Sept 1994 (elections)	Jan 1996
ODS	66	66	66	65	66	72	69	HZDS	74	65	54	61	61
KDS	10	10	10	10	6	-	-	SNS	15	8	9	9	9
ODA	14	14	15	17	16	16	13	ESWS	9	9	9	9	9
KDU- ČSL	15	15	15	16	24	24	18	MKDH	5	5	5	7	7
LB	35	35	35	24	23	23	-	SDL	29	28	28	18	18
ČSSD	16	16	18	21	24	22	58	KDH	18	18	18	17	16
LSU	16	14	13	-	-	-	-	DÚ	–	-	18	15	15
SPR-RSČ	14	11	8	6	5	5	18	NDS-NA	–	6	6	-	-
HSD-(S)MS	14	14	15	-	-	-	-	ZRS	–	-	-	13	12
KSČM	–	-	-	10	10	10	22	MPP	-	-	-	1	1
LSNS	–	5	5	5	6	6	-						
ČMUS	–	-	-	15	15	15	-						
Non-affiliated	–	-	-	11	5	7	-	Non-affiliated	-	11	3	-	2
Total	200	200	200	200	200	200	200	Total	150	150	150	150	150

These numbers clearly demonstrate the level of instability within the parliamentary parties. The phenomenon of party splits, typical for the Czechoslovak Federal Assembly from 1990 to 1992, was also observable in the successor Czech and Slovak parliaments. Although the scale of parliamentary party fragmentation decreased in comparison with the previous parliament,[2] it nevertheless shows that at least some of the Czech and Slovak parliamentary parties are continuously prone to fragmentation. Since parties are, in general, neither monolithic in organization nor homogeneous in composition, internal differences can of course be expected to arise. In our survey, 61 percent of the Czech MPs stated that there were subgroups or currents within their parliamentary party, and almost half of these deputies claimed to belong to one of the subgroups.[3] We did not record a single Czech parliamentary party where MPs failed to report the existence of subgroups. In the Slovak parliament, subgroups or currents were identified by 47 percent of MPs, of which 36 percent belonged to such (an) intra-party group(s). The only parliamentary party without subgroups was the Group of Independent MPs (KNP), a six- member splinter group from HZDS, which later developed into DU.

Studies of party factionalism in Czech (Kopecký, 1995b) and other Eastern European parties (Waller, 1995; Lewis, 1995) showed that during the early stages of the process of democratization and party formation in post-communist democracies, the occurrence of such subgroups within parliamentary parties often reflects the state of party disarray rather than any form of stable intra-party organization. The subgroups within parliamentary parties come to signal fissile tendencies in party structures, which reflect the instability of an emerging party system on one hand, and obviously reinforce it on the other hand. Rather than organized factions, the non-institutionalized party organizations, an unstructured (open) electoral field, and personalized politics, all have an impact on the fragmentation of parliamentary parties. In other words, it is the lack of electoral, ideological and organizational identity which makes many Czech and Slovak political parties susceptible to frequent splits and fusions, and the state of parliamentary party fragmentation demonstrated in Table 6.1 is a reflection of this.

The acquisition of a broadly organizational-based identity is undoubtedly one of the preconditions of the stabilization of individual parliamentary parties. Given that is normally a rather lengthy process, it would be perhaps premature to expect a low level of party fragmentation in the initial stages of party formation. The identity and organization building are nevertheless processes calibrated in a given institutional environment, which can significantly influence them. As we saw in chapter 3, the small changes of electoral systems were introduced in both countries to counter excessive fragmentation of political parties and to reward the bigger parties. It showed that the Czech and Slovak political elites proved apt at institutional engineering, and the rules concerning the formation of parliamentary parties did not remain unchanged either. Perhaps most important was the adoption of a more stringent rule on their minimum size. In the 1992-1996 Czech parliament, the minimum size of a parliamentary party was five members, meaning that only groups of MPs meeting this threshold could register with the chairmanship of the parliament and receive financial support from the parliamentary budget. The consequence was the creation of sometimes quite temporary parliamentary parties consisting of members of different parties, who hardly had anything in common other than the desire to obtain financial and logistical support. An identical rule on the minimum size of parliamentary parties existed in Slovakia between 1992 and 1996, and had similar effects.

When new standing orders were debated in the Czech parliament in 1995, the section concerning parliamentary parties became, unsurprisingly, a bone of political contention. The government parliamentary parties, which had not fragmented, supported restrictive measures. Small opposition parties (which were prone to fragmentation or were newly established as a result of it) fiercely opposed them. In the end, the decision to combat fragmentation was pushed through primarily by the incumbent coalition parties. Accordingly, from the 1996 parliamentary term on, the minimum size of a parliamentary party was increased to 10 MPs. Furthermore, if a new parliamentary party is to be established during parliamentary term, it can only consist of (at least 10) MPs who are no longer members of the party in which they were elected. This means, for example, that it is no longer possible to be a member of ODS without being a member of its parliamentary party and/or to join another parliamentary party. Finally, newly formed parliamentary parties are to be excluded both from financial support from the parliamentary budget (and will receive only an equipped office) and from participation in other organs of the parliament. This effectively means that the new standing orders provide for two classes of parliamentary parties: one which has contested elections and gets full rights; and one which is formed later in parliament and gets very limited rights. In addition, in Slovakia, as a result of new standing orders from October 1996, a larger number of MPs (at least 8) is now needed to form a parliamentary party.

There is no doubt that the adoption of such restrictive formal rules will make it less attractive, if not impossible, for individual MPs to leave their parliamentary parties and/or set up wholly new ones. In that sense, new institutional rules have certainly been behind decreasing parliamentary party fragmentation. However, it should be stressed that even before these rules were introduced, the life of MPs who left their parliamentary party was more difficult than that of those who remained. This relates to the design of standing orders in both parliaments, which have since 1990 designated parliamentary parties as the basic units of reference. The composition and rules of other parliamentary organs, such as the Organizational Committee in the Czech parliament, and the Presidium in the Slovak parliament, are derived from it or based on it. It is thus not only financial and logistical support which parliamentary parties can offer, but also strength in influencing decision-making in the whole parliamentary arena (see Kopecký, 1996).

Looking at the data in Table 6.2, we can see that MPs in both countries perceived the advantages of parliamentary party membership roughly in the terms described above. The large majority in both countries gave answers which have been coded as "collective power". This includes answers referring both to collective strength in pushing through policies and the collective forum; e.g. not just power which parliamentary party membership gives them, but also consultations with colleagues, forming opinions on issues, moral support and a sense of belonging. The second largest number of MPs referred to service and expertise provided by parliamentary parties which, as we shall see later, partly includes the services from the parties' central offices. Some MPs in both parliaments - albeit in small numbers - valued the possibility of

Table 6.2: Main advantages of membership of parliamentary party (first answer; in %)

	Czech Republic	Slovakia
Collective power	61.9	55.2
Service, expertise	19.0	20.8
Material and financial backup	1.8	0.0
Specialization	7.1	8.3
None	1.8	0.0
Unarrangeable answers	6.5	9.4
DK/NA	1.8	6.3
(N)	(168)	(9-96)

specializing in their policy field that parliamentary party membership gave them.

If we consider the answers on disadvantages of parliamentary parties (Table 6.3), the high number of the Czech MPs seeing 'no disadvantages' was striking. If disadvantages were perceived, in the case of the Czech MPs they could be found in the answers of 13 percent of MPs in the category 'party discipline', referring usually to the need to adapt one's own opinion to that of the majority. This was also the answer of 11 percent of the Slovak MPs. Yet, the answers of the Czech MPs contrast quite sharply with the Slovak MPs, a majority of whom did not want to answer, did not know, or gave uncodable answers. The cross-tabulation by party did not reveal a concentration of such answers in one parliamentary party which could, for example, signal tensions in it. Although the HZDS and the KDH MPs were slightly above the average of other parliamentary parties in these categories, we can only report that the Slovak MPs were in general more reluctant to provide expansive answers on this question. This could relate to the sensitivity of the issue at the time the interviews were carried out, given it was during and shortly after the major (parliamentary) party splits.

Table 6.3: Main disadvantages of membership of parliamentary party (in %)

	Czech Republic	Slovakia
Waste of time	6.0	10.4
Party discipline	13.1	11.5
None	57.1	26.0
Unarrangeable answers	17.3	21.9
DK/NA	6.6	30.2
(N)	(168)	(96)

Taking into account both (data on) MPs' evaluation of parliamentary party membership and the structure of parliaments, it comes as no surprise that defecting MPs usually formed new parliamentary parties or joined other parliamentary parties quite quickly, rather than staying non-affiliated. The prevailing climate, in normative as well as institutional terms, has been quite favorable to the operation of parliamentary parties in both parliaments. If we bring this to the picture of fragmentation of parliamentary parties, it only bolsters the point that the phenomenon of fragmentation hinges on the extent of party loyalty and identification of individual MPs with their party. As soon as that level is low, the propensity to fragmentation is likely to persist, regardless of the institutional restrictions, or general normative acceptance of a parliamentary party as the basic way of operation. In combination with stringent rules, it might even lead to a paradoxical situation in which parliamentary parties remain together out of necessity (i.e. do not fragment anymore), but, because of a lack of overarching loyalties of their members, become extremely uncohesive (for example, in voting on the floor).

Internal Organization of Parliamentary Parties and their Cohesion

The following evidence on voting patterns in the votes taken on the floor of the parliament does not support any hints about the lack of parliamentary party cohesion, however. Table 6.4 summarizes measurement of cohesion for the Czech parliamentary parties. The machine-readable data were made available from the voting machine installed in the parliament in 1993. No such machine were installed in the Slovak parliament when this study was conducted, and comparable data are thus not available.[4] The next few paragraphs will thus describe the voting cohesion of the Czech parliamentary parties only. However, there is now a new evidence to expect a similiar set of results in the Slovak parliament, especially after the 1994 elections (see Malová, 1998).

The measure of voting cohesion of the Czech parliamentary parties consists of two related parts: *average similarity* represents the average size of the majority of a parliamentary party voting one way or another. For instance: over a given period three votes were taken. On the first vote party A was split 75–25; the size of the majority is then 75 percent. On the second vote party A was unanimous: a 'majority' of 100 percent. On the third vote the party was split 50-50; this counts as a 'majority' of 50 percent. The average similarity is thus (75+100+50)/3 = 75. Abstentions (not absence!) are calculated as 'no' votes.[5]

The importance of the second part - *average participation* - stems from the way the first measurement is constructed. Because it takes into account only the votes of MPs who were actually registered to vote (by inserting a card into the electronic voting machine), the average participation on voting is an additional indicator of the parliamentary parties' degree of cohesion on the floor. If these two measurements are considered together, it helps to avoid situations in which we would misinterpret results: for example, party A with 10 members is very cohesive due to an average similarity of 90 percent, while this 90 percent would be made only by, say, three MPs with the other seven never showing up during the votes.

Table 6.4: Voting Cohesion of the Czech parliamentary parties (1992-1996)

	Average similarity	Average participation
Coalition parties:		
KDS	93.98	75.24
ODS	92.49	74.40
KDU-ČSL	91.24	75.24
ODA	90.65	66.43
Opposition parties:		
SPR-RSČ	96.73	47.41
KSČM	91.28	76.00
LSNS	90.46	49.19
LB	90.06	74.03
ČSSD	85.75	64.20
ČMUS	86.87	64.22
Parties no longer existing:		
LSU	86.91	63.84
HSD-SMS	86.67	57.45
ČMSS	86.14	63.27

The data show a fairly high level of voting cohesion among the Czech parliamentary parties on the floor.[6] In particular coalition parties, which also fared well in their of low level of fragmentation, have achieved a high level of voting cohesion (they scored high on average similarity as well as on average participation). On the other hand, the fragmentation of the opposition parliamentary parties, demonstrated in Table 6.1, was accompanied by a relatively low level of voting cohesion. This applies to the relatively stable opposition parties, like the ČSSD, as well as to some of those who lost members or were created after splits from other parliamentary parties (ČMUS, LSNS). On an empirical level, these findings characterize the Czech political scene between 1992 and 1996 quite well, complementing our findings in chapter 4. The right-of-center coalition government, consisting of four (parliamentary) parties, managed to govern without major upheavals and it was the opposition which appeared disunited and hence largely lacking any significant influence.

We should recall here both the data on the distances between individual parties presented earlier (Figure 4.1), as well as the analysis of parliamentary party influence on the work of parliamentary committees (section 4.2). It demonstrated that since 1992, there was an overall congruity among the coalition parties, a strong division between coalition and opposition parliamentary parties, and divisions among opposition parliamentary parties themselves. In other words, on the level of inter-party conflict, the votes were by and large structured between two blocks of parties in the parliament. Cross-alliances between coalition parliamentary parties and opposition parliamentary parties were rare.

What accounts for this high level of parliamentary party cohesion? Voting cohesion is an indicator of how individual legislators act together in the very last stage of a quite often complicated and lengthy legislative process. Voting cohesion is a result of parliamentary and intra-party decision-making processes, with many intervening interactions relevant to the shape of the final product. While we cannot work on the assumption that voting cohesion automatically implies party pressure (discipline), it is also true that low cohesion does not automatically mean an absence of party pressures. As the studies on cohesion stress, however, a number of factors can possibly affect cohesion, but only a few can be treated simultaneously (see Özbudun, 1970). Such studies tend to concentrate on the internal organization of parliamentary parties and viewing the Czech and Slovak parliamentary parties from inside certainly provides a clue as to the mechanisms by which parliamentary party cohesion is bolstered.

In response to the question "When your parliamentary party makes a decision, where does the main point of decision-making lie", 76 percent of the Czech and 81 percent of the Slovak MPs cited the parliamentary party meeting, as opposed to the parliamentary party leadership, parliamentary party experts, or somewhere else. This indicates that for the functioning of Czech and Slovak parliamentary parties the parliamentary party meeting is crucial, acting as a sort of collective decision-making arena. There the parliamentary party strategies are adopted and opposing views are discussed and eventually reconciled. Parliamentary party meetings are always held prior to the floor debates of the parliament. The floor debates in the Czech parliament last normally one week, preceded by two weeks of work in the committees, one week of work in the MPs' constituencies, and one week reserved for international working journeys (a five-week cycle). This is similar in Slovakia, except for the week for international working journeys (a four-week cycle). On a less regular basis, meetings of parliamentary parties are called during the committee stage of the legislative month, and also during the floor debates, especially when a new controversial amendment appears on the agenda.

All parliamentary parties elect their own leadership. The leadership of the parliamentary parties plays an important role in their representation in the various parliamentary bodies (like the Organizational Committee or the Presidium), in other party organs (see below), and in the organization of the meetings and debates of the parliamentary parties themselves. The power connected with the function of parliamentary party leader, such as the responsibility of conveying the positions of party executives to MPs and vice versa, or influence over agendas of meetings, obviously makes leaders more influential figures in internal organization of Czech and Slovak parties than an ordinary member. However, the answers of the MPs in both countries to the question concerning the main point of decision-making indicate that the role of the leaders is not overtly dominant: only 5 percent of MPs stated that the main point of decision-making within the parliamentary party lies with its leadership - a finding which seems to be well supported by the relatively small prestige associated with, and the minimal popular attention paid to, the position of parliamentary party leader in both countries. Thus, although we find differences between individual Czech and Slovak parties, there is no consistent evidence to suggest that parliamentary party leaders hold a commanding position in the internal decision-making of parliamentary party organizations, bar certain exceptions when this function is held by the leader of the party as a whole.

Somewhat surprising (again in both parliaments) was the generally low importance attributed by MPs to the role of parliamentary party experts in parliamentary party decision-making. The truth is that the majority of the Czech and Slovak parliamentary parties do not have a system of specialized internal party committees concentrating on specific subject areas. Yet, additional personal interviews indicated that specialization in a given policy area is usually carried out by one parliamentarian (or, in larger parliamentary parties, by a small group of MPs) responsible for a particular bill, who is spokesman of the parliamentary party on this bill, and who defends it in the committees. This MP, or a group of MPs, are then in a strong position to formulate party policy, being a functional equivalent to an intra-party committee, especially in small parties.[7] Consequently, recognized specialists in a particular policy field do advise their parliamentary parties and their advice is often followed by the rest of their colleagues in parliamentary party meetings. It is therefore the parliamentary party meeting where the main decision-making power lies, but the meetings frequently do no more than conform to the position established by a relatively narrow group of specialists. This might explain the puzzlingly low level of importance attributed to the role of parliamentary party experts in our survey.[8]

On balance, however, the relatively high influence of specialists - whether from committees, government, or parties' research departments - on parliamentary parties related primarily to relatively non-controversial and/or technical and highly specialized policy proposals. As we also saw in chapter 4, it related to certain policy attributes too, in that economic issues were dominated by the expertise of the governments (ministers as specialists), whereas issues related, for example, to the reform of state administration and constitutional matters seemed to induce remarkable activity among specialized individual MPs. In any case, as soon as a proposal generated strong disagreement between specialists and the rest of the parliamentary party - and this admittedly occurred on a number of issues dealt with in both countries - the position of parliamentary parties was established by majority voting. At least on important and highly politicized matters, MPs were and are supposed to conform to the collectively established party line. Particularly in the case of Czech coalition parliamentary parties, it became normal practice to have a co-ordinator on the floor who led the voting on a specific bill. The parliamentary party leadership was expected to ensure that there were enough MPs to secure a majority, assuming the role of whip - which was, at least apparently, less evident during the decision-making process inside the parliamentary parties. This has also become the custom in Slovakia, but in a detectable form only from March 1994, when Moravčík's broadly based cabinet took over after the successful vote of no-confidence in the Mečiar's led HZDS-SNS administration. Since then, especially larger parliamentary parties like HZDS, KDH and SDL have established procedures for overseeing their deputies, monitoring their performance in parliament on issues including party-line voting, general participation, work on committees, and activity on the floor (Malová and Krause, 1996).

What remains very difficult in our two countries, and obviously many other countries too, is to roll out a system of party sanctions (disciplinary measures) for individual MPs who deviate from the established party line or do not adjust to the organizational principles of the parliamentary party. Parliamentary party meetings of the Czech and Slovak parties are not public and, moreover, most of the parliamentary parties do not have formally written rules of proceedings which specify the conduct of their business.[9] Some forms of party sanctions are known from ODS in the Czech Republic and HZDS in Slovakia. The ODS parliamentary party statute stipulates, for example, that should an MP defect from a parliamentary party line, the leadership must be informed. It also assumes that on the major issues (so called three-line whip), a MP must follow the line of the parliamentary party, and should this not be the case, the regional party organization, which formally holds power over nominations, will be informed. In the case of HZDS, each of the nominated candidates before the 1994 elections were allegedly required to pledge compensation of five million Slovak crowns (about $160,000) to the party should they leave the parliamentary party while remaining in parliament.[10]

To be sure, such measures would have to be deemed unconstitutional in the current Czech and Slovak Republics, since both constitutions stipulate that MPs exercise their mandate personally, according to their conscience and convictions, and are not bound by any orders. This explains why any formal forms of disciplining measures, if existing at all, are kept strictly inside parties. However, since 1989, in the light of parliamentary party fragmentation, voices could be heard in both countries advocating the introduction of at least by-elections for those MPs changing parliamentary party affiliation during the parliamentary term. And, on numerous occasions, HZDS did not hesitate to test the constitutionally granted independence of the deputies' mandate, particularly in the now (in)famous Gauladier case.[11] The Czech and Slovak MPs themselves exhibited a remarkable division of opinion on the statement "an individual MP who decides to leave the party for which he was elected should give up his parliamentary seat". In the Czech Republic, 35 percent of MPs agreed or agreed completely with the statement. The percentage in Slovakia was even higher: 47 percent of MPs. In the Czech Republic, 51 percent of MPs disagreed or disagreed completely, in Slovakia it was 41 percent of MPs. These answers testify to the central problem which is felt in both countries with regard to the collective behavior of parliamentary parties. The focus of party elites' attention is on the performance of individual MPs within their parliamentary parties, i.e. whether an MP is loyal to the party line or deviates from it, but even more so on the threats of fragmentation, i.e. whether an MP stays with the party at all or forms a new (parliamentary) party.

In any event, it is clear that while parliamentary parties may seek to influence the opinions of individual representatives, both deputies' freedom of choice, as stipulated in the Czech and Slovak constitutions, and their normative commitments, can limit the parties' possibilities on this front. The fact that only 11 percent of the Czech, and 17 percent of the Slovak MPs were of the opinion that an MP should vote in accordance with the parliamentary party if his/her view is different indicates the limits of parties to demand full obedience in countries where unconditional party loyalty bears obvious negative connotations from the past.[12] As many as 50 percent of the Czech MPs, and 35 percent of the Slovak MPs considered voting according to one's own opinion the norm.

We can see from Table 6.5 that in none of the Czech parliamentary parties, except for the Republicans (SPR-RSČ), were MPs particularly in favour of following parliamentary party opinion. This said, the Czech coalition MPs seem to be less categorical in preferring their own opinion (59 percent stated that it would depend) than the opposition MPs, which fits well with the general tendency of coalition parliamentary parties to be more cohesive than their opposition counterparts. Hypothetically, the stance of individual deputies could vary with the issue on the agenda. Table 6.5 also summarizes answers by parliamentary party of those 65 Czech MPs who, in answer to the question on how an MP should vote in case of differing views, said "it depends", and who were, therefore, asked three follow-up questions.[13] As could be expected, the number of Czech parliamentarians agreeing to subordinate their view to that of the parliamentary party would increase with voting on economic and important constitutional issues. On the contrary, moral issues would probably be decided on an individual basis. We can also see that differences between coalition MPs and opposition MPs were not particularly big, and neither were the differences between MPs from different parliamentary parties.

The answers of Slovak MPs are summarized in Table 6.6. We can see that when Slovak MPs were asked three follow-up questions (45 MPs), similarly to the Czech MPs, in most parties the number of parliamentarians agreeing to subordinate their view to that of the parliamentary party would increase with voting on economic and constitutional issues. We can also see that MPs of the coalition parliamentary parties, HZDS and SNS, as with their Czech counterparts, gave more answers in the two categories 'it would depend' or 'parliamentary party' opinion, which contrasted with the answers

Table 6.5: How should an MP vote in case of a difference of opinion with his parliamentary party? (Czech Republic)

	All parties	Coalition parties	ODS	KDU-ČSL	ODA	KDS	Opposition parties	LB	ČSSD	LSU	SPR-RSČ	Others
In general												
Opinion of PP	10.7	4.8	5.8	-	9.1	-	16.5	2.9	7.1	11.1	75.0	26.3
Own opinion	50.0	36.1	25.0	33.3	63.6	75.0	63.5	82.9	57.1	77.8	-	52.6
It depends	39.3	59.0	69.2	66.7	27.3	25.0	20.0	14.3	35.7	11.1	25.0	21.1
(N)	(168)	(83)	(52)	(12)	(11)	(8)	(85)	(35)	(14)	(9)	(8)	(19)
Economic issues												
Opinion of PP	53.8	52.1	51.4	75.0	-	50.0	58.8	60.0	60.0	100.0	-	75.0
Own opinion	9.2	10.4	5.7	25.0	33.3	-	5.9	-	20.0	-	-	-
It depends	36.9	37.5	42.9		66.7	50.0	35.3	40.0	20.0	-	100.0	25.0
(N)	(65)	(48)	(35)	(8)	(3)	(2)	(17)	(5)	(5)	(1)	(2)	(4)
Constitutional issues												
opinion of pp	55.4	53.1	55.6	50.0	-	100.0	62.5	100.0	40.0	100.0	50.0	25.0
own opinion	16.9	18.4	16.7	37.5	-	-	12.5	-	20.0	-	-	25.0
it depends	27.7	28.6	27.8	12.5	100.0	-	25.0	-	40.0	-	50.0	50.0
(N)	(65)	(49)	(36)	(8)	(3)	(2)	(16)	(5)	(5)	(1)	(2)	(4)
Moral issues												
Opinion of PP	-	-	-	-	-	-	-		-	-	-	-
Own opinion	83.1	81.3	80.0	100.0	33.3	100.0	88.2	100.0	80.0	100.0	50.0	100.0
It depends	16.9	18.8	20.0	-	66.7	-	11.8	-	20.0	-	50.0	-
(N)	(65)	(48)	(35)	(8)	(3)	(2)	(17)	(5)	(5)	(1)	(2)	(4)

Table 6.6: How should an MP vote in case of a difference of opinion with his parliamentary party? (Slovak Republic)

	All parties	Coalition parties	HZDS	SNS	Opposition parties	SDL	KDH	Hungarian Parties	Others
In general									
Opinion of PP	16.5	30.2	32.4	16.7	5.6	-	6.7	22.2	30.0
Own opinion	34.0	14.0	8.1	50.0	50.0	60.0	46.7	55.2	50.0
It depends	49.5	55.8	59.5	33.3	44.5	40.0	46.7	22.2	20.0
(N)	(97)	(43)	(37)	(6)	(54)	(20)	(15)	(9)	(10)
Economic issues									
Opinion of PP	62.2	47.8	47.6	50.0	77.3	62.5	71.4	100.0	100.0
Own opinion	4.4	8.7	9.5		-			-	-
It depends	33.3	43.5	42.9	50.0	22.7	37.5	28.6	-	-
(N)	(45)	(23)	(21)	(2)	(22)	(8)	(7)	(9)	(5)
Constitutional issues									
Opinion of PP	62.2	65.2	66.7	57.1	59.1	62.5	57.1	100.0	40.0
Own opinion	20.0	13.0	14.3	28.6	27.3	25.0	28.6	-	40.0
It depends	17.8	21.7	19.0	14.3	13.6	12.5	14.3	-	20.0
(N)	(45)	(23)	(21)	(2)	(22)	(8)	(7)	(2)	(5)
Moral issues									
Opinion of PP	4.4	-			9.1		14.3	-	20.0
Own opinion	91.1	95.7	95.2	100.0	86.4	100.0	71.4	100.0	80.0
It depends	4.4	4.3	4.8		4.5		14.3	-	-
(N)	(45)	(23)	(21)	(2)	(22)	(8)	(7)	(2)	(5)

of MPs from opposition parliamentary parties. However, at least for Slovakia, this sounds somewhat contradictory, since it was precisely HZDS and SNS parliamentary parties whose fragmentation and lack of cohesion led to the fall of the government in March 1994. It was the opposition parties which appeared non-fragmented and largely cohesive, a quality which helped their governance between March and September 1994. One simply has to bear in mind here - and we shall see this again below - that the HZDS and SNS MPs interviewed were those who remained in their parliamentary parties after purges and defections: thus they were MPs who already proved their loyalty to their respective (parliamentary) parties.

In any event, the findings on deputies' normative commitments, and the differences between the two countries, bring us to an important point. In general, the experience of the Czech and Slovak parties suggests that when either the parliamentary party leaders or the executive leadership (see below) demanded too much party discipline, it usually led to the opposite of the desired effect - less cohesion on the floor and, even more often, parliamentary party fragmentation. This is especially apparent if the disputes involved larger groups of MPs, rather than more vulnerable and isolated individuals. Both the extreme-right wing SPR-RSČ in the Czech Republic and HZDS in Slovakia are a case in point here, as the parliamentary party splits (both in 1993) resulted from an attempt to instil party cohesion in the situation where a larger group of MPs were at odds with the leadership and the rest of the parliamentary party. After the purges and splits, the MPs who did not leave their respective parliamentary parties were much more willing to accept the standpoints of either the leadership or the parliamentary party, which, as we saw in Tables 6.5 and 6.6, seem also to be reflected in their normative commitments. Only the Republican MPs in the Czech Republic were, overall, of the opinion that the standpoint of the parliamentary party should be superior to an MP's own opinion, should there be a difference, and basically only in HZDS was the proportion of those likely to adhere to parliamentary party point of view so high in Slovakia.

On the other hand, parties like ODS gradually developed a more subtle intra-party mechanism of parliamentary party management which made the parliamentary party very cohesive, without any apparent signs of discontent, and without any apparent signs of disciplining measures. The same could be said about the other Czech coalition party KDU-ČSL, or KDH, SDL and the Hungarian minority parties, all opposition parties in Slovakia. What comes into force here is not only collective decision-making within these parties, but also, or above all, a sort of internal security they gain from passing a certain threshold of party organizational and ideological development. Although it would be perhaps too early to consider all these parties as having a firmly established identity, it seems that on both ideological and organizational grounds, they have all acquired a discernable face which embraces individual members and links them together into a congruent whole. Party discipline seemed often to be of secondary importance, since there was a general consensus among the (parliamentary) party members on where the party stands, and where it should go.[14]

Clearly, this is not to say that no disciplining measures are exercised in more stable parliamentary parties. At least on the level of day-to-day parliamentary party management, it appears clear that the measures of discipline (compulsory participation in voting and parliamentary party meetings) have been gradually developed and applied.[15] But they have been implemented along with a decline in reasons for splitting and defecting. This, of course, relates to the previous high parliamentary party fragmentation and internal party conflicts, which, finally, sorted out many of the unlikely party partnerships constructed in the Czech and Slovak Republics before the 1992 elections. In a comparative perspective, the natural process of sorting out was by and large completed for the Czech coalition parties before the 1992 elections, whereas HZDS and SNS in Slovakia had to undergo this process while holding power in the first Slovak post-divorce government. However, the Czech opposition parliamentary parties, some of them largely heterogenous in composition, continued their internal fighting through the whole of the 1992-1996 legislative term. With the exception of ČSSD, they all disintegrated, whereas the Slovak opposition parties, strong in their initial base, did not face any significant changes from 1992 to 1996.

In the final account of parliamentary party cohesion, it is very important to note that the Czech and Slovak parliamentary parties, and particularly the coalition ones, also significantly benefited from their position in power, increasing the potential for their members' career advancement and, in turn, providing benefits to be used as a reward for party loyalty. In fact, such rewards, which Damgaard (1995) in his analysis of Western European parliamentary parties calls positive sanctions, may have been even more important in controlling the behavior of individual Czech and Slovak MPs than punishments (negative sanctions). In other words, it was not punishment for deviant behavior, bur rather rewards for a good behavior that produced the MPs' compliance with their parliamentary parties. Two elements are important in this respect.

First, as was documented in the previous chapter in connection with ministerial recruitment, parliamentary parties in the Czech and Slovak Republics are one of the means by which an aspiring politician can enter the government. It has become expected that the path to the cabinet leads through parliament. Therefore, those who wish to obtain a cabinet appointment, or those who hold it and are entitled to vote in the parliament (Czech Republic), can be expected to vote with the parliamentary party and, more so, to actively form and consistently support the party and government position. Inside ODS, for example, there is an established career path mechanism, whereby an aspiring MP first becomes chairman of a parliamentary committee and is eventually promoted to a ministerial post in the corresponding policy field. Similarly in Slovakia between 1992 and 1994, Malová and Siváková (1996) report on two deputies who were promoted to ministerial and deputy ministerial posts after showing activity in their field of specialization within their parliamentary parties and parliamentary committees.

Second, the parliamentary parties are also one of the means to get appointments to high civil service positions. As it turns out, the civil service positions in both the Czech and Slovak Republics are, on both national and local levels, strongly linked to party and government patronage. Parliamentary party members are among the recruitment reservoirs, particularly those with a good record of expertise in certain areas. During 1992-1996 period in the Czech Republic, one KDS deputy worked for the Foreign Office, one ODS deputy served as a permanent delegate to the institutions of the European Union, another gained a high position in the diplomatic service, to name but a few examples.

However, it has been in the aftermath of the early 1994 elections in Slovakia, under the new Mečiar administration, that the resources of government participation appeared to become a chief asset in rewarding and promoting party loyalty. Although both HZDS and SNS turned out in 1994 to be somewhat more congruent in composition after the dramatic fragmentation of their previous parliamentary delegations, the arguably high cohesion achieved by their parliamentary parties, and that of the third coalition partner (ZRS), can in large part be attributed to the use of resources available from their complete takeover of power in the country. All sorts of important posts in the country's administration, from ministries to the local councils, were distributed on an unprecedented scale according to the loyalty that likely candidates showed to governing parties (see Leško, 1996; Mikloš, 1997; Mesežnikov, 1997). The MPs themselves were no exception in benefiting from the patronage and clientelistic networks such a move has brought. It has enhanced parliamentary party stability further than one could expect from parties, namely HZDS and ZRS, which still remain amalgams uniting a wide array of diverse interests.

Surely, if we take into account what has been stated about fragmentation (especially if we consider that it was the government parties in Slovakia which disintegrated between 1992 and 1994 while having the resources of the entire government their disposal), it appears clear that homogeneity, or what we have called here party identity, stands out as a crucial variable behind parliamentary party cohesion or a lack of it. In a country where MPs do not strongly identify with their party, and can relatively easily shift allegiances from one parliamentary party to another, both government patronage as well as party discipline tend to be of limited effectiveness as a means of achieving high party cohesion. Party and government patronage, as well as advancement in the parliamentary party hierarchy can facilitate the rise of a sense of common interest, or uphold an already existing base, but it cannot fully substitute for an underlying sense of belonging to a particular party organization. The same applies to the measures of discipline, especially in the form of negative sanctions.

All this suggests that a relatively high level of cohesion (and decreasing fragmentation) which can be observed among the Czech and Slovak parliamentary parties is a function of a broader process of party development, which links individual MPs and parties into a congruent whole. It also implies that parliamentary parties are becoming complex organizations, rather than just 'clubs of convenience' they were at the beginning of democratization processes. They appear to be in a position to monitor and sanction the behavior of their own members and, perhaps, even themselves become subjected to pressures from their own extra-parliamentary party organization. And this is the subject we wish to address in the next section: to what extent is the cohesion of the Czech and Slovak parliamentary parties influenced by their relationhip with the external party organizations? Are parliamentary parties themselves becoming embedded in a wider party structure? Have party executives outside parliament been able to influence behavior of their own parliamentary delegations?

Parliamentary Parties and Extraparliamentary Party Organizations

On the surface, the relationships between parliamentary parties and extra-parliamentary organizations or, as we shall analyze it here, between parliamentary

Table 6.7: Who should have the final say in case of conflicts between parliamentary party and party executive?

Czech Republic	All parties	Coalition parties	ODS	KDU-ČSL	ODA	KDS	Opposition parties	LB	ČSSD	LSU	SPR-RSČ	Others
Parliamentary party	33.3	25.3	26.9	25.0	27.3	12.5	41.2	62.9	42.9	22.2	25.0	15.8
National executive	22.6	25.3	21.2	41.7	27.3	25.0	20.0	17.1	35.7	11.1	12.5	21.1
It depends	34.5	41.0	42.3	25.0	36.4	62.5	28.2	17.1	21.4	55.6	12.5	47.4
DK/NA	9.5	8.4	9.6	8.3	9.1		10.6	2.9		11.1	50.0	15.8
(N)	(168)	(83)	(52)	(12)	(11)	(8)	(85)	(35)	(14)	(9)	(8)	(19)

Slovak Republic	All parties	Coalition parties	HZDS	SNS	Opposition parties	SDL	KDH	Hungar. parties	Others
Parliamentary party	34.0	27.9	27.0	33.3	38.9	50.0	33.3	44.4	20.0
National executive	15.5	14.0	16.2		16.7	5.0	40.0	22.2	-
It depends	39.2	46.5	45.9	50.0	33.3	40.0	20.0	11.1	60.0
DK/NA	11.3	11.6	10.8	16.7	3.8	5.0	6.7	22.2	20.0
(N)	(97)	(43)	(37)	(6)	(54)	(20)	(15)	(9)	(10)

Table 6.8: Frequency of party national executive instructions to parliamentary parties

Czech Republic	All parties	Coalition parties	ODS	KDU-ČSL	ODA	KDS	Opposition parties	LB	ČSSD	LSU	SPR-RSČ	Others
Often	17.3	18.1	21.2	3.3	-	37.5	16.5	8.6	35.7	11.1	12.5	21.1
Sometimes	57.1	53.0	61.5	33.3	36.4	50.0	61.2	74.3	57.1	55.6	75.0	36.8
Never	20.2	24.1	13.5	50.0	54.5	12.5	16.5	17.1	-	33.3	-	26.3
DK/NA	5.4	4.8	3.8	8.3	9.1	-	5.9	-	7.1	-	12.5	15.8
(N)	(168)	(83)	(52)	(12)	(11)	(8)	(85)	(35)	(14)	(9)	(8)	(19)

Slovak Republic	All parties	Coalition parties	HZDS	SNS	Opposition parties	SDL	KDH	Hungar. parties	Others
Often	17.5	30.2	27.0	50.0	7.4	-	13.3	11.1	10.0
Sometimes	59.8	59.2	56.8	16.7	66.7	75.0	66.7	77.8	40.0
Never	13.4	4.7	2.7	16.7	20.4	25.0	20.0	11.1	20.0
DK/NA	9.3	13.9	13.5	16.7	5.7	-	-	-	30.0
(N)	(97)	(43)	(37)	(6)	(54)	(20)	(15)	(9)	(10)

parties and party executives[16] in the contemporary Czech and Slovak Republics should not be expected to be very complex. Because parties originated at the parliamentary level and lacked personnel to fill emerging party and parliamentary positions, party executives were composed of, and were dominated by, parties' parliamentary delegations. Parliamentary parties and party executives were, in terms of personnel, virtually identical with the other. Furthermore, considering that the Czech and Slovak party executives usually include representatives of party on the ground (membership organization),[17] and that this party on the ground has hitherto been weak (see chapter 3), the situation we might expect is the primacy of parliamentary parties over the rest of the party organizations, rather than any sort of complex relationship.

Indeed, studying the functioning of the Czech and Slovak political parties after 1992, there would seem to be little counter-evidence to this picture. First of all, the ongoing enormous overlap of personnel between party executives and parliamentary parties was typical for virtually all of them. In the survey, 36 percent of the Czech and 39 percent of the Slovak MPs stated they had some function in the party's national executive.[18] Thus, many members of the national executives were seated in the parliament. This was the case for ODS, KDS, ČSSD, LB, ČMUS, and ODA in the Czech parliament, for SDL and DU in the 1992-1994 Slovak parliament, and has been the case in all Slovak opposition parties since 1994. In some extreme cases (mostly small parties and newly established ones emerging from the process of fragmentation of the existing parties on the parliamentary level, i.e. DU in Slovakia), the extent of overlap between the party in parliament and the party executive was so extensive as to render the question of their mutual relation virtually meaningless. One party unit could not be disentangled from the other.

In addition to this, the primacy of parliamentary parties is nicely illustrated by the answers of the Czech and Slovak MPs to the normative question "If your parliamentary party and the party's national executive differ in opinion, who, in your view, should have the final say?". We can see from Table 6.7 that the MPs in both countries were conscious of their position vis-a-vis the national executive: only 23 percent of the Czech, and 15 percent of the Slovak MPs thought that the national executive should have the final say in the case of difference with the parliamentary party opinion. On the other hand, 33 percent of the Czech and 34 percent of the Slovak deputies stated that the parliamentary party should have the final say, and 34 percent and 39 percent respectively answered that it depends. The cross-tabulation by party showed that in virtually all the Czech and Slovak parliamentary parties, a cumulative majority of MPs opined either that the final say should rest with the parliamentary party or that it would depend.

Nevertheless, there is also some puzzling evidence which goes against this picture of overwhelming primacy of parliamentary parties. It is confusing, for example, that a significant number of MPs gave the final say to the party executive in normative terms. If the parliamentary party *is* the party executive, as the hypothesis and the empirical evidence on the personnel overlap suggests, members of parliamentary parties may simply not have been concerned whether the party executive or parliamentary party should have the final say. However, empirical reality may be more complex than the hypothesized picture outlined above. For only a third of MPs in both countries had a function in their party executive in the first place. As stated, in small parties, or newly established parliamentary parties, there was undoubtedly such a large overlap that a simple explanation would easily hold. Yet, in bigger parties, the majority of MPs did not have any function in the executive, but yet many of them answered the normative question in favour of the party executive or stated that it depends.

Another puzzle emerges in the answers of Czech and Slovak MPs to the empirical question "How often does it happen that your party's national executive tries to instruct your parliamentary party?". The data assembled in Table 6.8 suggest that, in the Czech and Slovak parliaments, national party executives played *some* role vis-à-vis their parliamentary parties. The words 'to instruct', given in the survey question, in reality cover a range of actions, from soft reminders of the general party policy to commands on how parliamentary parties should vote. These data give us an indication on the perceived importance of party executives, on the differences between individual parties, and on differences between the two countries. Can we still talk about the strong primacy of parliamentary parties over party executives or, in the same vein, about the futility of disentangling parliamentary parties from party executives?

We contend the answer is 'no'. If we consider the influence of party executives on parliamentary parties in the broadest sense, in all bigger and longer established Czech and Slovak parties (ODS, ČSSD, KDU-ČSL in the Czech Republic, HZDS, SDL, KDH in Slovakia), they do matter in relation to the parliamentary parties in two important respects: determination of general party policies and, partly, the nomination of candidates. With regard to policies, the importance of party executives was largely confirmed by the answers of the Czech and Slovak MPs, of which 79 percent and 76 percent respectively stated that the party's national executive, as opposed to the parliamentary party, has the most say in party policy.[19] The general party policies are embodied in party programs and manifestos, which seem to be increasingly, though not exclusively, drafted outside of the parliamentary party domain. This is the first, and arguably very important limit on the primacy of parliamentary parties over their respective parties in central office. For example, before the 1996 elections in the Czech Republic, only in the newly emerged (and now defunct) Party of the Left Bloc was each expert MP supposed to contribute a part to the whole party electoral program. The rest of the parties, while involving some MPs, endowed various expert bodies outside of the parliament (answerable to national executives) with most of the work. The situation in most Slovak parties before the 1994 early elections was similar, although the process of drafting party programs was harder to analyze there due to the short time frame within which drafting took place.

The patterns of the drafting process closely relate to another important aspect of the relationship between parliamentary parties and party executives: the fact that the latter are not only an executive leadership (i.e. an executive committee), but also a bureaucratic machinery, including party administration and various expert teams in special party departments. With the growth of, and structural differentiation inside, Czech and Slovak parties, the central offices underwent a clear-cut process of change. The central office of the parties now provide a source of expertise, information and policy research needed for the parliamentary parties to conduct their work. In the early formative period, particularly in the former Federal Assembly, parties relied predominantly on the expertise of their own parliamentarians, who employed limited resources offered by the staff of the parliament. This has changed with the expansion of the central office staff, which has itself been stimulated by the increase in state subsidies and, crucially, the way the money is distributed. Although parliamentary parties receive a sum of money from the budget of the parliament, the party in central office is the principal supervisor, and principal receiver, of the bulk of state subsidies for political parties in the Czech and Slovak Republics. The subsidy to the parliamentary parties in both countries is disproportionally lower than the state subsidy to the central office, which is distributed according to the number of votes obtained in the parliamentary elections.[20]

As a result, in most Czech and Slovak parties, particularly the larger, more stable ones, the central office has been allowed to grow from small number of clerical staff into a professionalized bureaucratic machine (for more details see van Biezen, 2000). While MPs themselves sometimes work in the analytical departments of the central office, the parliamentary parties as a whole increasingly depend on the professionalized extra-parliamentary party apparatus, which is headed by the national executives.[21] Given that Czech MPs now also control enough resources to employ their own staff, and given that those who control extra-parliamentary party organs are sometimes members of parliamentary parties, any resulting imbalance of power can obviously be countered. However, the parliamentary parties also depend on the existence of the parties on the ground, at least for their claim to be a legitimate party representation, and parliamentary parties also depend on the fund-raising for the whole party. Their partial dependence on the party in central office can thus be firmly established. For the Czech and Slovak parties in central office increasingly perform precisely such activities like organizing, co-ordinating, and communicating with the party on the ground, organizing often expensive electoral campaigns, as well as organizing and supervising money donations.

With regard to the nomination of candidates, it is clear that, inasmuch as parliamentary parties can be treated separately from party executives, it is the latter who have the larger say as to the lists of candidates. Despite the existence of preferential votes in the Czech and Slovak electoral systems, the lists effectively determine the composition of parliamentary parties. This is the second limit on the primacy of parliamentary parties over the party in central office. We should remind ourselves here of the formal centralization of candidate selection in many of the Czech and Slovak parties analyzed in chapter 3. In practice, nominations in 1996 (and also 1998) in the Czech Republic showed that party executives employed their power to influence the composition of parliamentary parties in two fundamentally different ways. On one hand, there were cases where party executives challenged the list proposed by local and regional branches in order to place a new candidate or to promote onto the list the ones who did not obtain sufficient support on the ground. Such reshuffles and additions to the lists occurred in KDU-ČSL and ČSSD. On the other hand, the ODS Executive Council did not challenge any of the proposals of the party on the ground, in spite of the fact that some prominent MPs were turned down in the regions and, being disappointed, asked the national executive to promote them. The Executive Council refused to intervene, thus in a sense determining the composition of the parliamentary party in deciding to leave it up to the party membership. The important point is, therefore, that in both ways, the parliamentary party as such had little influence over nominations, which were either determined by the party on the ground alone, or the party on the ground in combination with the party executives.

The practice of nominations in the 1994 elections in Slovakia, however, appears to be somewhat different from that of the Czech Republic. Malová and Krause (1996) argue that the link between parliamentary parties and party executives has been so strong in Slovakia that the executive veto power over the local and regional nominations only acts to reinforce the domination of parliamentary parties. And since the party leaders, without exception, won the nominations to party lists from local and regional organizations, the power to challenge lists did not have to be exercised at all. In essence, therefore, their argument leads us, at least with regard to Slovakia, back to the general hypothesis from which we started this section: since parliamentary parties and party executives are the same thing, the party in public office (ministers and MPs) predominates over the rest of the party organization. Thus, at least with regard to nominations of candidates, we find a substantial difference between the two countries. How can this be explained?

We have a purely idiosyncratic explanation which takes into account the fact that between 1992 and 1996 party leaders (chairmen and vice-chairmen) of Czech parties occupied positions only in the party executive. This was due to the fact that, unlike the top Slovak party leaders, who were nominated in 1992 to the Slovak National Council, the Czech party leaders were at those same elections nominated to the Czechoslovak Federal Parliament. With the demise of the common state and therefore of their deputy mandate in the Federal Assembly, most of them concentrated solely on activities in the central office or, in the case of coalition parties, found a position in the new Czech government. The result was that in the Czech opposition parties like ČSSD, SPR-RSČ, and LB, there was a more or less constant tension between the parliamentary parties and the party executives, since the leaders tried to make their voices heard in parliamentary party matters. If we look again at Table 6.8, it was precisely in these Czech (opposition) parties where MPs indicated most frequently that their parliamentary parties are often instructed by party executives.

Party executives often tried to discipline parliamentary parties by binding them to a voting position on issues. These attempts produced conflicts which were unknown to the Slovak opposition parties (KDH, SDL, Hungarian parties), whose leaders were seated in the parliament (even though they were nominally not chairing parliamentary parties). Between 1992 and 1996, the Czech Social Democrats almost split over the question of parliamentary party management when the party leader (who did not have a seat in parliament) - repeatedly issued directives from party headquarters and was rebuffed by his own parliamentarians, many of whom were highly critical of his confrontational style. Also noticeable was the split of LB in 1993, which assumed the form of a conflict between a parliamentary party more accommodating of the political game being played with other parties, and the rigid party executive, which tried to radicalize their own parliamentary delegation. As a result, the parliamentary party LB split into LB, representing the rebellious MPs, and KSČM, epitomized by the MPs more linked and obedient to the party executive outside of the parliament. Reflecting on the conflict, the leader of the LB parliamentary party noted that "the wires of voting machines could sometimes be extended to the party headquarters".[22]

To be sure, the above does not mean that the Czech coalition parliamentary parties were spared of the influence of, and even conflicts with, the party executives. On the contrary, the fact that the party leaders came back from the Federal Assembly to find a place in the Czech government only reinforced the habitual practice in which coalition parties tended to use the national executive as a tool for influencing the parliamentary parties. The party executive served as a coordinating body between the party in government, the top party leadership (being normally party in government) and the parliamentary party, occasionally issuing recommendations to the parliamentary party on both voting position and legislative initiatives.[23] This was more true for ODS and KDS than for the rest of the coalition parliamentary parties (ODA and KDU-ČSL), which can be explained by the different degree of personnel overlap between the two party units (a larger separation in ODS and KDS) and, partly, by the size of parliamentary parties (ODS was numerically far bigger than the rest).

To conclude our inventory, the picture which emerges can be summarized in three points. First, despite the generally large personnel overlap between Czech and Slovak parliamentary parties and party executives, which evokes a picture of permanent contact between, if not an inseparability of, the two units, our evidence suggests that there are spheres where they can be conceived of as working autonomously. With regard to the formation of broad party policies and, partly, with regard to the nomination of candidates, it seems that party executives are becoming an important power player of their respective party organization, particularly in the bigger and longer established Czech and Slovak political parties. The issue at stake here, well worthy of further research, is the often neglected bureaucratic face of the party in central office which, by becoming more and more professionalized in most Czech and Slovak parties, offers indispensable resources outweighing the ones so far available to parliamentary parties.

Secondly, on the level of top party leadership, the Slovak parties appeared in general more overlapping with respect to composition of parliamentary party and party executives than most of their Czech counterparts between 1992 and 1996. With the exception of HZDS, this diversity fostered a relatively accommodative relationship between the two faces of party organizations in Slovakia. In the Czech Republic, where the top party leadership was, in many parties, separated from parliamentary parties, conflicts over who has the most say and who should follow whom surfaced repeatedly between 1992 and 1996. However, this may have been a temporary phenomenon, caused by the conjuncture in candidate nomination strategies in 1992 elections. Given that prior to the 1996 (and also 1998) elections in the Czech Republic the majority of party leaders were placed on the lists of candidates, we may very well witness their return to the parliament and, in turn, a return to the accommodating character of the relationship between parliamentary parties and party executives.

Third, the evidence presented on the Czech and Slovak parties again shows that the intra-party conflicts, in this case between parliamentary parties and party executives, are indeed difficult to contain by measures of discipline. The cases in point are Czech opposition parties between 1992-1996, where attempts to discipline parliamentary parties from national headquarters ended up in quite sharp conflicts, and even in party fragmentation. Clearly, the cause of these particular clashes was again a deeper lack of coherent party collectivity as such, which made accommodation difficult, if not, as in the case of LB, impossible. Yet, it must be emphasized that even where there were binding instructions and resolutions from party executives (councils) to parliamentary parties, this by no means turned out to be a one-way street. Rather, the occasional guidelines from party executives, usually representing the viewpoints of ministers, implied a search for a wider consensus within parliamentary parties, which retained the power of interpreting party policies and molding them into legislation.

Conclusions

We saw earlier in this study, particularly in chapter 3, that the internal organization of parliaments, the behavior of MPs in parliamentary committess, the distribution of committee chairs and positions, as well as the make-up of other parliamentary bodies such as Steering Committees, became subservient to party politics in both countries. The evidence from this chapter substantiates these findings on the direction of parliamentary institutionalization. In the web of complex relationships between individual MPs and their respective party organizations, the position of the Czech and Slovak parliamentary parties is clearly pivotal. Parliamentary parties in both countries basically act cohesively on the floor, perhaps to an extent that would not differentiate them from their counterparts in many Western European parliamentary democracies. In addition, the fragmentation which used to threaten the very existence of parliamentary parties has been decreasing in both parliaments. Parliamentary parties are, indeed, the most important organizational unit in the internal life of the Czech and Slovak parliaments.

This situation can partly be accounted for by the adoption of several new institutional rules, such as higher number of deputies needed to form a parliamentary party, which make it difficult for individual MPs to opearate outside of a party organization. It can also be explained by the measures of party discipline which some Czech and Slovak parties gradually started to apply on their members. The many attempts, particularly in Slovakia, to enhance parliamentary party cohesion through the use of party discipline, such as expulsions or even stripping of parliamentary mandates, took their toll, not least in terms of psychological pressure on individual MPs. However, our analysis also showed that equally important for the internal cohesion of parties has been an increase in the homogeneity of their representatives and the fact that previous party fragmentation helped to sort out many unviable friendships among the Czech and Slovak parliamentary elites.

Moreover, many Czech and Slovak parties have started distributing selective incentives to their members. These incentives, in such forms as rewards in career advancement within the party and state institutional hierarchy, figure far higher in our explanation of cohesion than any form of directives, expulsions of MPs, or attempts to legislate disobedient MPs out of parlimentary processes, however strong these may have been, particularly in Slovakia. Surely, as Saalfeld (1995) points out, in order to employ selective incentives, the party must be able to detect whether individual MPs comply with their obligations and norms or not. This is exactly the point. The Czech and Slovak parliamentary parties, especially those with the internal development directed toward the acquisition of organizational and ideological identity, gradually established monitoring mechanisms. Indeed, there is a clear sign of the growing organizational complexity of parties - the complexity of which provides social pressure to link the preferences of individual MPs to that of the collective within which they operated. Our findings on the changing position of parliamentary parties within parties as a whole can only reinforce the point. While parliamentary parties, often linked in personnel with executive leadership, remain pivotal units within their respective party organizations, shifts of power towards central offices in matters concerning formation of broad party policy, services, expertise and electoral activities can be clearly observed in the larger, longer established Czech and Slovak parties.

Notes

1. As in the previous chapters, the term "parliamentary parties" is used to describe party groups in the parliament (*Fraktionen* in German, *fràcties* in Dutch). In the Czech and Slovak terminology they are normally referred to as either *parlamentní kluby* (parliamentary clubs) or *poslanecké kluby* (clubs of deputies).

2. From eight initial parliamentary parties present after the 1990 general elections, the former Czechoslovak parliament ended up with about twice as many in April 1992.

3. The survey question was: "Would you say there are subgroups or currents within your parliamentary party?", followed by the questions "Do you belong to a particular one?", "Which one?".

4. Noticeable in this respect is the resistance of the Slovak MPs to the introduction of the machines to the parliament. It perhaps draws on the experience of the Czech colleagues, for whom the installation meant a greater monitoring and control from both the public as well as the parliamentary party leadership. Although the Slovak parliamentary parties supervise the behavior of their MPs without the voting machines (see below), it is probably more the public availability of such information which was not particularly appealing. In the Czech Republic, it took a considerable time and a great deal of hesitation before the parliament agreed on making voting records open to the public. It underscores the sensitivity with which political elites in both countries treat the question of party cohesion and discipline, obviously in close relation to the negative connotation such questions bear from the communist period.

5. For alternative measures of cohesion, see studies of Saalfeld (1990) and Lanfranchi and Lüthi (1995), both using the Rice index of cohesion, or the study of Raunio (1996), using the so-called index of agreement. The MPs voting 'I abstain' represent a methodological problem for any measurement of voting cohesion. We calculated abstaining MPs as those voting 'no'. It reflects the way abstentions show in the result of voting in the Czech parliament, as well as the way they are dealt with inside parliamentary parties. The Czech parliamentary rules state that when *announcing* the result of the vote, only the number of MPs who participated in the vote, and total votes cast for or against are publicly declared. Therefore, to abstain is a sort of neutral position, possibly important symbolically. However, from a power politics point of view, if a party decides to support a bill, being present on voting (by inserting one's card into the machine) but voting 'I abstain' basically means voting against the party. In a similar vein, if a party decides not to support a bill and an MP votes 'I abstain', it produces the same final effect as voting 'no'. The reason is that

an MP who votes 'I abstain' is present, and thus increases the number of votes needed to pass a resolution. As it normally occurred in the Czech parliament, coalition parliamentary parties decided to kill a dozen of opposition amendments, but because it would involve so much individual button pushing, coalition MPs often did not do anything but inserted their cards into the machine (thus increasing the quorum to pass the resolution) and played computer games or read newspapers. This explains why on the vast majority of votes (exception are only very rare votes by name), whips do not usually pester MPs to vote 'I abstain' if a party does not support a resolution. The whips only make sure that MPs are present on voting - that is, that they insert their cards to the voting machine.

6. It should be noted, though, the presented evidence fails to take into account the relative importance of issues. Due to the inclusion of virtually all votes (procedural questions, amendments, interpolations, final votes, votes on presidential suspensions) into the final measurement, serious intra-parliamentary party divisions on crucial issues may have been hidden by the flattening effect of a high level of cohesion on a large number of relatively minor questions.

7. This situation relates to the average size of parliamentary parties, which was relatively small compared to the number of specialized parliamentary committees (11 in both parliaments). Looking at Table 6.1, we can easily count that, in June 1992, seven out of nine parliamentary parties in the Czech parliament, and four out of six in the Slovak parliament, would not have more than one member on most intra-party committees.

8. In both countries, the specialists, or policy experts, are of course primarily MPs designated to a particular parliamentary committee. The phrasing of our question on the main decision-making point within the parliamentary parties therefore attempted to explore the influence of those MPs. This notwithstanding, it must be clearly emphasized that matters are complicated by the fact that the policy specialists of Czech and Slovak parliamentary parties are quite often also government ministers (in government parties) and working groups located within parties' central offices. Our survey question here does not provide many clues about this complex state of affairs. The experts' actual influence obviously depends on the position of parliamentary parties in relation to both party in government and party in central office. As we saw in the previous chapter, ministers' influence on parliamentary parties was in general quite high, finding its expression in more or less regular contacts between ministers and individual MPs and ministers and their parliamentary parties. The existence of the party working group (a kind of research center) has its roots in the developing division of labor between different parts of Czech and Slovak party organizations, and as such will be analyzed in the following section.

9. The exceptions were ODS and LB, both numerically by far the largest parties (at least in 1992) in the Czech parliament, and SDL and KDH in the Slovak parliament. The leaders of small parliamentary parties in both countries stated that, so far, a set of informal rules meets their needs.

10. Information from the Constitutional Watch on Slovakia, *East European Constitutional Review*, 4(2), 1995. The post-election rumours have it that similar pledges were required from the deputies of Sládek's Republicans in the Czech Republic (see *Respekt*, 16-19 December 1996). These measures of discipline are particularly interesting, because it

closely resembles the system of party discipline commonly applied in the First Czechoslovak Republic, where the MPs had to sign a letter of commitment to the party secretaries stating they would give up their seat should they leave the party for which they were elected.

11. Political turmoil hit Slovakia when the coalition majority in parliament voted on 4 December 1996 to remove the mandate of one deputy who quit the ruling HZDS accusing the party of failing to keep pre-election promises and of passing unconstitutional legislation. The matter was passed to the Constitutional Court, while the US and EU officials demanded that Slovakia restore Gauladier's mandate. The Constitutional Court concluded in August 1997 that the ruling coalition acted unconstitutionally in withdrawing the mandate and called on parliament to restore it. However, members of the ruling coalition boycotted two parliamentary sessions that were to decide the fate of Gauladier, arguing that judges of the Constitutional Court did not respect the rights of supreme state organs (parliament) to decide on such issues.

12. The question was: "If MP has to vote, but holds an opinion which is different from the one held by his parliamentary party, should he then vote in accordance with the opinion of the parliamentary party or should he follow his own opinion?"

13. The questions were: "How should an MP vote on economic issues? Should he vote in accordance with the opinion of the parliamentary club or should he follow his own opinion?"; "And what if there is a vote on important legislation concerning constitutional issues; should a MP then vote in accordance with the opinion of the parliamentary club or should he follow his own opinion?"; "And how should he vote on moral issues: in accordance with the opinion of the parliamentary club or should he follow his own opinion?".

14. Note that a dramatic split of ODS in January 1998, when about half of the MPs left the party to set up a new formation, was not the result of disciplining measures. Rather, the group of deputies left the party after the fall of their own party-led government, and after they lost both the battle over party's future direction and an unsuccessful attempt to replace Klaus as the party leader.

15. Note, for example, the reaction of the leader of ČSSD Miloš Zeman when three of his party deputies left for vacation, and their absence allowed the passage of undesirable legislation. The leader was quoted in *Právo* (August 10, 1996) saying "If any deputy is unable to bear the responsibility, there is only one honorable solution: to free his post for replacement". Later on, in December 1996, the social democrats' chairmanship decided to expel from the party three (other) MPs, who supported the governing coalition in the vote on the budget. This effectively meant the three 'rebels' also had to leave their parliamentary party. Similarly, the chairmanship of KDH in Slovakia recommended that its parliamentary party expel an MP (who was elected on the party list, but was not a party member) who in January 1995 had supported the HZDS-led coalition in an investiture vote. However, unlike in the case of Gauladier (HZDS), his subsequent expulsion did not mean he was forced out of the parliament.

16. Any analysis of the relationships between parliamentary parties and extra-parliamentary organizations faces the conceptual problem of what is exactly to be understood by the latter. From the beginning, the analysis of political parties in this study followed a distinction between the different faces of party organization: that of the 'party in public office', the 'party in the central office' (party executive), and the 'party on the ground' (Katz and Mair, 1994). This framework was carried a step further by breaking 'party in public office' into two separate units: parliamentary party and party in government. Within this framework we discussed first, in chapter 3, the development of Czech and Slovak parties on the ground - an aspect relevant to our concerns about representation. Interactions between parliamentary parties and party in government (for Czech and Slovak coalition parties) were analyzed in chapter 4. In this section, we shall concentrate on the relations between parliamentary parties and party executives (the party in central office).

17. The names, size and composition of the Czech and Slovak party executives obviously differ. For example, ODS has the Political Gremium, ČSSD has the Chairmanship, both KSČM and KDS have the Executive Committee, HZDS and SDL have the Board of Representatives, DU has the Political Bureau, and KDH has the Chairmanship. Party executives are relatively small bodies, meeting regularly, and formally making all decisions on the everyday business of the party as well as decisions concerning current political issues. They usually comprise the chairman and vice-chairmen of the party, party secretaries, MPs and ministers, and representatives of the constituency or local branches, all elected by the party Congress (for more details on the composition of party executives in both countries see Kroupa and Kostelecký, 1996; van Biezen,2000).

18. The open-ended question was "What is the highest function you have in the party's national executive".

19. The question was: "In your party, who has the most say in party policy, the parliamentary party or the party's national executive?"

20. In the Czech parliament, support for a parliamentary party includes an office in the building, a car, 20,000 CK (about $735) per month, plus an additional 2,500 CK (about $91) a month per member. In Slovakia, that some was even lower. Compare these figures with the amounts received by parties after the elections presented in Table 3.9 in chapter 3.

21. Note, for example, that the statute of SDL in Slovakia stipulates "close cooperation of the parliamentary party and the Council of the Office for Practical Politics". The latter is a party think tank located in the central office.

22. Interview with Jaroslav Ortman, the former chairman of the LB parliamentary party, in *Rudé Právo*, February 14, 1994.

23. This role of party executives as the coordinating body between parliamentary parties and the parties' government in Czech coalition parties could also be observed in Slovakia. In the case of HZDS, particularly between 1992 and 1994, the party executive was used as a means of communication between the parliamentary party and the party in government,

conceivably even more so than in the case of ODS. The explanation for this, as stated already in chapter 4, is that, unlike in the Czech Republic, once a member of parliamentary party in Slovakia becomes a part of party in government, (s)he is no longer a member of the parliamentary party. Ministers have to give up their seat in parliament. Partly as a consequence of such a separation of mandates, the party executive performed a coordinating function, committing the MPs to the party line via the participation of parliamentary party chairman in the executive meetings. Probably because of the relative failure of such politics, and the conflicts which arose from it, this seems to have changed from 1994 onwards. More than before, the ministers of the Mečiar II government developed stronger and more direct relationships with their party colleagues in parliament, participating regularly in parliamentary party meetings.

7 Conclusion: Growing Apart?

Introduction

It seems, at this point in the analysis, that the processes of parlimentary institutionalization produced very different results in the two countries studied in this book. The central problem this study intended to illuminate was a path of parliamentary institutionalization in two new democracies in East Central Europe. Our investigations have provided us with a wealth of material to show that this path has become divergent. It is worth mentioning that our conclusions have been reflected elsewhere as well. On July 16, 1997, the European Commission concluded its survey of Eastern European countries applying for EU membership. While inviting the Czech Republic, alongside Poland, Hungary, Slovenia and Estonia, to start accession negotiations, Slovakia was consigned to a group of other states - such as Bulgaria and Romania - not recommended for the first wave of enlargement. What is even more striking is that, unlike in the case of Bulgaria and Romania, which were excluded primarily on economic grounds, the Commission explicitly stated that Slovakia did not satisfy political criteria laid down by the Copenhagen European Council in 1993. Formally speaking, this means that the country did not achieve "stability of institutions guaranteeing democracy, the rule of law, human rights and respect for and protection of minorities".[1]

Indeed, following a series of demarches and critical letters from various international organizations and foreign governments, including the European Union, the exclusion of Slovakia from its main declared foreign policy goal has so far been the highest visible price the country has paid for its internal political developments. This may come as a surprise for many, given both the relatively short period of time that has elapsed since Czechoslovakia split into two sovereign republics, as well as the many traditions and inheritances commonly shared between the two new democracies. But it also presents analysts with an excellent pairing for comparative analysis of issues pertinent to the debates on democratization and the different outcomes that this multi-faceted and uncertain process of political change often produces. Serving as a conclusion of our study, this chapter will attempt such an exercise. The first section provides a summary of our main findings on the process of institutionalization of parliaments. The next section provides a closer look at the systemic level of emerging Czech and Slovak democracies and will assess the process of democratic consolidation. Using theoretical insights from the democratization literature, the third and final section then focuses on possible explanations of the different trajectories towards parliamentary institutionalization and democratic consolidation these two countries experienced.

Institutionalization of the Czech and Slovak Parliaments

Following Huntington, Sisson and others, the first chapter defined institutionalization of parliaments as the process of creation of formal and informal rules, procedures and regular patterns of behavior that ensures their capacity to reproduce themselves and enables these institutions to accommodate new changes in their external and internal environment in a manner not threatening their entire existence. The institutionalization of parliaments was understood in terms of its external and internal dimensions: the character of interaction between the parliament and its environment, such as constitutional structure, party political format, electoral systems or the structure of the executive; and the internal parliamentary structure, such as the character and operation of parliamentary committees and parliamentary parties. It was argued that both dimensions should be studied simultaneously, so as to capture the implications of the external relationship for the dynamic of parliament's internal development and vice versa.

Furthermore, we distinguished between two analytical dimensions: the direction of parliamentary institutonalization and the degree of parliamentary institutionalization. Central to the former were the questions regarding the type of parliament developing, specific formal and informal mechanisms regulating parliamentary processes, and the overall stage it has all reached. Central to the latter were the questions regarding the formation of cultural attributes, probing into the consensus of political elites on parliamentary and other rules, and elites' conformity with roles and procedural regulations. Throughout the empirical chapters, we explored characteristics of the Czech and Slovak parliaments and various institutions developing within and around them, and we drew our evidence from answers of MPs in both countries to empirical and normative questions about the functioning and desirability of these institutions. What can this evidence tell us?

Direction of institutionalization

If we look at the macro level - that is, at the rooting of the parliaments in the overall institutional structure - the most important characteristic is that the Czech and Slovak parliaments have been developing in the context of the parliamentary system of government over an extended period of time. This tradition of parliamentarism, established during the Czechoslovak pre-war First Republic, and retained, in the formal sense at least, by the communist regime has not changed in neither of the two independent republics since 1993. In fact, there was not even a significant challenge to this dominant constitutional conception, for none of the relevant Czech and Slovak political parties advocated an alternative system of government during the 1992 constitutional negotiations. This may come as a surprise, since the parliamentary system which existed in Czechoslovakia between 1989 and 1992 was seen by many observers and politicians as unacceptable, and was often held accountable for the split of the country into two separate republics. With the benefit of hindsight, it is apparent that what was unacceptable was not the principle of parliamentarism and the parliamentary system of government as such, but rather the accompanying federal arrangement, and the constitutionally rooted complicated power-sharing mechanism between the two constituent republics.

As we argued in great detail in chapter 2, the institutional system alone, which perfectly fits all characteristics of Lijphart's consociational system of institutions, could not be blamed for the split. It was the behavior of political elites and their parties, which were structurally encouraged to compete rather than to compromise, that led to the results of the 1992 elections, the subsequent talks between Klaus and Mečiar and, ultimately, into the peaceful partition of the common state. Nevertheless, the three post-communist years of experience with federal institutions, as well as the rapid pace of events surrounding the whole process of dissolution, had an impact on the shape of the new Czech and Slovak constitutions, and hence on the position of parliaments within the emerging structure of institutions. While the option of a parliamentary system of government was not disputed in principle, in both countries there were attempts to empower the cabinet, at the expense of both presidential as well as parliamentary prerogatives. The fact that the former Federal Government was often obstructed by a fragmented and divided Federal Assembly certainly played a role in this. In a similar vein, the actions of Havel, in attempting several times to strengthen the federal presidency, generated negative feelings towards a strong presidential executive, particularly in the Czech Republic. But it was also the emergence of two winners in the 1992 elections - the Klaus-led ODS in the Czech Republic and Mečiar's HZDS in Slovakia. Both were set to head their respective governments and, therefore, both were keen to strengthen the core executives at the expense of other institutions.

In many respects, the bargaining over the new Czech and Slovak constitutions showed that the momentary distribution of power among political actors (parties) involved in negotiations, as well as their calculations and future expectations, played a more decisive role in shaping the new constitutions than home-grown traditions or foreign models. The exigencies of 'real' politics came to be reflected in the balance of institutional structure. Since neither ODS nor HZDS had absolute majorities to push through their proposals, both parliaments and presidents emerged from constitutional bargaining with certain specified powers, because the then-opposition saw these institutions as a guarantee of their rights and an assurance of governmental (or majority) accountability. Overall, the Czech constitution appears more balanced in distributing powers among the legislative, executive and judiciary branches than does the Slovak constitution. The best way to explain this is in the value attached to constitutions in both countries. The Slovak constitution, drafted and adopted well before the decision to split Czechoslovakia, was produced hurriedly, as a symbol of national sovereignty rather than as a framework for government, with too many loose ends and unclear constitutional provisions. The Czech constitution, drafted in a longer process, and adopted after the decision to split the federation, undoubtedly carried a symbolic value too. Equally, certain controversial provisions, such as the territorial division of the country and the electoral law for the Senate, were left unresolved. Nevertheless, the Czech constitution was drafted primarily to be the 'rules of the game'. It was a bargain struck by (relatively crystallized) parties with clear preferences and conceptions to draw on.

At first sight, the differences in constitution-making process would not appear to have a major impact on the institutionalization of the relationship between the parliaments and, perhaps the most crucial actor of their external environment, the cabinet. Our analysis in chapter 4 showed that relationships between these two institutions have been developing in a broadly similar way in both countries. The similarity here is that in both countries the links between MPs and ministers are organized and structured by political parties, increasingly cohesive and disciplined, which makes parliament - government relations heavily dependent on party politics and the nature of the parliamentary majority. With the help of cohesive parties, Czech and Slovak governments have been able to pass most of their legislation. The main challenges to governments in clearly establishing themselves as the major source of legislation and policy initiatives usually came from within coalition parties, rather than from the opposition. Unlike in the pre-1994 period in Slovakia, when fragmentation undermined the party structure of parliament-government relations, the formation of a minority cabinet in the Czech Republic after the 1996 (and also 1998) elections changed little in the basic principles. For, while the political situation obviously gave more voice and leverage to the opposition, namely the Social Democrats, and also slightly enhanced the position of the previously (between 1992 and 1996) weak institutions like parliamentary committees, the fact is that parties have remained the major players in these relationships and, in the views of MPs (actually in both countries) are also expected to do so.

The internal organization of Czech and Slovak parliaments underlines this direction of institutionalization. Parties gradually consolidated their grip on individual members of parliament and, in this process, dramatically changed the picture of fragmentation, instability and MPs' free-riding behavior associated with Eastern European parliaments. Furthermore, the rules of the game within the parliament (i.e. Standing Orders) came to reflect a dominant conception which puts parties above individual MPs and other institutions within the parliament. The parliamentarians became, partly in institutional and almost fully in behavioral terms, the bearers of the party mandate; they came to be the creators and executors of party policy. The roll-call analysis presented in chapter 6 provided us with evidence of the behavior of deputies during the floor sessions of the Czech parliament, and there are many good reasons and much evidence to expect a comparable set of results in the Slovak parliament, especially after the 1994 elections (see Malová, 1998). Moreover, the behavior of parliamentarians in parliamentary committees, the distribution of committee chairs and positions, as well as the make-up of other parliamentary bodies such as Steering Committees, all reflect the subservience of the parliamentary machinery to party politics in both countries.

The rules that guide the relationships within parliaments, and in particular the changes that have been made to these rules, are another set of evidence of the direction of institutional development. The number of parties represented in the Czech and Slovak parliaments has been decreasing since the first post-communist elections in 1990 - not least because relatively modest tinkering with electoral laws made it more difficult for smaller competitors to challenge the dominant position of the bigger and established players. Furthermore, the formation of parliamentary party groups during the parliamentary term has been made more complicated for those wishing to defect from the party for which they were elected. By increasing the number of deputies needed to form a parliamentary party, and by curbing the rights of such newly formed groups in the legislative process, elites in our two countries demonstrated that you need a clear electoral mandate to be entitled to form a parliamentary party group, and that fission and fusion during the term is seen as illegitimate and undesirable once the parties are elected.

The attempts to deny office space and other material privileges might partly explain the higher level of cohesion Czech and Slovak parliamentary parties display, as well as their lower level of fragmentation. Nevertheless, our analysis showed that this process also has something to do with the developments of political parties at the level of their organization. In other words, increased parliamentary party cohesion has also been a function of internal party politics, rather than only a function of the changes in formal institutional rules. The many attempts, particularly in Slovakia, to enhance parliamentary party cohesion through the use of party discipline, such as expulsions or even stripping of parliamentary mandates, surely took their toll, not least in terms of psychological pressure on individual MPs. However, equally important for the internal cohesion of parties has been an increase in the homogeneity of their representatives and the fact that longer-established parties could start distributing selective incentives to their members, whether in the form of patronage (often leading into clear cases of corruption and party financial scandals) or, particularly in the case of opposition parties deprived of privileges associated with the tenure in office, in the increasingly routine and complex process of candidate selection. It is needless to say that, in the case of many long-standing Czech and Slovak parties, the previous fragmentation also helped to sort out the many unviable internal friendships, thus making parties more homogeneous and ultimately stronger. Therefore, paradoxical as it may sound, the splits, mergers, expulsions and partial organizational discontinuities that hit some of the Czech and Slovak parties, especially at the later stage of their development, actually became a symbol of their growing maturity and collective organizational strength, rather than, as we would expect, the epitome of their institutional weakness.[2]

The growing strength of parties also made an impact on the institutionalization of the links between parliament and society. Our analysis in chapter 3 strongly suggested that the party dominates the representation and, consequently, it is the party rather than the individual MP who provides the crucial link between citizens and state institutions. Although there is not yet a definite pattern in the formation of direct links between Czech and Slovak MPs and their local constituencies and matters have been developing rapidly in the recent years as the result of changing formal rules - representatives in both countries apparently do see their roles of representing local constituencies or professional and social interests as largely subordinated to the roles associated with the execution of the party mandate. Increased professionalization of the political class, as well as the fact that MPs owe their careers to political parties, is unlikely to push the party out of its current dominance in the sphere of representation. Moreover, the current shape of electoral systems provides another structural incentive underpinning the existing system. Czech and Slovak MPs, most of whom lack the tradition of and experience with constituency work, are elected in relatively large districts, under a system where the initial position on the list of candidates is more important in the electoral process than popularity with the local electorate.

It is worth pointing out in this respect that the hold of Czech and Slovak parties over their MPs, as well as their ability to organize the functioning of parliaments and relationships between parliaments and governments, has not been reproduced in their penetration of the society at the grass-roots level. Our findings support Ágh's (1996) view that most of the Eastern European parties have been stronger in their governing and other institutional roles than in their societal roles (on Western developments see Katz and Mair, 1995). In other words, the parties' linkage function - that is, their capacity to act as a vent for citizens activity, as well as their ability to forge solid links with their constituencies - have clearly been weak. Although Czech and Slovak parties themselves did not exert much effort to mobilize on the ground, especially in periods between successive electoral campaigns, it appears that the citizens' consistently low interest in getting involved in political and civil society organizations is the main explanation for this phenomenon. Moreover, parties also display weak direct links with other civil society actors, such as trade unions, professional organizations or non-governmental organizations. Part of this is, again, due to the weakness (normative-moral, organizational and financial) of post-communist civil society itself, rather than to strategic decisions of party elites to keep the autonomy of civil society organizations intact (see Kopecký and Barnfield, 1999). But the resulting effect is worth further consideration in democratization theory, because the political process, and primarily the legislative process, have been virtually snapped up in both countries by governments and their parliamentary majority, with civil society actors, even those affected by particular policies, largely excluded from it.

The strength of parties also had an impact on the institutionalization of presidents in the executive-legislative relations, and their position in the overall political architecture in both countries. As shown earlier, the attempts of presidents, and in particular that of Havel in the Czech Republic, to institutionalize their charisma did not work, since both presidents were given mostly ceremonial prerogatives in the two constitutions, with governments favoured as the dominant element of executive power. However, as could be expected, the political role the presidents played had a major influence on the way formal rules worked in practice. Although the formal institutional position has differed only slightly between the two countries, the formation of presidential roles stirred up numerous controversies on the political scenes, with significant consequences for the institutionalization of the relationship between parliaments and governments on one hand, and presidents on the other. As shown in chapter 6, the Czech Republic emerged as a more settled entity in this respect. While Havel's position and influence in the domestic political process clearly differed from period to period (from a relatively marginal role in 1992-1996, to the position of arbiter and broker after 1996), and while his political involvements were never to everybody's liking, the overall position of Czech president shows signs of stability and acceptance among politicians. Much of this stands in sharp contrast to Slovakia, where personal and political conflicts between Mečiar and his government(s) and then-president Kováč put the whole institutional shape of the presidency into question. In line with numerous other attempts to institutionalize a strong majority rule (see below), the ruling elite in Slovakia toyed with ideas of instituting a presidential system at first (in 1993), to proceed later with drastic cuts in presidential prerogatives under the existing parliamentary system, effectively blocking the election of a new president after Kováč's term expired, and fiercely resisting the opposition's attempts to pass legislation enabling presidential elections by popular vote.

In sum, the general direction in which the Czech and Slovak parliaments become institutionalized strongly resembles a European parliamentary context, with a predominance of political parties in parliamentary and political processes. Parliaments in both countries operate in the context of party government (for more details see Kopecký, 2001), with all the repercussions that model entails. Katz (1986:43) defined party government as a model which "makes government accountable to the general public by entrusting it to individuals organized into parties that owe their positions to electoral approbation" and consisting of three key characteristics: all major governmental decisions must be taken by people chosen in elections conducted along party lines; policy is decided within a governing party or a coalition of governing parties; ministers and the prime minister must be selected within their parties and be responsible to the people through their parties. As we saw throughout the chapters, both countries very neatly approximate this definition on all three dimensions. Not only is party control of the whole government apparatus strong in narrow institutional terms (a condition referred to as *partyness of government* by Katz), but this also applies to the role of parties in the overall polity (referred to as *party governmentness* by Katz), i.e. their exercise of social power in the political system.

The Czech and Slovak political systems consequently allow relatively little exercise of independent authority beyond party reach. This is true on the level of the state bureaucracy and, worryingly, also in part of the judiciary (especially in Slovakia), which is controlled by parties in both countries through party-sympathy and patronage-driven system of appointments. An individual MPs' position is linked to a party too, through the latter's controlled mechanisms of recruitment. We already noted that, in the realm of the self-organized social sphere commonly referred to as "civil society", Czech and Slovak parties did not quite succeed in relegating independent groups to the status of affiliated and ancillary organizations through the processes of organizational encapsulation, nor did they attempt to do so. Parties nevertheless managed to establish a monopoly of control over the decision-making process, whereby civil society actors' relative autonomy vis-à-vis parties is checked by their marginal input to the political process. Policy demands originating from within civil society are channelled to the political arena on the basis of either a multi-party strategy, or through personal contacts with MPs, ministers and bureaucracy, and their fate ultimately depends on subsequent decisions within parties, governments and parliaments. Deviations from the ideal-typical definition of party government do exist, however. The independent power exercised by constitutional courts, or the partial relegation of policy-making power to the instituted system of tripartite bargaining between major interest groups, are perhaps the two most important examples. Still, the party (in all relevant aspects) is a crucial variable in understanding the operation of contemporary parliaments and political systems in both countries.

Party government in the Czech and Slovak republics should be seen as a developing entity or political strategy, rather than something of a given and historically pre-determined nature. Chapter 2 showed that individual MPs, strong personalities, shifting coalitions cutting across party lines and many other variables inimical to the concept of party government played an important role at the beginning of democratization in the former Czechoslovakia. Why, then, did both countries come to party government? This question is especially pertinent given that competing models of democratic governance were considered (for example, "anti-political politics" with broad and diffuse interest representation) and the whole idea of 'party' encountered strong normative opposition in the aftermath of the communist breakdown, particularly among the former dissidents (notably Havel). And, one has to ask about the prospects for party government to persist in both countries.

As for the explanation, it is clear from the above that structural attributes of the Czech and Slovak political systems, such as a parliamentary system of government, PR electoral systems, or the dominance of the party in the system of representation, are highly conducive to a strong party government. If we can assume, on the basis of inference from the empirical chapters, that dramatic changes in these structural attributes are unlikely in the future, then the persistence of party government in some form seems also guaranteed in both countries. However, the key question inevitably must be why such structural attributes exist in the first place, and why the party as a political tool became so attractive to the Czech and Slovak political elites. The answer is not simple, yet Katz's suggestion that "the strongest conditioning factor for party government at the present is to have had party government in the past" may help us in this respect (see Katz, 1986:55). Although we saw in chapter 2 that it is problematic to attribute the choice of a parliamentary system of government, and that of a PR electoral system, solely to the democratic traditions of the First Republic, it is striking to see that the role models of politicians from this period, together with many political symbols and rhetoric, were carried over to the post-communist period, particularly in the Czech Republic. Needless to say, the First Republic had the party government *par excellence*.

Moreover, and perhaps most importantly, the highly contingent decision from the 1989 Round Table talks to carry on with the old communist constitution, which mandated a form of parliamentary system of government, set the process of party government formation in motion. For it was then that the few ambitious politicians, such as Klaus in the Czech Republic, and Mečiar and Čarnogurský in Slovakia, came to appreciate that a strong party organization was the best way to pursue their interests, both policy and personal, and their advances in the political field made it abundantly clear for others that avoiding a party strategy would mean depriving themselves of a vital instrument for achieving their political ends. Differences between parties and politicians alike were apparent, but overall this process of learning was quite rapid, so the constitution-making process in 1992 only reflected an already established dominant conception of democracy which, in turn, became embodied in these two new constitutions.

Degree of institutionalization

The Czech and Slovak parliaments started in 1992 with very similar structures and these structures have remained largely unchanged in 1998. However, and crucially, this structurally similar context is clearly differentiated by the extent of majority rule application; that is, by the behavioral, normative or cultural characteristics underpinning these formal structural and organizational attributes. If we situate the institutionalization of Czech and Slovak parliaments within the context of the party government model - and there are good reasons to do so - then the concern with majority rule becomes important. For, "[I]n the party government conception, the fundamental democratic principle is majority rule" (Katz, 1986:49). As we saw, elites in both countries showed that majority rule is a norm which drives the formal institutional apparatus, with occasional attempts at institutional engineering which would help to cement a momentary political dominance into a permanent state of affairs, sanctioned by explicitly codified rules. In that respect as well, the Czech and Slovak differed little from each other and, for that matter, differed little from other countries in post-communist Europe (see Bale and Kopecký, 1998).

Nevertheless, it also became apparent from the preceding chapters that the manner in which the 'winners' tended to treat the 'losers' has consistently differed between the two countries, and this is crucial for our understanding of why very similar institutions or indeed institutional regimes based on similar customs and norms may in fact operate in such different fashions. In Slovakia, especially after the 1994 elections, we witnessed a systematic attempt by the governing majority to eliminate all rules ensuring horizontal accountability between political institutions, as well as a strong inclination to ignore existing rules and norms where formal changes proved impossible. The Czech elites, on the other hand showed more restraint in this respect, attempting fewer formal institutional manipulations, and respecting established customs and conventions.

This difference has a bearing on the systemic level of the Czech and Slovak Republics; that is, on the consolidation of their new democracies.

Sartori (1987:31) argues that "[T]he current objections to the identification of democracy to sheer (and hence absolute) majority rule apply, more often than not, to the special case of the highly divided and intensely conflictual societies". Arguably, Slovakia is such a "conflictual society" and we return to this issue in the next two sections. Here it is important to point out that (the varying extent of) majority rule application also has a significant bearing on the level or degree of institutionalization of parliaments in both countries, in that it left the Slovak parliament less institutionalized after almost 10 years of democratization than the same institution in the Czech Republic. If one agrees with Jepperson in that "one can perhaps best conceive of degrees of institutionalization in terms of relative vulnerability to social intervention", and in that "[A]n institution is highly institutionalized if it presents a near insuperable collective action threshold" (Jepperson, 1991:151), our contention will become more obvious. In contrast to the Czech parliament, the Slovak parliament operates in a comparatively more expandable and unstable institutional framework, and both its formal and informal internal arrangements, as well as the formal and informal relationships with the external environment, are heavily dependent on what the majority actually chooses to do. Hence contingent rather than structured or institutionalized relationships are common.

It should be stressed that this dependence goes well beyond simply the governing style of a particular majority. It is certain that the actual changes of ruling elites in the Czech Republic put a mark on the way parliamentary processes turn out to work in practice. The minority government that was formed after the 1996 (and also 1998) elections, for example, transformed the previously strong and largely unrestrained, dominance of the ruling majority into a more consensual power-sharing style of governance. This, in turn, threw various formal and informal arrangements, such as mechanisms of filling leadership posts in the parliament's chairmanship and committees or electoral system, into question, leading to re-adjustments and a great deal of inter-party bargaining, especially after the 1998 elections. But it is equally certain that in none of the political periods or legislative terms did the Czech Republic witness such a fundamental conflict over formal parliamentary and constitutional rules, as well as informal intra-parliamentary arrangements, as in Slovakia, where virtually every political issue immediately opened debates about the entire institutional framework.

It may sound paradoxical that the comparatively lower degree of institutionalization of the Slovak parliament is parallelled by an increase in parliament's prerogatives within the country's institutional architecture.

While the parliament acquired additional powers after 1994, namely over the president and Constitutional Court, the latter institutions saw a corresponding decline in their power and influence. It underscores the point that nominal formal procedures alone have little to do with the process of institutionalization, and that what matters in this respect is not just the power of the institution within the entire system, but rather the fact that constant changes and elite interventions to these powers and procedures prevent it from becoming routinized, embedded and integrated within that system. Unlike in the case of the Czech parliament, the problem for the Slovak parliament (and democracy) is that any change in the elite or its composition might spell a switch from one institutional form to another, organized around different normative principles, rules or valued behaviors. Where Czech party elites appear to display a common understanding of these basic principles and behaviors, which, in turn, underline relatively stable institutional patterns, the Slovak elite is engaged in a heavy dispute over them.

All this means that, at present, the Slovak parliament is not only less institutionalized than the Czech parliament, i.e. it provides a lower collective action threshold, but also that the mechanisms which ensure its reproduction against the actions of those actors interested in surpassing such a threshold differ substantially between the two parliaments. Despite the numerous changes the Czech parliament witnessed in its formal rules of conduct since 1989, or perhaps even thanks to some of these changes, parliamentary processes are now for the most part routinely reproduced by highly formalized rules, with an elaborated system of mechanisms and sanctions for controlling and enforcing them. The rules of the Slovak parliament were, needless to say, changed on many occasions too. However, it is striking to see that, in comparison to the Czech parliament, the newest version of Slovak parliamentary rules are deliberately formulated in a rather vague form, thus opening up the possibility of various interpretations and potential flexibilities appropriated according to the exigencies of the moment. This makes parliamentary processes subject less to strongly formalized and clear procedures than to informal, and hence less transparent, less accountable, and less predictable modes of interactions (see Malová, 1998).

To be sure, the Czech parliament is not lacking in grey areas governed by informal rules either, and the system of party discipline is just one example of a sphere largely beyond the reach of formalized parliamentary rules. But the point here is that party discipline and other sets of informal regimes and practices jelled with a system of relatively developed formalized rules to produce a parliament capable of adapting to significant environmental changes (for example, the new government constellations after the 1996 and 1998 elections), without following these environmental shocks with dramatic alterations of internal structures or undermining the existing rules of the game. In contrast, the predominance of informal rules governing the Slovak parliament primarily reflects the weakness of the formal rules which before 1994 ensured the universality and transparency of parliamentary processes, as well as the more comprehensive rights of the parliamentary opposition. Rather than effecting a highly developed and reproducible organizational pattern, the informal rules and regimes which either replaced or complemented existing formal rules of parliamentary processes in Slovakia appear as a set of instruments in the hands of a particular governing elite, designed to ensure its unrestricted majority rule, and hence as a set of rules which is ephemeral in character.

We now return to the starting point of this discussion: a consideration of the process of constitution-making in both countries, and the possible consequences it had on the process of institutionalization of parliaments. Although the Slovak constitution was poorly and hastily drafted, leaving many provisions unclear and open to interpretation, this fact did not seem to influence the general direction of institutionalization of parliament (i.e. development of a strong party government in both countries). Still, there are grounds to suggest that the constitution has influenced the stage this process has reached (i.e. the degree of institutionalization). Since constitutional provisions, namely those regulating the position of the president and relations between parliament and government, were of inferior quality, some scholars argue that the battle over institutional rules was inevitable, and thus that the whole process of constitution-making lies behind much of the troubles in contemporary Slovakia (see Zifčák, 1995; Malová, 1998). However, this argument tends to ignore that many such provisions were poorly defined in the Czech Republic as well and that, from a comparative perspective, it is more interesting to see that this did not lead into them being subjected to such a bitter conflict as in Slovakia. Constitution-making analysis will therefore not help us much in explaining different degrees of institutionalization of parliaments. The next sections should shed more light on this issue.

Consolidation of Czech and Slovak Democracies

As was established in the first chapter, institutionalization and consolidation point to different levels of analysis, despite their close conceptual relationship. Institutionalization referred in this study to a sub-system level of analysis of a particular institution or institutional system. Consolidation referred to a systemic level of analysis, examining the characteristics of the regime as a whole. Our previous considerations of parliamentary institutionalization, and in particular of differing degrees of institutionalization, in the Czech and Slovak Republics raise the suspicion that the degree of consolidation of democracy differs between the two countries as well. This view is supported by the pivotal position of parliaments in political processes in general since, as we argued in the first chapter, parliaments are those institutions around which most crucial questions involving styles of democracy revolve. However, parliament is also only one institution or partial institutional regime, albeit a large one. Our conclusions, which are valid for complex networks of interactions between parliaments and other (select) institutions, might not be quite the same as for the political system as a whole. Therefore, if we wish to make a more grounded statement on democratic consolidation, we need to consider further whether these different degrees of parliamentary institutionalization are also reflected on the systemic level. We can do so using the concepts of democratic consolidation introduced at the beginning of this study.

We distinguished between two different conceptualizations of democratic consolidation. The first one, represented by the works of Linz (1990), Burton, Gunther and Higley (1992), Diamondouros, Puhle and Gunther (1995) or Valenzuela (1992), speaks of consolidated democracy, in an ideal-typical and minimal sense, as a regime in which all politically significant groups adhere to established democratic rules of the game. Democracy is defined in minimalist terms, as a set of institutions and procedures that guarantee competitive politics. This procedural democracy encompasses competitive elections held at regular intervals and based on universal suffrage; citizens enjoying basic freedoms of speech, press and organization; and the existence of formalized (in a written or unwritten constitution) and legally binding procedures that regulate the powers of government and divisions among its branches. Consolidated democracy, in minimal terms, is thus defined in terms of the behavioral compliance of political actors with such established rules. Compliance is a sufficient indicator of consolidation, and non-compliance is a sufficient indicator of non-consolidation.

The second notion, represented by the work of Linz and Stepan (1996), is based on a more substantive definition of democratic consolidation (and democracy). Democracy is consolidated when, first, "no significant national, social, economic, political, or institutional actors spend significant resources attempting to achieve their objectives by creating a nondemocratic regime or turning to violence or foreign intervention to secede from the state"; when, second, "a strong majority of public opinion holds the belief that democratic procedures and institutions are the most appropriate way to govern collective life in a society..."; and, third, "when governmental and non-governmental forces alike, throughout the territory of the state, become subjected to, and habituated to, the resolution of conflict within the specific laws, procedures, and institutions sanctioned by the new democratic process" (Linz and Stepan, 1996:6). Therefore, political actors must not only comply with democratic rules of the game, but these rules must also be seen as legitimate by the actors themselves and by a large section of public opinion. In addition, there are five definitional pre-requisites for consolidation to exist: the existence of a free and lively civil society; the existence of a relatively autonomous political society; the subjection of political actors to the rule of law; and the operations of a usable bureaucracy and an institutionalized economic society.

How, then, do the new Czech and Slovak regimes fare in light of these definitions? If we take the minimal definition of consolidation and democracy as the starting point, the conclusion seems to be that both countries are consolidated democracies - a view widely shared among many observers of post-communist and Czech and Slovak politics (e.g. Skalnik-Leff, 1996; Comisso, 1997). In nominal terms, all the necessary institutions based on competitive politics and universal suffrage have successfully been introduced and sustained in the Czech and Slovak Republics. Genuinely competitive elections take place on a regular basis, allowing representation of citizens' views. The rules governing the electoral processes have, so far, been democratic and international observers were satisfied with the manner in which past elections were conducted in both states. These elections determine who holds power and they have always been marked by the presence of a wide choice of alternatives to incumbents. From 1989 to the current date, different parties have alternated in power in both countries. Basic freedoms of speech, press and organization are guaranteed, and written constitutions limit governments and provide for the division of powers between executive, legislative and judicial branches in a manner perfectly consistent with procedural requirements of democracy. Moreover, despite the attempts in both countries to enact legislation favouring the incumbents, such as changes to electoral laws or laws regulating party finances and access to state-controlled media,[3] it is important (from a minimal procedural point of view) that these legislative acts were adopted by constitutionally sanctioned bodies and procedures. They can be changed through similar bodies and procedures, and are universal in character. One can certainly question the reasons, morality and political brinkmanship which lie behind many such attempts, and we shall do this below, but it is clear that they do not violate the picture of procedural democracy. It is at least apparent that similar showdowns of institutional manipulation and skewing of incumbents' power and resources to their own advantage are not uncommon in long-established western democracies, and are certainly common to both countries under scrutiny here, as well as to their neighbors in the region.

Understandably, then, there is also no obvious evidence to suggest that the main political actors in both countries are not complying with minimal procedural requirements of democracy. Even if we take into account supposedly non-democratic or marginal political forces, such as the extreme-right Republicans and conservative Communists in the Czech Republic, or Hungarian parties in Slovakia, there are precious few indications that their behavior is in contradiction with nominal and minimal democratic procedures, and that they try to subvert the democratic process in their respective countries by advocating non-democratic regimes or secession from the state. Such rhetoric may be part of political battles and conflicts, often employed by the mutually identifiable political opponents, but what matters here is that these conflicts have so far been subjected to resolution through essentially democratic procedures. Simply put, in minimalist terms, the Czech and Slovak democracies appear as consolidated democracies.

What is clearly worrisome in this respect, however, is that even the application of the minimalist definition to our two countries might actually provide us with the sense of difference in the degree of democratic consolidation between them. The effective cancellation of Gauladier's deputy mandate (discussed in chapter 6) and the installation of Hruška as an MP (discussed in chapter 4) - both acts implemented against the rulings of the Constitutional Court - as well as the unilateral cancellation of the 1997 referendum on direct presidential elections by the authorities (discussed in chapter 5) - also against the recommendations of the Court and the Central Referendum Commission - are cases in point here. Arguably, these three political issues alone are the first serious signs of erosion of democratic consolidation in Slovakia even in elementary minimalist terms - issues for which we would certainly not find a comparable equivalent in the Czech Republic.

Indeed, these are also the most oft-cited instances which, for some observers, appear to render Slovak democracy as non-consolidated in behavioral terms. Szomolányi (1997:21), for example, refers to the political style and behavior of (ruling) elites and argues that Slovakia is "...an unconsolidated, unstable democracy. It remains a democracy because elementary, yet fragile democratic institutions persist. But implementation of democratic procedures is often thwarted by the policies of the power holders...The process of regime change has thus neither led to democratic consolidation nor the establishment of an authoritarian regime". Similarly, Elster, Offe and Preuss (1998:287) conclude their survey of Eastern European countries with a note that "[A]lready the basic criterion of what we called vertical consolidation - the distinction of political struggles under constitutional rules and disputes about such rules - is not safely guaranteed." Moreover, after adding another criterion of democratic consolidation to their evaluation, extending well beyond minimalist procedural concerns, the authors conclude that Slovakia failed to consolidate its democracy, whereas "...the Czech Republic fares extraordinary well" (p.279). In other words, whichever more elaborated criteria one is using, there is a fair established general tendency in the comparative literature (and among foreign governments and policy-makers) to consign the Czech Republic unequivocally to the category *democracy* or *consolidated democracy* (usually together with Poland, Hungary and Slovenia), whereas Slovakia is now regularly put into the contrasting category such as *border democratic* (see Gastil, 1994), *partly-free regime* (see Karatnycky, 1997), *nationalist-populist regime* (Carpenter, 1997), or a "*special case with doubts over its status*" (see Lewis, 1997:5).

In the light of this, the reader will undoubtedly expect that even a cursory application of Linz and Stepan's more substantial conceptualization of democratic consolidation will give us reasons why Slovakia's process of democratization is evaluated as it is. And there are indeed many such reasons. As was apparent with our assessment of the process of parliamentary institutionalization, the key problem of Slovak democracy lies in the application of the majority rule principle and the subsequent overall pattern of political activity. Linz and Stepan (1996:10) stress in their definition the indispensability of "the rule of law" and "spirit of constitutionalism" for democratic consolidation. This involves the understanding that political actors abide by rules because they see them as legitimate, not just because they see them as 'strategically' more convenient than some other alternative. A striking feature of the political activity overall in Slovakia is that while elementary democratic procedures still remain largely intact, not least because of a great deal of skilful brinkmanship with legal loopholes on the side of the HZDS-led government and the fact that the country has been subjected to severe international pressures, its broader pattern is characterized by a sharp meta-institutional and national-identity conflict on the one hand, and deeply personalized politics revolving around Prime Minister Mečiar on the other hand. The political stakes in contemporary Slovak politics have been gradually raised and provide for a sharp elite polarization and disunity (see Gould and Szomolányi, 1998), whereby opposition and government forces alike perceive each other as illegitimate. The political conflict revolves around dogged and protracted struggles over constitutional matters, rights of opposition, and the rights of minorities, with the heaviest artillery of rhetoric and means employed in these exchanges.

In the post-1994 elections and under the reign of the HZDS/SNS/ZRS government, this structure of conflict produced symptoms barely compatible with the spirit of constitutionalism or rule of law. The constitution itself was many times subjected to alterations for clear partisan advantage (mostly without success thanks to the qualified majority requirements). Horizontal accountability between state institutions was drastically cut by either revisions in prerogatives and/or changes of personnel in the key institutions initially designed to check on the government's power, such as the National Property Fund, Supreme Control Office, Slovak Information Service, or public television and broadcasting. The obstructionist behavior of governmental authorities (for example, the removal of supposedly informed investigators in police investigations of the Slovak president's son kidnapping) undermined trust in the independence of state bureaucracy. Moreover, the combination of the government's institutional manipulations and brinkmanship with the underlying confrontation between Slovak's political elites resulted in a strange and vicious dynamic of conflict resolution: the government proposes a law; this law is usually passed without any amendments or opposition input in parliament; the president vetoes it, usually at the behest of the opposition; a parliamentary (governmental) majority reapproves it in the original form, and then either the president or the opposition use their right to ask the Constitutional Court to judge on the law's compatibility with the constitution. The Court thus became the only key Slovak institution able to challenge the government - a sort of second assembly - and the outcomes of legislative activity normally depend on the subsequent ability or will of the government majority to avoid, reinterpret or violate the Court's rulings.

These negative aspects of the current Slovak regime have inevitably been reproduced as well in the other "arenas of consolidated democracy". Although a great deal of freedom and independent political and social activity is exercised on the local level and among the increasingly modern, organized and action-capable societal groups, research by Malová (1997) suggests that the autonomy of civil society has been severely circumscribed by concerted actions of the Slovak ruling elite. Many legislative acts involving for example foundations, universities or local governments have attempted to squeeze civil society actors out of existence, and where such state actions run into the resilience of better organized and co-ordinated actors (like trade unions), the ruling HZDS exercised the 'divide and rule' strategy, granting privileged access to politically loyal groups or creating their own party-affiliated groups competing with those who opted for independence and disobedience. In a similar vein, the cancellations of voucher privatization and its replacement by direct sales, as well as the government's total control over the bodies responsible for privatization of state property, are clear indications of the changing agenda of economic transformation. These acts in themselves are neither undemocratic, nor do they necessarily change Slovakia's general direction toward a market economy. But they created serious impediments to the development of a universal legal and regulatory framework essential for the existence of "economic society", which would institutionalize market exchanges and separate them from the state apparatus and political actors. Instead, the evidence suggests that the ruling Slovak elites systematically engaged in patronage-oriented allocation of economic benefits, turning privatization into pork-barrel politics rewarding those inside and close to ruling parties (see Leško, 1996; Mikloš, 1997; Mesežnikov, 1997).

Evidently, if we consider Slovakia against the more demanding criteria of democratic consolidation, it will appear that, after almost 10 years of democratization, the new regime displays more signs of unconsolidated than consolidated democracy. However, this should not obscure the fact that, measured against the same demanding definition of democratic consolidation, the Czech Republic will hardly be able to qualify as a fully consolidated democracy either. What clearly separates the country from its eastern neighbor is a significantly more developed and widely respected system of horizontal and vertical accountability between institutions, as well as the overall pattern of political activity which takes place within these institutions. The protracted wars between different state bodies, such as those which occurred in Slovakia between the president and the parliament and government, are basically unknown in the Czech Republic or, when clashes occur, at least they do not lead to subsequent attempts to eliminate rival institutions from the political landscape. The Czech constitution has also gained a widespread acceptance among elites and public alike, at least inasmuch as that blatant and overt attempts to manipulate it to partisan advantage were mitigated by a sort of 'constitutional conservatism' which has been gaining momentum ever since the document was adopted in the winter of 1992. Thus, although various constitutional reforms have been advocated since that date (the protracted process of establishing of the Senate being the most obvious example), and may well be advanced in the future (note the debates on electoral system and presidential prerogatives after the 1998 elections), the reluctance of elites to reopen such negotiations has usually led to either discharging amendments from political agenda, or cautiously subjecting them to a wider inter-party debate. Equally, although strong majority rule has been a guiding principle of parliamentary processes and the laws that regulate them, this has not resulted in severe imbalances in favour of ruling majorities or the exclusion of the opposition from supervisory and oversight bodies, such as parliamentary committees and commissions, or the Independent Control Office.[4]

In truth, however, the picture will become bleaker if one checks on civil or economic societies - the other arenas of consolidated democracy identified by Linz and Stepan. In contrast to a prudent and settled political society, most visibly represented to the outside world by the skilful leadership of Havel and Klaus, the character and legal regulatory framework necessary for civil and economic societies remains the subject of political battles, leaving both arenas lagging behind the relatively well-developed and stable forms of governance and state management. Political controversies involving the decentralization of government through the creation of regions, which was reluctantly pursued by various governments, as well as the battles involving laws on non-profit associations and labor codes, all testify to the desire, however subtly pursued, of (some) elites to effectively exercise control and monopoly over areas that could potentially challenge their existing dominance.[5] After an analysis of the poorly developed civil society in the Czech Republic, Green and Skalnik-Leff (1997:84) observe that "[T]his stunting of the political process - an unevenness in the evolution of democratic institutions and processes - carries risks for the management of future political controversy." Indeed, the political crisis that hit the Czech Republic at the end of 1997 may be partly attributed to accumulated deficits in the development of associational life and the deficient legal framework for allowing civil society organized access to the state and policy-making processes (see Pehe, 1997). This crisis also showed that, despite the neo-liberal rhetoric and supposed 'rolling back of the state', the policies of the Czech government(s) towards economic society were quite interventionist and, given the now-known scale of illegal party funding and corruption (see chapter 3), also involved elements of pork-barrel politics.

Even taking all this into account, in comparison to Slovakia, many of the Czech Republic's violations and deviations from the more substantive standards of consolidated democracy do not grossly impinge on mutually balanced and accountable relationships between institutions, and do not produce a bitter, zero-sum conflict between the country's political elites. Although plagued by numerous scandals, the Czech Republic has not witnessed attempts to forestall police investigations of these events and the following criminal prosecutions, or attempts to undermine several non-party or all-party investigations into the matters of public concern (Krause, 1998). Equally, while the civil society received an arguably indifferent treatment from the state and party elites, all the ongoing processes and debates surrounding its future development are subject to open contestation on the political scene, without the danger of slipping into the same type of super-charged and chronic controversy over democracy that characterizes Slovakia. In sum, democratization in the Czech Republic seems to have produced a democratic system which, due to its internal incentives and structural underpinnings, guarantees that its deficiencies may be corrected over time, by means of peaceful evolution. In contrast, democratization in Slovakia has produced a democratic system operating with internal incentives and a structure of conflict that profoundly endangers its elementary pluralist character, a system requiring a radical rupture with its political practices if it is to progress in the future.

These considerations point to advantages and disadvantages of minimalist and substantive definitions of democratic consolidation. Minimalist definitions can produce a reasonably unambiguous statement, and hence remain potentially attractive for use in large cross-national comparative studies as a basic cut-off point which will separate countries into different categories of regimes. A more substantive consideration, in contrast, will almost inevitably leave us with an ambiguous impression about the degree of democracy and of consolidation, or will lead into the creation of numerous labels and terms for describing a democratic system(s) under scrutiny, i.e. "democracy with adjectives" (Collier and Levitsky, 1997). Our examination based on one such standard suggests that the two cases of new democratic regimes considered in this study differ primarily in the degree of their democratic consolidation; that is, they satisfy certain parts of definitions better than others, but not all of them at the same time. We contend, though cannot prove here, that this is likely to be the case for many Eastern European countries towards the end of the first decade of their democratization processes.

The general theoretical implication is that the notion of consolidation should not be defined with excessive expectations, particularly in the context of the post-communist legacy which is much less favorable for democratization than the legacy left by non-democratic regimes in Southern Europe and Latin America. If defined excessively, democratic consolidation is very likely to be fully unattainable even in the most advanced countries of East Central Europe for years to come. Several 'deficiencies' of democracy in the region, such as relatively thin civil society or higher level of elite conflict, can then mistakenly be interpreted as the signs of non-consolidation, rather than the source of futher pressures for evolutionary change normal in established democracies. Therefore, democratic consolidation should be linked to a minimal procedural definition of democracy and should not refer to any notions relating it to the deepening of democracy. Democracy can certainly be divided according to different types and degrees of institutionalization (e.g. O'Donnell, 1996), or different ways it is organized. However, these problems and classifications should be part of the (broader) study of the functioning of democracy rather than the (more narrow) study of the consolidation of democracy.

As for the interpretation of the Czech and Slovak Republics, we were concerned in this study with the development of formal and informal institutional structures centered around parliaments, because of the presumed key importance of these in the process of political change. Our explorations pointed to divergent patterns in the degree of parliamentary institutionalization and, to finish this section, we suggest that they also point to a different degree of democratic consolidation. Slovakia has experienced great difficulties in erecting a stable and widely respected elementary institutional framework of democracy and, in our view, this in itself is a sufficient indication to label the country as an unconsolidated democracy. The opposite is true for the Czech Republic, and this is the reason why we label the country as a consolidated democracy (see Table 7.1 at the end of this chapter). The inevitable question now is what accounts for these differences. We suggest that differences we established in both the degree of parliamentary institutionalization, as well as the degree of democratic consolidation, can be explained within a single explanatory framework.

Toward an Explanation

Explanations of democratization and its different patterns can roughly be clustered around three sets of variables: *structural*, such as the level of socioeconomic development, patterns of modernization and industrialization, and prevailing cultural patterns, all of which can be linked to the modernization paradigm; *institutional*, such as designs of executive-legislative relations and electoral systems; and *elite/behavioral*, such as the power constellation of elites, patterns of competition between the elites, or even very particular and contingent policy decisions. The elite/behavioral variables are especially prominent in democratization theories emphasizing strategic choices and leadership processes.

The principal distinction between these three sets of variables lies in the degree of determinism or intentionality with which they influence present outcomes (Elster, Offe and Preuss, 1998). The structures are the long-term cultural, economic and social preconditions which shape the present trajectories of democratization. Structural variables generate constraints and opportunities for political actors in a fashion that is relatively independent from their action. They are the lasting determinants, often stemming from the distant past or country-specific historical experiences. Elite/behavioral variables, on the other hand, emphasize a considerable amount of freedom from structures. They refer to the character of competition and the way politics is played out. Strategies of elite actors and their mutual relationships during and shortly after the breakdown of regimes are crucial in shaping democratization pathways. Intentionality, contingency and immediate action are here considered more important than long-term structures and rigid determinants. Institutional variables can be placed close to the structural variables. Institutions may reflect long-term cultural and social patterns and, at the same time, provide constraints on elite behaviour. Because of their capacity to shape political behaviour, they act as independent variables.[6]

Within these broad categories, several (overlapping) explanations have already been proposed to account for different patterns of democratization in Eastern Europe in general, and in the Czech and Slovak Republics in particular. Most frequently, these have included individual factors, or a modest variation of factors such as: different modes of extrication from communism, i.e. radical breakaway and the presence of large counter-elites as opposed to a mere transformation of old elites; different levels of modernization; different levels of stability of communist rule, i.e. the presence or absence of internal revolts against the communist regimes; the relative strength of civil societies in different countries; and different historically induced cultural traditions, i.e. either the prevalence of the Ottoman, or the dominant influence of Austro-Hungarian and Northern European traditions (Lewis, 1997; see also Munck and Skalnik-Leff, 1997).

The trouble is, however, that many of these factors, at least if considered on their own terms, will not yield sufficient explanatory power to illuminate our two cases. The Czech and Slovak Republics, rather than displaying marked differences, appear to share many historical, institutional, social and cultural characteristics, including most obviously the same type of communist regime. The mode of extrication from communist regimes and the relative strength of their civil societies are similar as well. Broad opposition popular movements (OF in the Czech Republic and PAV in Slovakia) were involved in the breakdown of the Czechoslovak communist regime, and both groups also dominated round-table talks and the subsequent first free elections in the respective parts of the then-federal state; elements of opposition civil societies were present in both countries under communism (groups around Charter 77). Although civil society was perhaps weaker in the Slovak than in the Czech part (e.g. Mansfeldová, 1998), it is clear that both were relatively weak in comparison with Poland or Hungary (although stronger than in Bulgaria or Albania).

Structural and Institutional Explanations

The other three broad explanations which figure prominently in democratization literature (and in the comparative literature on East Central Europe) - economic, cultural, and, what we term here 'aggregate institutional' - will not fully bear the burden of explanation for our two cases either. Firstly, although large historical disparities in socioeconomic development (measured in related indices of modernization such as the degree of industrialization, technological development, and levels of education and urbanization) between the Czech lands and Slovakia persisted until the end of WWII, they were evened out by the rapid and concerted communist-led modernization and industrialization of Slovakia. The result of these policies was that, toward the end of the 1980s, Czech and Slovak societies became very similar in macro-economic terms (see Musil, 1993). Certainly, the application of the unifying Soviet model of modernization and industrialization, which was driven by strategic and military reasons, bore all the hallmarks of a centrally planned economy and its attendant distortions. In comparison to the Czech lands, the communists grafted heavy industries - in particular armament factories - onto the originally rural-based Slovak economy. The first Czechoslovak post-communist government's pursuit of radical shock-therapy reform brought an end to redistributive economic measures, and large parts of these industries and obsolete factories collapsed, putting a heavy burden on Slovak economic transformation.

These key disadvantages in the structure of the Slovak economy were thus the main reasons behind the steeper decline in production and higher rate of unemployment in Slovakia compared to the Czech lands, and certainly played a role in the split of the country at the end of 1992 by loading Czecho-Slovak disputes with the sense of economic inequalities between the two constituent republics (see chapter 2). However, contrary to general expectations, and despite the rhetoric of Mečiar's governments about halting shock-therapy policies, Slovakia continued these radical economic policies after the split and has been performing well by all basic macroeconomic indicators, such as GDP growth, inflation, trade deficit, balance of payments, and levels of unemployment (Mikloš and Žitnanský, 1998). In fact, from 1994 onward, the country not only outperformed the Czech Republic, which now appears to be backsliding from its initially impressive achievements in radical economic reforms (at least rhetorically championed under the banner of big-bang reforms by Klaus's governments), but also the many supposed front runners of consolidation in the region (see Mikloš, 1997; Carpenter, 1997). Therefore, while the improved performance of the Slovak economy coincides with the persistent, if not worsening problems in democratic consolidation, the Czech Republic appears to confirm the opposite linkage.[7]

Secondly, there is little evidence from the Czech and Slovak Republics to support propositions about their deep cultural differences (see Kusý, 1995), and in particular the "civic" as opposed to "traditionalist" cultures prevailing in the respective republics (see Carpenter, 1997; and, more general, Jowitt, 1992). As we saw in chapter 2, many (sociological) studies pointed to a different electoral climate in both republics before the split of Czechoslovakia. These differences in attitudes between Czechs and Slovaks on the mass level were related to views concerning the common state, the desirability of radical reforms, views on unemployment and the role of the state in the economy, or views concerning the traditions of the First Republic and the legacy of the war period (Wolchik, 1994). However, even accepting that these differences could partly account for the upsurge in popularity of nationalist forces in Slovakia, and hence have led to split of the Federation, it was already doubtful what changes these attitudes would undergo after that event, given that they were related primarily to the issue of Czecho-Slovak coexistence, and often evaluated on the basis of a highly select number of individual surveys. Indeed, Krause's (1997) systematic analysis of mass-level opinions in the Czech and Slovak Republics (based on the results of more than 25 surveys between 1990 and 1995) is tellingly entitled "Different but not *that* Different". The author concludes his analysis of several important dimensions of popular attitudes with a note that:

> "Slovaks and Czechs are different but the similarities in their opinions far exceed the differences.....even when the difference in mean between the two populations exceeds 15 percentage points an overwhelming share of the two populations (over 82%) hold an identical set of opinions. On nearly all questions cited here, the difference in means is considerably smaller than 15 percentage points and on many questions the Slovak and Czech populations are extremely similar" (Krause, 1997:30).

Moreover, when the attitudes of the Slovaks are compared to those of a larger pool of East Europeans, they are generally closest to those of the Czechs and (far) more similar to attitudes of the citizens of consolidated democracies (like Hungary and Poland), than to those of other problematic democracies, such as Bulgaria or Romania, let alone Russia (see Rose 1994; Markowski 1997; Rose 1997). A relevant example is provided by Rose (1997: 104), who presents data on popular support for authoritarian alternatives (army, communist regime, strong leader, reject all) in seven Central East European countries and Russia. For all different alternatives, popular support in Slovakia is very low, almost similar to the Czech Republic (and virtually identical to Hungary), far below the scores in Bulgaria or Russia. And finally, irrespective of comparisons, ever since the fall of communism, a significant majority of the Slovak population has consistently supported parliamentary democracy, while only a small minority preferred authoritarianism or the old communist regime (see Rose and Haerpfer 1993, 1994, 1996).

To be sure, this is not to deny that important differences exist on the mass level, and that these may bear upon the possible explanation of divergent patterns of parliamentary institutionalization and democratic consolidation observed in this study (see below). But the relative insignificance of attitudinal differences between the two populations requires us to further explore how these microstructures and characteristics are channelled (and perhaps retrospectively reinforced) by Czech and Slovak elites to produce significant differences in political outcomes on the macro level. In other words, we need to look beyond overgeneralized and simplistic accounts of either socioeconomic or cultural differences to account for our divergent patterns. We need to link these differences to a clear focus on elites.

Thirdly, it is important to note again that differences in political outcomes cannot be rooted in 'aggregated institutional' explanations. By this we mean explanations pointing to different institutional frameworks and their possible effects on institutionalization and consolidation; that is, the well-established debates concerning the pay-offs between presidential and parliamentary systems, the PR and majoritarian electoral systems, and the various combination of these basic institutional pillars of modern democracies. For, as we saw in this study, both countries have long operated with fundamentally similar institutional frameworks. There is room to argue that subtle differences in the formulation of power balance between the executive and legislative branches, like for example a stronger fusion of a governmental mandate with that of an MP mandate in the Czech Republic, may bear upon slightly different manners of parliamentary institutionalization, and in particular the nature of contacts between ministers and MPs (see chapter 4). But from a broader comparative perspective, there is virtually no difference in the shape of the macro-institutional structure of both countries. It would appear highly problematic to trace divergent outcomes of democratic consolidation to these types of institutional effects.

Elite/Behavioral Variables: The Character of Party Competition

What, then, accounts for differences between the Czech and Slovak Republics? To start to answer, we suggest that it is the character of political competition that is the key explanation which, in turn, derives from the presence and dominance of nation- and identity-related questions in Slovakia, and the almost total absence of these in the Czech Republic. Given that elites in both countries operate within political parties, it follows that it is the specific nature of party competition which shapes different outcomes in parliamentary institutionalization and democratic consolidation. This differing nature of party competition derives from a simultaneous process of state and nation building in Slovakia, acting as the source of fundamental political and institutional conflicts, as against the largely resolved character of these issues in the Czech Republic, where political conflicts focus on issues of a less divisive nature.

Though written for a different time and territory, the famous cleavage model of Lipset and Rokkan (1967) captures the difference in party competition in the contemporary Czech and Slovak Republics. In terms of their *a-g-I-l* paradigm, political competition in the Czech Republic is predominantly situated at the moderate *a* end of the functional dimension, pointing to interest-specific oppositions, while in the Slovak Republic political competition is situated at the more extreme *I* end of that dimension, i.e. ideological oppositions in 'friend-foe' terms, as well as on the *g* end of the territorial axis, i.e. oppositions within the national established elite. In other words, the crucial factors to account for our differences lies in ethnonational geography, problems of nationhood and statehood and politics of national identity: variables which, due to their politically less salient character, received almost no systematic academic attention during transitions in Southern Europe and Latin America (Linz, 1993; Linz and Stepan, 1996), but came to the forefront of analysis during transitions in Eastern Europe, with many authors arguing that this is a specificity which sets this region's democratization apart (see Offe, 1991; Bunce, 1995a,b).

Indeed, it requires no more than a cursory glance at political elites and party systems in both countries to demonstrate the manner in which issues associated with nationhood and statehood formation bear on political outcomes. Given our empirical considerations on democratic consolidation cited above, we repeat that the fundamental flaw in the way Slovak nascent democratic institutions function can be directly linked to the behavior of political elites which operate within them. Unlike the Czech political elites, who are united behind basic democratic principles and rules of the game, the Slovak elites are divided to the point that the overall political and institutional structure is dominated by two almost irreconcilable camps of opponents (each with its own divisions and conflicts), espousing diametrically opposing conceptions of democratic rules and procedures and views on politics. Most importantly, ever since Mečiar's first ousting from governmental office - during his reign as the leader of the Slovak government during the federal years (see chapter 2) - and ever since the formation of his HZDS in 1991, elite divisions and rival positions have been framed as struggles over the 'right and proper' defence of Slovak national identity and interests. These divisions, personal as well as institutional, gained momentum over several parliamentary terms and governmental changes and reached a level of elite antagonism that endangered the entire democratic political order. Skalnik-Leff (1996:48) captures the problem accurately by pointing out that:

> "socioeconomic and national-identity issues that resonate through the political crisis are not mere cleavage politics..., potentially susceptible to elite bargaining and accommodation. They have become instead elements in a politics of hyperbolic 'life or death' struggle over the meaning of Slovak independence".

Nowhere has this become more apparent than in the structure of party competition. The now well empirically grounded research shows that the Czech Republic's party system competition is of a uni-dimensional nature, with the dominant conflict structured alongside a socioeconomic dimension (see Kitschelt, 1994; Huber and Inglehart, 1995; Krause, 1996a; Markowski, 1997; Evans and Whitefield, 1998). The Czech parties compete primarily on positions clustered around questions of market liberalism/economic populism. The other existing dimensions (nationalism and religion), while important for individual parties (SPR-RSČ and KDU-ČSL), play a significantly less important role in shaping the overall competition. The composition of government coalitions has so far been a perfect embodiment of these demarcations, with either right-of-center governments of ODS, ODA, KDU-ČSL (1992, 1996), or the left-of-center minority government of ČSSD (1998) taking on the respective roles of government and opposition.

In contrast, the Slovak party system can be characterized by several dimensions of competition, of which a dimension clustered around national and collective identity questions appears to be the most important in structuring the party political conflict (see Krause, 1996b, 1998). While other dimensions exist, most notably a socioeconomic dimension, they mainly provide potential for disagreements among parties within the two blocks, rather than potential for structuring the conflict between the two blocks. The composition of government coalitions has reflected these dimensions of competition, for example, in the party marriages of HZDS, SNS, and later ZRS in Mečiar's governments (1992, 1994), which were largely united on national and identity questions but potentially divided on socioeconomic ones. On the other hand, Moravčík's temporary government from 1994 (and also post-1998 Dzurinda's government), consisted of a similarly ideologically diverse set of SDL, KDH, and DU (with the tacit support of Hungarian parties), and was united mainly against Mečiar and his allies.

Thus, if one is to choose strictly between structural/institutional and elite/behavioral variables, then the burden of explanation for different outcomes in democratic consolidation and parliamentary institutionalization in the Czech and Slovak Republics can be put on elite/behavioral variables. Rather than deep cultural differences between the two countries on the mass level, differences in economic performance, differences under the previous communist regime, or differences in formal institutional structures, it is the elites and party systems which function in a different way, and which account for different political outcomes. In part, these differences can be explained by specific decisions taken by political actors in the early years of post-communist transformation, when party and elite competition in both countries started to gain momentum. In particular, it can be explained by the decision of VPN leaders to allow a significant number of former communists to enter the movement's organization and assume high parliamentary and governmental posts, as a compensation for dissident reluctance to participate in high politics. This move diluted the movement's unity and its strongly pro-reform and pro-federal character (see Učeň, 1998 for more details).

This was partly true for OF too, simply because the pervasive nature of the Czechoslovak communist regime made experienced non-communist elites something of a scarcity in both parts of the Federation. But the group which eventually seized power within OF and other state institutions was centered around a group of liberal economic technocrats (many of them former party members) led by Klaus, who largely succeeded in remodelling emerging institutions in accordance with a highly individualistic liberal blueprint, and who framed social and political conflict in terms of a struggle for allocation of economic resources. Even the arguments for the necessity for separation with the Slovaks, used by the Czech elites around 1992, were based mainly on general economic issues and practical considerations of the governance within the Federation, rather than on strong concerns about national identity. In contrast, the conflict within VPN started as a struggle over the defense of Slovak national interests (and the right to claim legitimacy as either a founder of the new Slovak state or a committed federalist), and later developed into a meta-conflict between the two blocks of Slovak political parties over the meaning and norms of democracy and political participation. It developed as a simultaneous conflict over both the state as well as the nation.[8] In both countries, the logic of electoral politics and mobilization then led to the closure (and also intensification) of these basic incipient frames into relatively stable patterns of competition, both leading into different patterns of parliamentary institutionalization and democratic consolidation.

These considerations nevertheless return our explanations to structural concerns. Our analysis shows that, over time, the Slovak elites framed the political conflict quite independently of pre-existing social divisions, and it is in this sense that we ascribe primacy to elites, rather than to political cultures, macro-institutions or socioeconomic development (structural variables). However, if it is the nature of elite and party competition which accounts for differences in political outcomes, then the dominance of national and identity related questions in Slovak post-communist politics, and the almost total absence of these in the Czech politics, is an historical artefact and, therefore, of a structurally given nature. Disputes over Slovak nationhood and statehood date back to political activities during the First Republic where, after the unification of formerly Hungarian-dominated and agrarian Slovakia with the much wealthier industrialized Czech and Moravian lands, calls for greater autonomy and the rise of Slovak separatist movements (Hlinka's People's Party) occurred in the context of Czech domination and the unitary nature of the interwar state. At that time, the debate on national issues already served as the most fundamental divide between the then-small Slovak elites - a divide which also run through the history of the Slovak Communist Party after World War II (see Skalnik-Leff, 1988; Rothschild, 1992; Mamatey and Luža, 1973).

Given the multinational character of the First Republic, the divisions within Czech elites were no less urgent in this respect. Yet theirs was the easier situation since the Czech elites considered the Czechoslovak state to be their own creation and, in addition, were 'relieved' of significant national tensions after World War II, when the sizeable German minority was expelled from the state on the basis of a commonly adjudged complicity with the Nazi regime. After the split of Czechoslovakia in 1992, this made the Czech Republic one of the most homogeneous countries in the region, with relatively well established traditions and myths of statehood and nationhood, reinforced by the elite and exemplified by the citizens' and elites' strong identification with democracy in the First Republic.[9] The Czech Republic and its elite considered themselves from the outset as the successor to the Czechoslovak state, primarily adjusting itself to the changed reality (i.e. changing from a federal into a unitary state). Slovakia, in contrast, emerged as a state without a sustained historical experience of statehood. The institutional framework had to be built from scratch, the state's international position was far from clear. Moreover, the country also inherited a large and politically mobilized Hungarian minority (about 11 percent of the population), geographically concentrated in the border area with the 'guardian' Hungarian state - a state associated in Slovakia with a long history of national oppression. All these 'structurally embedded' problems created a perfect 'political opportunity structure' for the skillful populist Mečiar, whose polarizing power politics gradually led Slovakia away from the path of democratic consolidation.

Implications

Our arguments have two major implications. The first one is that the Czech Republic is very unlikely to regress into the pattern of elite and party competition typical for contemporary Slovakia, because there is little such regressive potential either at the mass level or in historical circumstances for the elites to exploit. The republic's relative ethnic homogeneity, together with (perceived) established traditions of statehood and nationhood, are primary reasons for this optimism. Czech elites would have to exert a great deal of political skill and activity to reopen issues which are largely considered settled. The processes of European integration looming on the horizon may possibly reopen issues of national identity and sovereignty, offering further opportunity to test these propositions, for the first time since the split of Czechoslovakia at the end of 1992. But at the moment, the case of the Czech Republic clearly shows that states which are both ethnically and culturally homogeneous, and which lack a significant external national problem (e.g. a sizeable active minority living outside its borders), provide more favorable conditions for the establishment of democracy - a point already emphasized in Rustow's 1970 seminal article on transitions.

Therefore, we suggest that there is possibly a hierarchy of conflicts, and that those democratizing countries where the state-and nation-building processes are not solved or, as in the case of Slovakia, overlap in practical politics, are less likely to successfully consolidate their emerging democratic systems. This is not to say that social and political conflicts centered around redistributive issues, i.e. socioeconomic dimension, are less divisive: the modern history of countries like Austria teaches us that class conflicts too can assume a strongly divisive and democracy endangering character. But the imminent danger of conflicts over "who we are" (Offe, 1991), and who should constitute the political community by having the right of citizenship, lies in these conflicts' propensity to fuse with other conflicts over the basic rules and procedures of the game. Such a fusion renders institutional settings vulnerable to political interventions and engineering and, ultimately, undermines one of the crucial elements of democratic consolidation and parliamentary institutionalization.

The second important implication is that Slovakia is not doomed to failure because there is relatively little, especially on the mass level, which holds the current pattern together. In other words, there is nothing inevitable about the Slovak path of democratization, and any fatalistic predictions based on the belief in Slovakia's backwardness, cultural inferiority, or fundamental lack in modernization are misplaced. This may be why, in so much contemporary writing on democratization in the region, Slovakia is considered as a sort of uneasy 'borderline case'. It is striking that the Slovak case is characterized by a relatively mild conflict on the mass level, and a severe and fundamental conflict on the party-elite level. This suggests that Slovak elites indeed "failed the people" (Szomolányi, 1997), at least in that the uncompromising and damaging character of party/elites conflict has largely been in contradiction with the absence of sharpness or polarization among those who elect these elites.

Fortunately, the events that occurred shortly before this book was completed give rise to some optimism. It is possible to argue that a significant victory scored by the anti-Mečiar opposition in the 1998 elections might bring Slovakia back onto its earlier path of democratic consolidation. If anything, Mečiar's electoral defeat indicates that he was unable to adapt the 'political opportunity structure' in a way that would enable his party to consolidate a permanent monopoly. Obviously, the processes of state- and nation-building in Slovakia are not completed yet. A great deal of skillful leadership and negotiating will be needed to offset some of the negative effects of previous years of political polarization and to ensure that the opposition's victory is not merely a further turn of the wheel. However, because Slovakia's troubles are less the result of deep problems with its (mass) political culture or socioeconomic modernity, than the result of distinct challenges of state- and nation-building, there is a clear hope for the future. As the country moves further from the communist regime (and the Federation), and as a new generation of voters and political activists who have not experienced anything but the new Slovak state come to politics, the intital anxieties are disappearing. Mobilization tactics based on "the 'threats' to the nation" (Fischer, 1999) do not seem to be anymore as successful as they had been in previous years.

In the most general sense, then, the comparison of political processes in the Czech and Slovak Republics, together with the explanation we put forward to explain their diversity, feeds directly into attempts to build a coherent and broad understanding of the complex relationships between state- and nation-building and processes of democratic consolidation. These processes now increasingly feature as part of the explanations for the diversity of outcomes in Eastern Europe's democratization (see Linz and Stepan 1996; Snyder and Vachudová, 1997); yet, for various reasons, this remains perhaps the least developed theoretical perspective, especially in the comparative literature dealing with East-Central Europe (see Kopecký and Mudde, 2000). There is a need for a comparative study of post-communist countries which face significant problems of state- and nation-building, and which differ in their degree of democratic consolidation. Slovakia can provide the case of a country where such circumstances led to a slowing down of democratic consolidation. Perhaps most importantly, Slovakia is also a reminder of the complexity of these processes. For the country's crisis has evidently been a crisis of a new state (state-building), rather only natural translation of its allegedly strong 'ethnic cleavage' (nation-building).

Furthermore, the analysis of the Czech and Slovak Republics clearly underscores the importance of elites in the political process in general, and during the democratization processes in particular. Our study speaks volumes for Sartori's (1976) general observation which links structuring of party systems to endogenous preferences and actions of parties, rather than only to exogenously induced societal structures (see also Lipset and Rokkan, 1967; Mair, 1997b). Indeed, even if often criticized for their inability to produce a coherent theory or testable hypotheses, democratization theories which emphasize strategic choices and leadership processes (i.e. the Latin American and Southern European 'transitology' and 'consolidology') are built on precisely these assumptions of elite and political autonomy. By doing so, they point to the real possibility that conflicts that dominate in a given polity may derive from the interests and behavior of those engaged in political competition, rather than only from objective social conditions.

However, our analysis also suggests that we need better conceptual tools to reveal the complexity of interactions between structures, institutions and agents in order to fully appreciate their relative explanatory weight. Behavior of elites cannot properly be understood without the context in which these actors develop their political strategies. Institutions cannot properly be understood without the context in which they are crafted and put into work. Our comparison of Czech and Slovak Republics suggests one such single contextual variable - incomplete processes of state- and nation-building. Given the turbulent history of ethnonational conflicts and regime changes in the region, this may well be a contextual variable that is highly relevant only for the analysis of post-communist democratization. But the strength with which it asserted itself in shaping the path of democratization in the Czech and Slovak Republics, particularly in the phase of consolidation, suggests that social and cultural structures, like identities and habits, or the shape of formal and informal institutional structures within which democratization starts, matter a great deal for the long-term success of transformation.

Table 7.1: Parliamentary Institutionalization and Democratic Consolidation in the Czech and Slovak Republics

	Czech Republic	Slovakia
parliamentary institutionalization	party government context; parliamentary processes driven by moderate majority rule; mix of complementary formal and informal rules effects developed and reproducible organizational pattern; relatively high degree of institutionalization	party government context; parliamentary processes driven by strong majority rule; informal rules prevail over formal, vulnerable and irregular organizational pattern; low degree of institutionalization
democratic consolidation	consolidated democracy; respected and developed system of horizontal and vertical accountability between institutions; rules of the game settled; moderate elite conflict;	unconsolidated democracy; elementary vertical accountability respected, but horizontal accountability between institutions poor; rules of the game subject of violations and sharp political battle; high level of elite conflict;
explanations	complex interaction between structures, institutions and agents; complete process of state and nation-building: moderate level of elite and party system system competition revolves around principles of economic redistribution;	complex interaction between structures, institutions and agents; ongoing simultaneous process of state and nation building: sharp level of elite and party system competition revolves around meaning of Slovak independence, norms of democracy and participation;

Notes

1. See *European Council in Copenhagen* (1993).

2. Note that studies that focused on the first democratic parliaments in Eastern Europe consider parliamentary party fragmentation largely in terms of their organizational weakness and immaturity (see Ágh, 1995; Olson, 1997).

3. Slovakia has often been criticized and labelled an unconsolidated democracy because of the attempts of Mečiar's ruling elite to exercise an iron grip on the country's media. The changes in the personnel of the Slovak Councils for Radio and Television Broadcasting, and their replacement with the party symphatizers of the government after the 1994 elections, received particular attention by observers. However, this should not obscure the fact that, despite these and other attempts of various post-communist governments in Slovakia to subordinate state media to their own advantage, a good deal of freedom and independent TV, radio and press exists, and these attempts at subordination or control are by no means specific to Slovakia (see Školkay, 1997).

4. The position of the Communists and the Republicans is a partial exception here, because both parties have been considered by the rest of parliamentary representation as "anti-system opposition". However, while this categorically excluded both parties from potential government coalitions or regular consultative meetings with the president, it did not exclude them from participation in parliamentary committees, investigatory commissions, question times, or even intra-parliamentary party negotiations.

5. The exchanges between Klaus and Havel are the best known embodiment of the continuos battle over the character of civil society in the Czech Republic. Klaus, echoing the well-known arguments of Mancur Olson, equates civil society with the rise of new bureaucracies and particularistic (as opposed to general and aggregated) interests, as a threat to the smooth functioning of modern states and markets. Havel, on the other hand, believes in the positive effects of associational life in general, defending civil society as a means to strengthen people's participation in government, as well as a means to control it. See Havel, Klaus and Pithart (1996).

6. However, institutions are also subject to purposive action, thus acting as dependent variables. It can be argued that the emphasis laid on institutions among the proponents of elite orientated democratization theories stems precisely from their pre-occupation with rules of the game and the shape of institutions which emerge during and shortly after the period of authoritarian breakdown. These institutions embody purposive action of elites involved in transitions.

7. It should be noted, though, that the post-Meciar period has shown that Slovakia's economy is in a worse state than originally thought. However, the same is true of the post-Klaus Czech economy. See the various reports in *Business Central Europe*, most notably November 1998 (survey on the Czech Republic) and May 1999 (survey on Slovakia).

8. For the relationship between the processes of state-building and nation-building see (Linz, 1993).

9. It should be noted, though, that the presence of Moravian parties (HSD-SMS and its splinter groups) in the Czech parliaments until the 1996 elections, demanding greater autonomy for this historical region of the country, provides a ground to suggest that also the Czech Republic might not have been spared of national and identity related tensions. The fact that latent Moravian sentiments were not mobilized into a politically divisive issue can be attributed to the organizational weakness of parties which tried to do so, as well as to the skilful overtaking (and defusing) of this issue by the established parties, such as KDU-ČSL.

Appendix: Survey Information

Aggregate Sampling and Response Information

	Czech Republic	Slovak Republic
original population	200	150
research population (excl. ministers)	194	150
sample	-	100
response (#)	168	97
response (% of sample)	-	97%
response (% of research population)	87%	65%

Sampling and Response Information in Slovakia

Slovakia	Seats		Sample		Interviews		
party	#	%	#	%	#	% of sample	% of population
KDH	18	12.00	15	15.00	15	100.00	83.33
HZDS	66	44.00	37	37.00	37	100.00	56.06
KNP	8	5.33	6	6.00	6	100.00	75.00
SDL	28	18.67	20	20.00	20	100.00	71.43
MKDH	5	3.38	4	4.00	4	88.33	80.00
Spoluzitie	9	6.00	6	6.00	5	83.33	55.56
SNS	15	10.00	12	12.00	10	-	66.67
independent	1	0.67	-	0.00	-		0.00
Total	150	100.00	100	100.00	97	97.00	64.67

Fieldwork

	first interview	last interview
Czech Republic	September 1993	December 1993
Slovakia	November 1993	March 1994

Length of interviews (in minutes)

	average	longest	shortest
Czech Republic	51	115	20
Slovakia	44	75	20

Bibliography

Ágh, Attila (1993). "The 'Comparative Revolution' and the Transition in Central and Southern Europe", *Journal of Theoretical Politics*, 5(2), 231-252.

Ágh, Attila (1995). "The Experience of the First Democratic Parliaments in East Central Europe", *Communist and Post-Communist Studies*, 28(2), 203-214.

Ágh, Attila (1996). "The End of the Beginning: The Partial Consolidation of East Central European Parties and Party Systems", *Budapest Papers on Democratic Transition*, No. 156 (Budapest: University of Economics).

Almond, Gabriel and Sidney Verba (1963). *The Civic Culture* (Boston: Little Brown).

Andeweg, Rudy B. (1992). "Executive-Legislative Relations in the Netherlands: Consecutive and Coexisting Patterns", *Legislative Studies Quarterly*, 17, 161-182.

Andeweg, Rudy (1997). "Role Specialisation or Role Switching? Dutch MPs between Electorate and Executive", *The Journal of Legislative Studies*, 3(1), 110-127.

Andeweg, Rudy B. and Lia Nijzink (1995). "Beyond the Two Body Image: Relations between Ministers and MPs", in Herbert Doring (ed.), *Parliaments and Majority Rule in Western Europe* (Frankfurt: Campus-Verlag), 152-178.

Baerwald, Hans H. (1979). "Committees in Japanese Diet", in John D. Lees and Malcolm Shaw (eds.), *Committees in Legislatures: A Comparative Analysis* (Durham: Duke University Press), 327-360.

Bale, Tim and Petr Kopecký (1998). "Can Young Pups Teach an Old Dog New Tricks? Lessons for British Reformers from Eastern Europe's New Constitutional Democracies", *The Journal of Legislative Studies*, 4(2), 149-169.

Bartolini, Stefano (1983). "The Membership of Mass Parties: The Social Democratic Experience, 1889-1978", in Hans Daalder and Peter Mair (eds), *Western European Party Systems: Continuity and Change* (London: Sage), 177-220.

Baylis, Thomas A. (1996). "Presidents versus Prime Ministers: Shaping Executive Authority in Eastern Europe", *World Politics*, 28(3), 297-323.

Beneš, Václav L. (1973). "Czechoslovak Democracy and its Problems 1918-1920", in Victor S. Mamatey and Radomír Luža (eds.), *A History of the Czechoslovak Republic 1918-1948* (Princeton: Princeton University Press), 39-98.

Biezen, Ingrid van (2000). *The Development of Party Organizations in New Democracies: Southern and Eastern Europe* (PhD Thesis, Leiden University, forthcoming).

Bogdanor, Vernon, ed., (1985). *Representatives of the People? Parliamentarians and Constituents in Western Democracies* (Aldershot: Gower).

Bogdanor, Vernon (1992). "The problem of the Upper House", in Hans W. Blom, Wim P. Blockman s and Hugo de Schepper (eds.), *Bicameralisme: Tweekamerstelsel vroeger en nu* ('s-Gravenhage: Sdu Uitgeverij Koninginnegracht), 411-422.

Brokl, Lubomír (1992). "Mezi listopadem 1989 a demokracií: antinomie naší politiky", *Czech Sociological Review*, 28(2), 150-164.

Brokl, Lubomír and Zdenka Mansfeldová (1994). "The Czech Republic", Political Data Yearbook 1994, *European Journal of Political Research*, 26 (3/4), 269-277.

Broklová, Eva (1992). *Československá Demokracie: Politický Systém ČSR 1918-1938* (Praha: Slon).

Bunce, Valeria (1995a). "Comparing East and South", *Journal of Democracy* 6 (3), 87-100

Bunce, Valeria (1995b). "Should Transitologists Be Grounded?", *Slavic Review* 54 (1), 111-127.

Burton, Michael, Richard Gunther and John Higley (1992). "Introduction: Elite Transformations and Democratic Regimes", in John Higley and Richard Gunther (eds.), *Elites and Democratic Consolidation in Latin America and Southern Europe* (Cambridge: Cambridge University Press), 1-37.

Bútorová, Zora (1993). "Premyslené 'ano' zániku ČSFR?", *Sociologický Časopis*, 29(1), 88-103.

Calda, Miloš (1996). "The Roundtable Talks in Czechoslovakia", in Jon Elster (ed.), *The Roundtable Talks and the Breakdown of Communism* (Chicago: University of Chicago Press), 135-177.

Calda, Miloš and Mark Gillis (1995). "Czech Republic: Is Legislative Illegitimacy the Price of Political Effectivness?", *East European Constitutional Review*, 4(2), 67-70.

Carpenter, Michael (1997). "Slovakia and the Triumph of Nationalist Populism", *Communist and Post-Communist Studies*, 30 (2), 205-220.

Cigánek, František et.al (1992). *Kronika demokratického parlamentu* (Prague: Cesty).

Collier, David and Steve Levitsky (1997). "Democracy with Adjectives: Conceptual Innovation in Comparative Research", *World Politics*, 49(April), 403-451.

Close, David, ed., (1995). *Legislatures and the New Democracies in Latin America* (Boulder: Lynne Rienner Publishers).

Comisso, Ellen (1997). Is the Glass Half Full or Half Empty? Reflections on Five Years of Competitive Politics in Eastern Europe", *Communist and Post-Communist Studies*, 30 (1),1-21.

Cox, Gary W. and Mathew D. McCubbins (1993). *Legislative Leviathan: Party Government in the House* (Berkeley: University of California Press).

Dahl, Robert (1971). *Polyarchy: Participation and Opposition* (New Haven: Yale University Press).

Damgaard, Erik, ed., (1994). *Parliamentary Change in the Nordic Countries* (Oslo: Scandinavian University Press).

Damgaard, Erik (1995). "How Parties Control Committee Members", in Herbert Doring (ed.), *Parliaments and Majority Rule in Western Europe* (Frankfurt: Campus-Verlag), 308-325.

Dellenbrant, Jan Ake (1993). "Parties and Party Systems in Eastern Europe", in Stephen White, Judy Batt and Paul G. Lewis (eds.), *Developments in East European Politics* (London: MacMillan Press), 147-162.

Diamandouros, P. Nikiforos, Hans-Jürgen Puhle and Richard Gunther (1995). "Conclusion" in: Richard Gunther, P. Nikiforos Diamandouros and Hans-Jürgen Puhle (eds.), *The Politics of Democratic Consolidation: Southern Europe in Comparative Perspective* (Baltimore: The Johns Hopkins University Press), 389-414.

Di Palma, Giuseppe (1990a). *To Craft Democracies. An Essay on Democratic Transition* (Berkeley: University of California Press).

Di Palma, Giuseppe (1990b). "Parliaments, Consolidation, Institutionalization: A Minimalist View", in Ulrike Liebert and Maurizio Cotta (eds.), *Parliament and Democratic Consolidation in Southern Europe: Greece, Italy, Portugal, Spain and Turkey* (London: Pinter Publishers), 31-51.

D'Onofrio, Francesco (1979). "Committees in the Italian Parliament", in John D. Lees and Malcolm Shaw (eds.), *Committees in Legislatures: A Comparative Analysis* (Durham: Duke University Press), 61-101.

Dvořáková, Vladimíra and Jiří Kunc (1992). *O přechodech k demokracii* (Prague: Slon).

Ehlau, Heinz and John C. Wahlke (1959). "The Role of the Representative: Some Empirical Observations on the Theory of Edmund Burke", *American Political Science Review*, 53 (September), 742-756.

Elster, Jon (1995). "Transition, Constitution-Making and Separation of Czechoslovakia", *European Journal of Sociology*, 36, 105-134.

Elster, Jon, Claus Offe and Ulrich K. Preuss (1998). *Institutional Design in Post-Communist Democracies: Rebuilding the Ship at Sea* (Cambridge: Cambridge University Press).

Evans, Geoffrey and Stephen Whitefield (1998). "The Structuring of Political Cleavages in Post-Communist Societies: the Case of the Czech Republic and Slovakia", *Political Studies*, 46 (1), 115-139.

Flores Juberías, Carlos (1992). "The Breakdown of the Czecho-Slovak Party System", in Györgi Szoboszlai (ed.), *Flying Blind. Emergind Democracies in East-Central Europe* (Budapest: Hungarian Political Science Association), 147-176.

Fisher, Sharon (1995). Kidnapping Case Continues to Complicate Political Scene", *Transition*, 2(13), 40-43/64.

Fisher, Sharon (1999) "Strengthening National Identity: The Politics of Language and Culture in Post-Independence Slovakia and Croatia", paper presented at the 4th Annual ASN Convention, New York, 15-17 April 1999.

Frye, Timothy M. (1992). "Ethnicity, Sovereignty and Transitions from Non-Democratic Rule", *Journal of International Affairs*, 45(2), 599-623.

Gallacher, Michael and Michael Marsh, eds., (1988). *Candidate Selection in Comparative Perspective: Secret Garden of Politics* (London: Sage).

Gastil, Raymond D. (ed.) (1994). *Freedom in the World: Political Rights and Civil Liberties, 1993-1994* (New York: Freedom House).

Geddes, Barbara (1995). "A Comparative Perspective on the Leninist Legacy in Eastern Europe", *Comparative Political Studies*, 28(2), 239-274.

Gerlich, Peter (1973). "The Institutionalization of European Parliaments", in Allan Kornberg (eds.), *Legislatures in Comparative Perspective* (New York: David McKay Company), 94-111.

Gould, John A. and Soňa Szomolányi (1998). "Elite Fragmentation, Industry and the Prospects for Democracy: Insights from New Elite Theory", in John A. Gould and Soňa Szomolányi (eds.). *Slovakia: Problems of Democratic Consolidation and the Struggle for the Rules of the Game.* (www.cc.columbia.edu/sec/dlc/ciao/ book/gould21.html).

Green, Andrew T. and Carol Skalnik Leff (1997). "The Quality of Democracy: Mass-Elite Linkages in the Czech Republic", *Democratization* 4 (4), 63-87.

Havel, Václav (1992). *Vážení občané: Projevy červenec 1990 - červenec 1992* (Prague: Lidové noviny).

Havel, Václav, Václav Klaus and Petr Pithart (1996). "Civil Society After Communism: Rival Visions I", *Journal of Democracy*, 7(1), 12-23.

Hibbing, John R. (1988). "Legislative Institutionalization with Illustrations from the British House of Commons, *American Journal of Political Science*, 32(4), 681-712.

Hibbing, John R. and Samuel C. Patterson (1994). "Public Trust in the New Parliaments of Central and Eastern Europe", *Political Studies*, 42(4), 570-592.

Henderson, Karen (1995). "Czechoslovakia: The Failure of Consensus Politics and the Break-up of the Federation", *Regional and Federal Studies*, 5(2), 111-133.

Herzmann, Jan (1992). "Volby v kontextu vývoje veřejneho mínení 1989-1991", *Czech Sociological Review*, 28(2), 165-183.

Holmes, Stephen (1993/1994). "The Postcommunist Presidency", *East European Constitutional Review*, 2+3(4+1), 36-39.

Hopkin, Jonathan (1995). "The Institutionalisation of New Political Parties: A Framework for Analysis", *Muirhead Papers*, No. 9, University of Birmingham.

Huber, John and Ronald Inglehart (1995). Expert Interpretations of Party Space and Party Locations in 42 Societies", *Party Politics*, 1(1), 73-111.

Huntington, Samuel (1968). *Political Order in Changing Societies* (New Haven: Yale University Press).

Huntington, Samuel (1991). *The Third Wave: Democratization in the Late Twentieth Century* (Norman: University of Oklahoma Press).

Ilonszki, Gabriella (1996). "From Marginal to Rational Parliaments: A Central European Regional View", in Attila Ágh and Gabriella Ilonszki (eds.), *Parliaments and Organized Interests: The Second Steps* (Budapest: Hungarian Centre For Democracy Studies).

Jičínský, Zdeněk (1993). *Československý parlament v polistopadovém vývoji* (Praha: NADAS-AFGH)

Jičínský, Zdeněk (1995). "Československý parlament v letech 1990-1992", *Politologická Revue*, 1(June), 3-12.

Jičínský, Zdeněk and Jan Škaloud (1996). "Transformace politického systému k - demokracii", in Vlasta Šafaříková et. al (ed.), *Transformace České společnosti 1989-1995* (Praha: Doplněk), 50-113.

Jepperson, Ronald L.(1991). "Institutions, Institutional Effects, and Institutionalism", in Walter W. Powell and Paul J. DiMaggio (eds.), *The New Institutionalism in Organizational Analysis* (Chicago: Chicago University Press), 143-163.

Jørgensen, Knud Erik (1992). "The End of Anti-politics in Central Europe", in Paul G. Lewis (ed.), *Democracy and Civil Society in Eastern Europe* (London: MacMillan Press), 32-60.

Jowitt, Ken (1992). *The New World Disorder: The Leninist Extinction* (Berkeley: University of California Press).

Karatnycky, Adrian (1997). "Freedom on the March", *Freedom Review*, 28 (1), 5-29.

Katz, Richard S. (1990). "Party as Linkage: A Vestigial Function?", *European Journal of Political Research*, 18, 143-161.

Katz, Richard S. (1986). "Party Government: A Rationalistic Conception", in Francis G. Castles and Rudolf Wildenmann (eds.), *The Future of Party Government: Visions and Realities of Party Government* (Firenze: European University Institute), 31-71.

Katz, Richard S. and Peter Mair (1994). "The Evolution of Party Organizations in Europe: Three Faces of Party Organization", *American Review of Politics*, 14 (Winter), 593-617.

Katz, Richard S. and Peter Mair (1995). "Changing Models of Party Organisations and Party Democracy: The Emergence of the Cartel Party", *Party Politics*, 1(1), 5-28.

King, Anthony (1976). "Modes of Executive-Legislative Relations: Great Britain, France and West Germany", *Legislative Studies Quarterly*, 1(1), 11-36.

Kitschelt, Herbert (1992). "Political Regime Change: Structure and Process-Driven Explanations?", *American Political Science Review*, 86(4), 1028-1034.

Kitschelt, Herbert (1994). "Party Systems in East Central Europe: Consolidation or Fluidity". Paper presented at the 1994 annual APSA meeting, New York, 1-4 September.

Klaus, Václav (1994). "Novoroční projev v Praze dne 1. ledna 1993", in Lubomír Brokl *et al* (ed.), *Česká Republika v roce 1993* (Praha: Sociologický ústav), 71-74.

Kopecký, Petr (1995a). "Developing Party Organizations in East-Central Europe: What Type of Party is Likely to Emerge?", *Party Politics*, 1(4), 515-534.

Kopecký, Petr (1995b). "Factionalism in Parliamentary Parties and Democratization in the Czech Republic: A Concept and Some Empirical Findings", *Democratization*, 2(1), 138-151.

Kopecký, Petr (1996). "The Organization and Behaviour of Political Parties in the Czech Parliament: From Transformative Towards Arena Type of Legislature", in Paul G. Lewis (ed.), *Party Structure and Organization in East-Central Europe* (Aldershot: Edward Elgar), 66-88.

Kopecký, Petr (2000). "From 'Velvet Revolution' to Velvet Split: Consociational Institutions and the Disintegration of Czechoslovakia", in Michael Kraus and Allison K. Stanger (eds.), *Irreconcilable Differences? Explaining Czechoslovakia's Dissolution*. (Lanham: Rowman and Littlefield), 69-86.

Kopecký, Petr (2001). "Building Party Government: Political Parties in the Czech and Slovak Republics", in Paul Webb and Stephen White (eds.), *Political Parties in New Democracies* (Oxford: Oxford University Press, forthcoming).

Kopecký, Petr, Pavel Hubáček and Petr Plecitý (1996). "Politické strany v českém parlamentu (1992-1996): organizace, chování a vliv", *Czech Sociological Review*, 32(4), 439-456.

Kopecký, Petr and Edward Barnfield (1999). "Charting the Decline of Civil Society: Explaining the Changing Roles and Conceptions of Civil Society in East Central Europe", in Jean Grugel (ed.), *Democracy Without Borders: Transnationalization and Conditionality in New Democracies* (London: Routledge), 76-91.

Kopecký, Petr and Cas Mudde (2000). "What Has Eastern Europe Taught us About the Democratisation Literature (and vice versa)?", *European Journal of Political Research*, 37(4), 517-539.

Kornberg, Allan and Lloyd D. Musolf (1972). "On Legislatures in Developmental Perspective", in Allan Kornberg and Lloyd D. Musolf (eds.), *Legislatures in Developmental Perspective* (Durham: Duke University Press), 3-32.

Kroupa, Aleš and Tomáš Kostelecký (1996). "Party Organization and Structure at National and Local Level in the Czech Republic Since 1989", in Paul G. Lewis (ed.), *Party Structure and Organization in East-Central Europe* (Aldershot: Edward Elgar), 89-119.

Krause, Kevin (1996a). "Dimensions of Party Competition in Slovakia", *Slovak Sociological Review* 1, 169-186.

Krause, Kevin (1996b). "The Political Party System in the Czech Republic: Democracy and the 1996 Elections", *Czech Sociological Review*, 32 (4), 423-438.

Krause, Kevin (1997). "Different but not *that* Different", on *www.nd.edu/~kkrause/papers*.

Krause, Kevin (1998). "Democracy and the Political Party Systems of Slovakia and the Czech Republic", on *www.nd.edu/~kkrause/papers*.

Krejčí, Oskar (1994). *Kniha o volbách* (Prague: Victoria Publishing).

Kresák, Peter (1994). The Regulation of Mutual Relations between the National Council of the Slovak republic and the Government in the Constitution of the Slovak Republic", in Irena Grudzinska Gross (ed.), *Constitutionalism and Politics* (Bratislava: European Cutural Foundation), 320-323.

Krivý, Vladimír (1993). "Slovenská a česká definícia situace", *Sociologický Časopis*, 29(1), 73-87.

Kusý, Miroslav (1995). "Slovak Exceptionalism", in Jiří Musil (ed.). *The End of Czechoslovakia* (Budapest: CEU Press), 139-155.

Lafranchi, Prisca and Ruth Lüthi (1995). "Cohesion of Party Groups and Interparty Conflict in the Swiss Parliament: Roll Call Voting in the National Council", paper presented at the ECPR Joint Sessions, Bordeaux.

Leško, Marian (1996). *Mečiar a Mečiarizmus* (Bratislava: VMV).

Lewis, Paul G. (1995). "Poland and Eastern Europe: Perspectives on Party Factions and Factionalism", *Democratization*, 2(1), 102-124.

Lewis, Paul G. (1997). "Theories of Democratization and Patterns of Regime Change in Eastern Europe", *Journal of Communist Studies and Transition Politics*, 13 (1), 4-26.

Lewis, Paul G. and Radzislawa Gortat (1995). "Models of Party Development and Questions of State Dependence in Poland", *Party Politics*, 1(4), 599-608.

Liebert, Ulrike (1990). "Parliament as a Central Site in Democratic Consolidation: A Preliminary Exploration", in Ulrike Liebert and Maurizio Cotta (eds.), *Parliament and Democratic Consolidation in Southern Europe: Greece, Italy, Portugal, Spain and Turkey* (London: Pinter Publishers), 3-30.

Lijphart, Arend (1977). *Democracy in Plural Societies: A Comparative Exploration* (New Haven: Yale University Press).

Lijphart, Arend (1990). *Parliamentary versus Presidential Government* (Oxford: Oxford University Press).

Lijphart, Arend (1992). "Democratization and Constitutional Choices in Czechoslovakia, Hungary and Poland: 1989-1991", *Journal of Theoretical Politics*, 4(2), 207-223.

Lijphart, Arend (1994). *Electoral Systems and Party Systems: A Study of Twenty-Seven Democracies 1945-1990* (Oxford: Oxford University Press).

Lijphart, Arend and Carlos C. Waisman, eds., (1996). *Institutional Design in New Democracies. Eastern Europe and Latin America* (Boulder: Westview Press).

Linz, Juan J. (1990). "Transitions to Democracy", *The Washington Quarterly*, 13(3), 143-164.

Linz, Juan J. (1993). "State Building and Nation Building", *European Review*, 1(4): 355-369.

Linz, Juan J. (1994). "Presidential or Parliamentary Democracy: Does it Make a Difference?", in Juan J. Linz and Arturo Valenzuela (eds.), *The Failure of Presidential Democracy: Comparative Perspectives*, Volume 1 (Baltimore: The John Hopkins University Press), 3-90.

Linz, Juan and Alfred Stepan (1996). *Problems of Democratic Transition and Consolidation: Southern Europe, South America, and Post-Communist Europe* (Baltimore: Johns Hopkins University Press).

Lipset, Seymour Martin (1960). *Political Man: The Social Basis of Politics* (London: Heinemann).

Lipset, Seymour M. and Stein Rokkan (1967). "Cleavage Structures, Party Systems and Voter Alignments: An Introduction", in Seymour M. Lipset and Stein Rokkan (eds), *Party Systems and Voter Alignments* (New York: The Free Press), 1-63.

Lipset, Seymour Martin, Seong Kyoung-Ryung and John Charles Torres (1993). "A Comparative Analysis of the Social Requisites of Democracy", *International Social Science Journal*, 136, 155-175.

Loewenberg, Gerhard and Samuel C. Patterson (1979). *Comparing Legislatures* (Boston: Little Brown).

Longley, Lawrence D. (1996). "Parliaments as Changing Institutions and as Agents of Regime Change: Evolving Perspectives and a New Research Framework", *The Journal of Legislative Studies*, 2(2), 22-44.

Machonin, Petr (1992). "Česko-Slovenské vztahy ve světle dat sociologického výzkumu", in Fedor Gál et al (eds.), *Dnešní Krize Česko-Slovenských Vztahů* (Praha: Slon), 73-87.

Mainwaring, Scott (1992). "Transitions to Democracy and Democratic Consolidation: Theoretical and Comparative Issues", in Scott Mainwaring, Guillermo O'Donnell and J. Samuel Valenzuela (eds.), *Issues in Democratic Consolidation: The New South American Democracies in Comparative Perspective* (Notre Dame: University of Notre Dame Press), 294-341.

Mainwaring, Scott and Timothy R. Scully (1995). *Building Democratic Institutions: Party Systems in Latin America* (Stanford: Stanford University Press).

Mair, Peter (1990). "Electoral Payoffs of Fission and Fusion", *British Journal of Political Science*, 1(3), 251-276.

Mair, Peter (1991). "Electoral Markets and Stable States", in Michael Moran and Maurice Wright (eds.), *The Market and the State* (London: MacMillan), 119-136.

Mair, Peter (1994). "Party Organizations: From Civil Society to the State", in Richard S. Katz and Peter Mair (eds), *How Parties Organize: Change and Adaptation in Party Organizations in Western Democracies* (London: Sage), 1-22.

Mair, Peter (1997a). Party System Change: *Approaches and Interpretations* (Oxford: Oxford University Press).

Mair, Peter (1997b). "E.E. Schattschneider's The Semisovereign People", *Political Studies*, 45(5), 947-954.

Malová, Darina (1993) "Effect of Cultural Factors on the Promotion of the Relations of the Czech and Slovaks", in Dušan Kováč (ed.), *History and Politics* (Bratislava: Czecho-Slovak Committee of the European Cultural Foundation), 129-134.

Malová, Darina (1994a). "Constitutionalism in Postcommunist Transition: Self-Limiting Activities of the State", in Irena Grudzinska Gross (ed.), *Constitutionalism and Politics* (Bratislava: European Cutural Foundation), 339-349.

Malová, Darina (1994b). "The Relationship between the State, Political Parties and Civil Society in Postcommunist Czecho-Slovakia: Initial Patterns of the Transition", in Soňa Szomolányi and Grigorij Mesežnikov (eds.), *The Slovak Path of Transition to Democracy?* (Bratislava: Slovak Political Science Association), 111-158.

Malová, Darina (1995a). "Parliamentary Rules and Legislative Dominance", *East European Constitutional Review*, 4(2).

Malová, Darina (1995b). "The Development of Hungarian Political Parties during the Three Election Cycles (1990-1994) in Slovakia", in Soňa Szomolányi and Grigorij Mesežnikov (eds.), *Slovakia: Parliamentary Elections 1994* (Bratislava: Slovak Political Science Association), 200-219.

Malová, Darina (1997). "The Development of Interest Representation in Slovakia After 1989: From 'Transmission Belts' to 'Party-State Corporatism'", in Soňa Szomolányi and John A. Gould (eds.). *Slovakia: Problems of Democratic Consolidation and the Struggle for the Rules of the Game*. Bratislava: Slovak Political Science Association, 93-112.

Malová, Darina (1998). "Slovakia: From the Assertion of Informal Institutional Rules to Violations of the Constitution ", unpublished paper, Robert Schuman Centre, European University Institute, Florence.

Malová, Darina and Kevin Krause (1996). "Parliamentary Party Groups in Slovakia", paper presented at the ECPR Joint Sessions, Oslo.

Malová, Darina and Danica Siváková (1996). "The National Council of the Slovak Republic: Between Democratic Transition and National State-Building", *The Journal of Legislative Studies*, 2(1), 108-132.

Mamatey Victor S. and Radomír Luža (eds.) *A History of the Czechoslovak Republic 1918-1948* (Princeton: Princeton University Press).

Mansfeldová, Zdenka (1996). "Tripartita jako model prostředkování zájmu v politickem systemu České Republiky", *Working Paper 96:5* (Prague: Institute of Sociology of the Czech Academy of Sciences).

Mansfeldová, Zdenka (1998). "Zivilgesellschaft in der Tschechischen und Slowakischen Republik", *Aus Politik und Zeitgeschichte*, B 6-7: 13-19.

Markowski, Radoslaw (1997). "Political Parties and Ideological Spaces in East Central Europe", *Communist and Post-Communist Studies,* 30 (3), 221-254.

Mathernová, Katherina (1993). "Czecho?Slovakia: Constitutional Disappointments", in A.E.D. Howard (ed.), *Constitution Making in Eastern Europe* (Washington: Woodrow Wilson Center Press), 57-91.

Mattson, Ingvar and Kaare Strøm (1995). "Parliamentary Committees", in Herbert Doring (ed.), *Parliaments and Majority Rule in Western Europe* (Frankfurt: Campus-Verlag), 249-307.

Mendillow, Jonathan (1992). "Public Party Funding and Party Transformation in Multiparty Systems", *Comparative Political Studies*, 25(1), 90-117.

Mesežnikov, Grigorij (1997). "The Open Ended Formation of Slovakia's Party System", in Soňa Szomolányi and John A. Gould (eds.), *Slovakia: Problems of Democratic Consolidation and the Struggle for the Rules of the Game* (Bratislava: Slovak Political Science Association), 35-56.

Mikloš, Ivan (1997). "Economic Transition and the Emergence of Clientelist Structures in Slovakia", in Sona Szomolányi and John A Gould (eds.), in Soňa Szomolányi and John A Gould (eds.) *Slovakia: Problems of Democratic Consolidation and the Struggle for the Rules of the Game* (Bratislava: Slovak Political Science Association), 57-92.

Mikloš, Ivan and Eduard Žitňanský (1998). "The Economy", in Martin Bútora and Thomas W. Skladony (eds.). *Slovakia 1996-1997. A Global Report on the State of Society* (Bratislava: Institute for Public Affairs), 103-115.

Miller, William, Stephen White and Paul Heywood (1998). *Values and Political Change in Postcommunist Europe* (Houndmills: MacMillan Press).

Mishler, William and Richard Rose (1994). "Support for Parliaments and Regimes in the Transition Toward Democracy in Eastern Europe", *Legislative Studies Quarterly*, 19, 5-32.

Moore, Barrington Jr. (1965). *Social Origins of Dictatorship and Democracy* (Boston: Beacon).

Mudde, Cas (2000). "Extreme Right Parties in Eastern Europe", *Patterns of Prejudice*, 34(1), 5-28.

Munck, Gerardo L. (1994). "Democratic Transitions in Comparative Perspectives", *Comparative Politics*, 26(3), 355-375.

Munck, Gerardo and Carol Skalnik Leff (1997). "Modes of Transition and Democratization: South America and Eastern Europe in Comparative Perspective", *Comparative Politics*, 29 (3), 343-362.

Musil, Jiri (1993). "Czech and Slovak Society: Outline of a Comparative Study", *Czech Sociological Review* 1 (1), 5-21.

Müller, Wolfgang C. (1993a). "The Relevance of the State for Party System Change", *Journal of Theoretical Politics*, 5(4), 419-454.

Müller, Wolfgang C. (1993b). "Executive-Legislative Relations In Austria: 1945-1992", *Legislative Studies Quarterly*, 18, 467-494.

Nelson, Daniel (1982). "Communist Legislatures and Communist Politics", in Daniel Nelson and Stephen White (eds.), *Communist Legislatures in Comparative Perspective* (London: MacMillan Press), 1-13.

Norton, Philip (1990). "General Introduction", in Philip Norton (ed.), *Legislatures* (Oxford: Oxford University Press), 1-16.

Norton, Philip and David M. Olson (1996). "Parliaments in Adolescence", *The Journal of Legislative Studies*, 2(1), 231-243.

O'Donnell, Guillermo (1996). "Illusions about Consolidation", *Journal of Democracy*, 7(2), 34-51.

O'Donnell, Guillermo and Philippe C. Schmitter (1986). *Transitions from Authoritarian Rule: Tentative Conclusions about Uncertain Democracies* (Baltimore: John Hopkins University Press).

Offe, Claus (1991). "Capitalism by Democratic Design: Democratic Theory Facing Triple Transition in East Central Europe", *Social Research*, 58(4), 865-892.

Olson, David M. (1993a). "Dissolution of the State: Political Parties and the 1992 Election in Czechoslovakia", *Communist and Post-Communist Studies*, 26(3), 301-314.

Olson, David M. (1993b). "Political Parties and Party Systems in Regime Transformation: Inner Transition in the New Democracies of Central Europe", *The American Review of Politics*, 14 (Winter), 619-658.

Olson, David M. (1994a). "The Sundered State: Federalism and Parliament in Czechoslovakia", in Thomas Remington (ed.), *Parliaments in Transition* (Westview Press), 97-123.

Olson, David M. (1994b). "The New Parliaments of New Democracies: The Experience of the Federal Assembly of the Czech and Slovak Federal Republic", in Attila Ágh (ed.), *The Emergence of East Central European Parliaments: The First Steps* (Budapest: Hungarian Centre of Demoracy Studies Foundation), 35-47.

Olson, David M. (1997). "Paradoxes of Institutional Development: The New Democratic Parliaments of Central Europe", *International Political Science Review*, 18(4), 1997.

Özbudun, Ergun (1970). "Party Cohesion in Western Democracies: A Causal Analysis", *Sage Professional Papers in Comparative Politics*, Series 01, No.001 (Beverly Hills: Sage Publications), 303-388.

Özbudun, Ergun (1987). "Institutionalizing Competitive Elections in Developing Societies", in Myron Weiner and Ergun Özbudun (eds.), *Competitive Elections in Developing Countries* (AEI: Duke University Press), 393-422.

Packenham, Robert (1970). "Legislatures and Political Development", in Allan Kornberg and Lloyd D. Musolf (eds.), *Legislatures in Developmental Perspective* (Durham: Duke University Press), 521-582.

Padgett, Stephen (1996). "Parties in Post-Communist Society: the German Case", in Paul G. Lewis (ed), *Party Structure and Organization in East-Central Europe* (Aldershot: Edward Elgar), 163-186.

Panebianco, Angelo (1988). *Political Parties: Organization and Power* (Cambridge, Cambridge University Press).

Pehe, Jiří (1992a). "Czechs and Slovaks Define Postdivorce Relations", *RFE/RL Report*, 1(45), 7-11.

Pehe, Jiří (1992b). "Czechoslovak Parliament Votes to Dissolve Federation", *RFE/RL Report*, 1(48), 1-5.

Pehe, Jiri (1997). "Czechs Fall From Their Ivory Tower", *Transitions* 4 (3), 22-27.

Plasser, Fritz, Peter A. Ulram and Harald Waldrauch (1998). *Democratic Consolidation in East-Central Europe* (Houndmills: MacMillan Press).

Plecitý, Petr (1995). "Konsensuální nebo konkurenční parlament?", *Parlamentní Zpravodaj*, 1(4), 152-153.

Polsby, Nelson (1968). "The Institutionalization of the U.S. House of Representatives", *American Political Science Review*, 62, 144-168.

Polsby, Nelson W. (1975). "Legislatures", in Fred I Greenstein and Nelson W. Polsby (eds.), *Handbook of Political Science*, Volume 5: Governmental Institutions and Processes (Cambridge: Addison-Wesley), 257-319.

Pravda, Alex (1978). "Elections in Communist States", in Guy Hermet, Richard Rose and Alain Rouqié (eds.), *Elections Without Choice* (London: MacMillan Press), 169-195.

Pridham, Geoffrey and Paul G. Lewis, eds., (1996). *Stabilising Fragile Democracies: Comparing New Party Systems in Southern Europe and Eastern Europe* (London: Routledge).

Przeworski, Adam (1991) *Democracy and the Market: Political and Economic Reforms in Eastern Europe and Latin America* (Cambridge: Cambridge University Press).

Przeworski, Adam and Fernando Limogni (1997). "Modernization: Theories and Facts", *World Politics*, 49(2), 155-183.

Raunio, Tapio (1996). *Party Group Behaviour in the European Parliament* (PhD. Dissertation, University of Tampere).

Reschová, Jana and Syllová, Jindřiška (1996). "The Legislature of the Czech Republic", *The Journal of Legislative Studies*, 2(1), 82-107.

Rose, Richard (1994). "Postcommunism and the Problem of Trust", *Journal of Democracy*, 5(3), 18-31.

Rose, Richard (1995). "Mobilizing Demobilized Voters", *Party Politics*, 1(4), 549-563.

Rose, Richard (1997). "Where Are Postcommunist Countries Going?", *Journal of Democracy*, 8(3), 92-108.

Rose, Richard and Christian Haerpfer (1993). *Adapting to Transformation in Eastern Europe: New Democratic Barometer II.* (Glasgow: Centre for the Study of Public Policy, Studies in Public Policy 212).

Rose, Richard and Christian Haerpfer (1994). *New Democratic Barometer III: Learning from What is Happening* (Glasgow: Centre for the Study of Public Policy, Studies in Public Policy 230).

Rose, Richard and Christian Haerpfer (1996). *New Democratic Barometer IV: A 10-Nation Survey* (Glasgow: Centre for the Study of Public Policy, Studies in Public Policy 262).

Rothschild, Joseph (1992). *East Central Europe between the Two World Wars* (Seattle: University of Washington Press, 7th edition).

Ruschemeyer, Dietrich, Evelyne Huber Stephens and John D. Stephens (1992). *Capitalist Development and Democracy* (Cambridge: Polity Press).

Rustow, Dankwart A. (1970). "Transitions to Democracy: Towards a Dynamic Model", *Comparative Politics*, 2(3), 337-365.

Saalfeld, Thomas (1990). "The West German Bundestag after 40 years: The role of Parliament in a 'Party Democracy'", in Philip Norton (ed.), *Parliaments in Western Europe* (London: Frank Cass), 68-89.

Saalfeld, Thomas (1995). "On Dogs and Whips: Recorded Votes", in Herbert Doring (ed.), *Parliaments and Majority Rule in Western Europe* (Frankfurt: Campus-Verlag), 528-565.

Sartori, Giovanni (1976). *Parties and Party Systems: A Framework for Analysis* (Cambridge: Cambridge University Press).

Sartori, Giovanni (1987). *The Theory of Democracy Revisited* (New Jersey: Chetham House).

Sartori, Giovanni (1994). *Comparative Constitutional Engineering: An Inquiry into Structures, Incentives and Outcomes* (London: McMillan Press).

Scarrow, Susan E. (1994). "The 'Paradox of Enrollment': Assessing the Costs and Benefits of Party Membership", *European Journal of Political Research*, 25(1), 41-60.

Schmitter, Philippe (1994). "Dangers and Dillemas of Democracy", *Journal of Democracy*, 5(2), 57-74.

Schmitter, Philippe (1995). "Organized Interests and Democratic Consolidation in Southern Europe", in Richard Gunther, P. Nikiforos Diamandouros, and Hans-Jurgen Puhle (eds.), *The Politics of Democratic Consolidation: Southern Europe in Comparative Perspective* (Baltimore: The Johns Hopkins University Press), 284-314.

Schmitter, Philippe C. and Terry Lynn Karl (1992). "The Types of Democracy Emerging in Southern and Eastern Europe and South and Central America", in Peter M. E. Volten (ed.), *Bound to Change: Consolidating Democracy in East Central Europe* (New York: Institute for East West Studies), 42-68.

Schumpeter, Joseph A. (1976). *Capitalism, Socialism, and Democracy* (London: Allen and Unwin).

Segert, Dieter (1995). "The East German CDU: An Historical or Post-communist Party?", *Party Politics*, 1(4), 589-598.

Shaw, Malcolm (1979). "Conclusion", in John D. Lees and Malcolm Shaw (eds.), *Committees in Legislatures: A Comparative Analysis* (Durham: Duke University Press), 361-434.

Shugart, Matthew Soberg and John M. Carey (1992). *Presidents and Assemblies: Constitutional Design and Electoral Dynamics* (Baltimore: The Johns Hopkins University Press).

Schedler, Andreas (1998). "What is Democratic Consolidation", *Journal of Democracy*, 9, 91-107.

Sisson, Richard (1973). "Comparative Legislative Institutionalization: A Theoretical Exploration", in Allan Kornberg (eds.), *Legislatures in Comparative Perspective* (New York: David McKay Company), 17-38.

Skalnik Leff, Carol (1988). *National Conflict In Czechoslovakia: The Making and Remaking of a State, 1918-1987* (Princeton: Princeton University Press).

Skalnik Leff, Carol (1996). "Dysfunctional Democratization? Institutional Conflict in Post-Communist Slovakia", *Problems of Post-Communism*, 43 (5), 36-50.

Školkay, Andrej (1997). "The Role of the Mass Media in the Post-Communist Transition of Slovakia", in Soňa Szomolányi and John A Gould (eds.) *Slovakia: Problems of Democratic Consolidation and the Struggle for the Rules of the Game* (Bratislava: Slovak Political Science Association), 187-207.

Smith, Peter H. (1991). "Crisis and Democracy in Latin America", *World Politics*, 43, 608-634.

Snyder, Tim and Milada A. Vachudova (1997). "Are Transitions Transitory? Two Types of Political Change in Eastern Europe Since 1989", *East Euroepan Politics and Societies*, 11 (1), 1-35.

Stanger, Allison K. (1999). "The Price of Velvet: Constitutional Politics and the Demise of the Czechoslovak Federation", in Michael Kraus and Allisan K. Stranger (eds.), *Irreconcilable Differences? Explaining the Dissolution of Czechoslovakia*. (Rowman and Littlefield, forthcoming).

Szomolányi, Soňa (1997). "Identifying Slovakia's Emerging Regime", in Soňa Szomolányi and John A Gould (eds.) *Slovakia: Problems of Democratic Consolidation and the Struggle for the Rules of the Game* (Bratislava: Slovak Political Science Association), 9-34.

Taagepera, Rein and Matthew S. Shugart (1989). *Seats and Votes: The Effects and Determinants of Electoral Systems* (New Haven: Yale University Press).

Tatár, Peter (1994). "The Circumstances of the Preparation and Acceptance of the Slovak Constitution", in Irena Grudzinska Gross (ed.), *Constitutionalism and Politics* (Bratislava: European Cutural Foundation), 318-319.

Tóka, Gábor (1996). "Parties and Electoral Choices in East Central Europe", in Geoffrey Pridham and Paul G. Lewis (eds.), *Stabilising Fragile Democracies: Comparing New Party Systems in Southern Europe and Eastern Europe* (London: Routledge), 100-125.

Tsebelis, George and Jeanette Money (1997). *Bicameralism* (Cambridge: Cambridge University Press).

Učeň, Peter (1998). "Implications of Slovakia's Party System Development for the Process of European Integration", unpublished paper, European University Institute, Florence.

Ulč, Otto (1974). *Politics in Czechoslovakia* (San Francisco: W.H. Freeman).

Valenzuela, J. Samuel (1992). "Democratic Consolidation in Post-Transitional Settings: Notion, Process, and Facilitating Conditions", in Scott Mainwaring, Guillermo O'Donnell and J. Samuel Valenzuela (eds.), *Issues in Democratic Consolidation: The New South American Democracies in Comparative Perspective* (Notre Dame: University of Notre Dame Press), 57-104.

Valko, Ernest (1994). "On the Constitution of the Slovak Republic", in Irena Grudzinska Gross (ed.), *Constitutionalism and Politics* (Bratislava: European Cutural Foundation), 315-317.

Vanhanen, Tatu (1997). *Prosepects of Democracy: A Study of 172 Countries* (London: Routledge).

Vermeersch, Jan (1994a). *De rode herinnering: Sociaal-demokraten in Praag* (Leuven: Garant).

Vermeersch, Jan (1994b). "Social Democracy in the Czech Republic and Slovakia", in Michael Waller, Bruno Coppieters and Kris Deschouwer (eds.), *Social Democracy in a Post-Communist Europe* (Ilford: Frank Cass), 119-135.

Waller, Michael (1993). *The End of the Communist Power Monopoly* (Manchester: Manchester University Press).

Waller, Michael (1995). "Making and Breaking: Factions in the Process of Party Formation in Bulgaria", *Democratization*, 2(1), 152-167.

Waller, Michael (1996). "Party Inheritences and Party Identities", in Geoffrey Pridham and Paul G. Lewis (eds.), *Rooting Fragile Democracies: Comparing New Party Systems in Southern Europe and Eastern Europe* (London: Routledge), 23-43.

Weiner, Myron (1987). "Empirical Democratic Theory", in Myron Weiner and Ergun Özbudun (eds.), *Competitive Elections in Developing Countries* (AEI: Duke University Press), 3-34.

Wightman, Gordon (1994). "The Czech and Slovak Republics", in Stephen White, Judy Batt and Paul G. Lewis (eds.), *Developments in East European Politics* (London: MacMillan), 51-61.

Wolchik, Sharon L. (1991). *Czechoslovakia in Transition* (London: Pinter).

Wolchik, Sharon L. (1994). "The Politics of Ethnicity in Post-Communist Czechoslovakia", *East European Politics and Societies*, 8 (1), 153-188.

Wyman, Matthew, Stephen White, Bill Miller and Paul Heywood (1995). "The Place of 'Party' in Post-communist Europe", *Party Politics*, 1(4), 535-548.

Zemko, Milan (1995). "Political Parties and the Election System in Slovakia", in Soňa Szomolányi and Grigorij Mesežnikov (eds.), *Slovakia: Parliamentary Elections 1994* (Bratislava: Slovak Political Science Association), 40-55.

Zielonka, Jan (1994). "New Institutions in the Old East Block", *Journal of Democracy*, 5(2), 87-104.

Zifčák, Spencer (1995). "The Battle over Presidential Power in Slovakia: How Constitutional Ambiguity Shapes Political Life", *East European Constitutional Review*, 4(3), 61-65.

Index

ballot structure 57, 58, 60

candidate selection 58, 71, 196, 211, 249
Chamber of Deputies 43, 44, 54, 56-59, 76, 104, 107, 145, 147, 155
Chamber of Nations 28, 30, 56, 78
Chamber of People 30, 56, 57, 63
civil society 7, 8, 90-92, 212-214, 221, 225-228, 230, 250, 251, 253, 254
closed lists 60
Communist Party xiii-xv, 6, 23, 25-29, 55, 76, 81-84, 87, 237, 258
consociational system 30, 31, 46, 208
consolidation of democracy x, 6, 8, 10, 11, 220, 228
constitution 17, 22, 25, 26, 28-31, 34, 36-46, 53, 67, 70, 104, 106-108, 119, 128, 131, 134, 136, 145-160, 162, 164-166, 209, 215, 216, 219, 220, 224, 226, 248, 252, 254, 255, 260
constitution-making 22, 34, 39, 45, 53, 164, 209, 216, 219, 248
cultural differences 231, 233, 235
culture 1, 3, 14, 107, 138, 140, 239, 246, 248, 260
Czech National Council 43, 56-58, 63, 76, 131, 146

democratic consolidation ix-xi, 1, 3, 4, 7-9, 17-19, 22, 207, 220-223, 225, 227, 228, 231-241, 247-249, 252-255, 257-260
dissidents 25, 26, 102, 215
districts 27, 53, 56, 58, 65-67, 91, 131, 212

elite behavior 1, 3, 9, 150
executive-legislative relations v, 38, 96, 97, 124, 140, 145, 146, 154, 165, 166, 213, 229, 250

Federal Assembly 24-31, 34-36, 39-42, 45, 54, 56-59, 63, 78, 98, 104, 131, 132, 135, 174, 195, 197, 198, 208, 256
federation 29, 31, 33-37, 39-41, 45, 46, 54, 104, 108, 132, 149, 209, 231, 236, 239
First Republic vii, 27, 39, 43-45, 55, 58, 60, 62, 67, 107, 208, 215, 231, 237

government formation 18, 104, 107, 108, 110, 116, 146, 147, 153, 215

Havel, Václav 249
Hungarian parties 36-38, 60, 71, 87, 103, 116, 128, 130, 197, 222, 235

Index v, 178, 262
investiture vote 108, 115, 128, 188

Klaus, Václav 251

legislative veto 155-157, 163
local party 72, 73, 78, 131

majority rule 30, 31, 123, 138, 160, 162, 213, 216, 217, 219, 223, 226, 241, 246, 248, 255, 258
Mečiar I government 102, 103, 106, 107, 109, 114, 115, 128, 135, 151-154, 156
Mečiar II government 103, 109, 115, 117, 127, 136, 137, 140, 159, 160, 166, 198
minority government 89, 103, 128, 146, 217, 235
modernization 3, 124, 229, 230, 239

nation-building 236, 238-241

Organizational Committee 122, 176, 181

parliamentary committees xi, 14, 18, 30, 36, 96, 104, 105, 117, 118, 120-124, 129, 130, 137, 139, 171, 180, 182, 189, 207, 210, 226
parliamentary culture 14
parliamentary institutionalization 3, v, ix-xi, 1, 4, 9, 11-19, 22, 53, 145, 172, 200, 206, 207, 220, 223, 228, 232, 233, 235, 236, 238, 241
parliamentary parties v, viii, ix, xi, 14, 18, 34, 39, 59, 60, 78, 98, 100-102, 105, 108, 110, 112-114, 116, 117, 120-122, 128, 130, 133, 134, 138, 139, 149, 157, 171-184, 187-190, 192-201, 207, 211, 251
parliamentary system 37, 53, 99, 150, 167, 208, 215
party cohesion 18, 101, 171, 178, 180, 187, 188, 190, 200, 211
party competition 3, xi, 10, 84, 233, 235, 237, 238, 251
party discipline 171, 177, 183, 187, 188, 190, 200, 211, 218, 219
party executive ix, 71, 114, 193, 194, 197, 198
party fragmentation 60, 172, 174, 176, 183, 187, 188, 199, 200, 211
party government 114, 116, 213-216, 219, 241, 247, 250, 251
party leadership 128, 171, 178, 180, 182, 198, 199
party membership viii, 75, 81-85, 176, 177, 196
preferential votes 57, 60-62, 65, 66, 106, 196
presidency 35, 39, 40, 146, 150, 151, 154, 159, 161, 165-167, 208, 213
Presidium 108, 116, 137, 138, 146, 176, 181
private member bills 125, 133, 134

referendum 30, 36, 44, 159, 160, 164, 222
representation v, vii, 2, 24, 27, 29, 30, 53, 54, 58-60, 63, 67-70, 72-74, 87, 90-92, 128, 131, 138, 181, 193, 196, 211, 212, 215, 221, 226, 254
role models 53, 54, 72, 215
Round Table 23-26, 55, 153, 215

Senate 40-42, 44, 45, 54, 56, 104, 117, 145, 155-157, 159, 209, 226
Slovak National Council 24, 34, 36, 37, 54, 56-60, 79, 84, 131, 133, 197
Standing Orders 119, 120, 122-125, 128, 131, 132, 135-139, 175, 176, 210
state subsidies 78, 80, 86, 195
state-building 236, 240
suspensive veto 40, 44, 155-157

threshold 28, 29, 57-65, 80, 175, 188, 218